# 365

## Favorite Brand Name ™

# COOKIE

### ▪ R E C I P E S ▪

PUBLICATIONS INTERNATIONAL, LTD.

**Microwave Cooking:** Microwave ovens vary in wattage. Use the cooking times as guidelines and check for doneness before adding more time.

# 365
## Favorite Brand Name ™
# COOKIE
## ▪ R E C I P E S ▪

# Treasured Cookie Classics

## 1 ORIGINAL NESTLÉ® TOLL HOUSE® CHOCOLATE CHIP COOKIES

2¼ cups all-purpose flour
1 teaspoon baking soda
1 teaspoon salt
1 cup (2 sticks) butter, softened
¾ cup granulated sugar
¾ cup packed brown sugar
1 teaspoon vanilla extract
2 eggs
2 cups (12-ounce package) NESTLÉ® TOLL HOUSE® Semi-Sweet Chocolate Morsels
1 cup chopped nuts

**COMBINE** flour, baking soda and salt in small bowl. Beat butter, sugars and vanilla in large mixer bowl. Add eggs one at a time, beating well after each addition; gradually beat in flour mixture. Stir in morsels and nuts. Drop by rounded tablespoon onto ungreased baking sheets.

**BAKE** in preheated 375°F. oven for 9 to 11 minutes or until golden brown. Cool on baking sheets for 2 minutes; remove to wire racks to cool completely.

*Makes about 5 dozen cookies*

**PAN COOKIE VARIATION:** Prepare dough as above. Spread into greased 15½×10½-inch jelly-roll pan. Bake in preheated 375°F. oven for 20 to 25 minutes or until golden brown. Cool in pan on wire rack. Makes 4 dozen bars.

**SLICE AND BAKE COOKIE VARIATION:** Prepare dough as above. Divide in half; wrap in waxed paper. Chill 1 hour or until firm. Shape each half into 15-inch log; wrap in waxed paper. Chill for 30 minutes.* Cut into ½-inch-thick slices; place on ungreased baking sheets. Bake in preheated 375°F. oven for 8 to 10 minutes or until golden brown. Cool on baking sheets for 2 minutes; remove to wire racks to cool completely. Makes about 5 dozen cookies.

*\*May be stored in refrigerator for up to 1 week or in freezer for up to 8 weeks.*

*Original Nestlé® Toll House® Chocolate Chip Cookies*

## TREASURED COOKIE CLASSICS

## 2 ULTIMATE SUGAR COOKIES

1¼ cups granulated sugar
  1 BUTTER FLAVOR* CRISCO® Stick or
    1 cup BUTTER FLAVOR CRISCO
    all-vegetable shortening
  2 eggs
¼ cup light corn syrup or regular pancake
    syrup
  1 tablespoon vanilla
  3 cups all-purpose flour (plus
    4 tablespoons), divided
¾ teaspoon baking powder
½ teaspoon baking soda
½ teaspoon salt
    Granulated sugar or colored sugar
    crystals

*Butter Flavor Crisco is artificially flavored.*

**1.** Place sugar and shortening in large bowl. Beat at medium speed of electric mixer until well blended. Add eggs, syrup and vanilla; beat until well blended and fluffy.

**2.** Combine 3 cups flour, baking powder, baking soda and salt. Add gradually to shortening mixture, beating at low speed until well blended.

**3.** Divide dough into 4 equal pieces; shape each piece into disk. Wrap with plastic wrap. Refrigerate 1 hour or until firm.

**4.** Heat oven to 375°F. Place sheets of foil on countertop for cooling cookies.

**5.** Sprinkle about 1 tablespoon flour on large sheet of waxed paper. Place disk of dough on floured paper; flatten slightly with hands. Turn dough over; cover with another large sheet of waxed paper. Roll dough to ¼-inch thickness. Remove top sheet of waxed

paper. Cut into desired shapes with floured cookie cutters. Place 2 inches apart on ungreased baking sheet. Repeat with remaining dough.

**6.** Sprinkle with granulated sugar.

**7.** Bake one baking sheet at a time at 375°F for 5 to 7 minutes or until edges of cookies are lightly browned. *Do not overbake.* Cool 2 minutes on baking sheet. Remove cookies to foil to cool completely.
*Makes about 3½ dozen cookies*

## 3 ALMOND CREAM CHEESE COOKIES

  1 (3-ounce) package cream cheese,
    softened
  1 cup butter, softened
  1 cup sugar
  1 egg yolk
  1 tablespoon milk
⅛ teaspoon almond extract
2½ cups sifted cake flour
  1 cup BLUE DIAMOND® Sliced Natural
    Almonds, toasted

Beat cream cheese with butter and sugar until fluffy. Blend in egg yolk, milk and almond extract. Gradually mix in flour. Gently stir in almonds. (Dough will be sticky.) Divide dough in half; place each half on large sheet of waxed paper. Working through waxed paper, shape each half into 12×1½-inch roll. Chill until very firm.

Preheat oven to 325°F. Cut rolls into ¼-inch slices. Bake on ungreased cookie sheets 10 to 15 minutes or until edges are golden. (Cookies will not brown.) Cool on wire racks.        *Makes about 4 dozen cookies*

*Ultimate Sugar Cookies*

## 4 HERSHEY'S CLASSIC CHOCOLATE CHIP COOKIES

2¼ cups all-purpose flour
1 teaspoon baking soda
½ teaspoon salt
1 cup (2 sticks) butter, softened
¾ cup granulated sugar
¾ cup packed light brown sugar
1 teaspoon vanilla extract
2 eggs
2 cups (12-ounce package) HERSHEY'S Semi-Sweet Chocolate Chips
1 cup chopped nuts (optional)

1. Heat oven to 375°F.

2. Stir together flour, baking soda and salt. In large bowl, beat butter, granulated sugar, brown sugar and vanilla with electric mixer until creamy. Add eggs; beat well. Gradually add flour mixture, beating well. Stir in chocolate chips and nuts, if desired. Drop by rounded teaspoons onto ungreased cookie sheet.

3. Bake 8 to 10 minutes or until lightly browned. Cool slightly; remove from cookie sheet to wire rack. Cool completely.

*Makes about 5 dozen cookies*

**"PERFECTLY CHOCOLATE" CHOCOLATE CHIP COOKIES:** Add ⅓ cup HERSHEY'S Cocoa to flour mixture.

**PAN RECIPE:** Spread batter into greased 15½×10½×1-inch jelly-roll pan. Bake at 375°F 20 minutes or until lightly browned. Cool completely. Cut into bars. Makes about 48 bars.

**ICE CREAM SANDWICH:** Press one small scoop of vanilla ice cream between two cookies.

**HIGH ALTITUDE DIRECTIONS:** Increase flour to 2⅔ cups. Decrease baking soda to ¾ teaspoon. Decrease granulated sugar to ⅔ cup. Decrease packed light brown sugar to ⅔ cup. Add ½ teaspoon water with flour. Bake at 375°F 5 to 7 minutes or until top is light golden with golden brown edges.

## 5 NAOMI'S REVEL BARS

1 cup plus 2 tablespoons butter or margarine, softened, divided
2 cups packed brown sugar
2 eggs
2 teaspoons vanilla
2½ cups all-purpose flour
1 teaspoon baking soda
3 cups uncooked rolled oats
1 package (12 ounces) semisweet chocolate chips
1 can (14 ounces) sweetened condensed milk

Preheat oven to 325°F. Lightly grease 13×9-inch pan.

Beat 1 cup butter and brown sugar in large bowl. Add eggs; beat until light. Blend in vanilla. Combine flour and baking soda; stir into creamed mixture. Blend in oats. Spread ¾ of the oat mixture evenly into prepared pan. Combine chocolate chips, milk and remaining 2 tablespoons butter in small heavy saucepan. Stir over low heat until chocolate is melted. Pour chocolate mixture evenly over oat mixture in pan. Dot with remaining oat mixture.

Bake 20 to 25 minutes or until edges are browned and center feels firm. Cool in pan on wire rack. Cut into 2×1½-inch bars.

*Makes 3 dozen bars*

*Naomi's Revel Bars*

## 6  GINGERSNAPS

2½ cups all-purpose flour
1½ teaspoons ground ginger
1 teaspoon baking soda
1 teaspoon ground allspice
½ teaspoon salt
1½ cups sugar
2 tablespoons margarine, softened
½ cup MOTT'S® Apple Sauce
¼ cup GRANDMA'S® Molasses

1. Preheat oven to 375°F. Spray cookie sheet with nonstick cooking spray.

2. In medium bowl, sift together flour, ginger, baking soda, allspice and salt.

3. In large bowl, beat sugar and margarine with electric mixer at medium speed until blended. Whisk in apple sauce and molasses.

4. Add flour mixture to apple sauce mixture; stir until well blended.

5. Drop rounded tablespoonfuls of dough 1 inch apart onto prepared cookie sheet. Flatten each slightly with moistened fingertips.

6. Bake 12 to 15 minutes or until firm. Cool completely on wire rack.

*Makes 3 dozen cookies*

## 7  IRRESISTIBLE PEANUT BUTTER COOKIES

1¼ cups firmly packed light brown sugar
¾ cup creamy peanut butter
½ CRISCO® Stick or ½ cup CRISCO all-vegetable shortening
3 tablespoons milk
1 tablespoon vanilla
1 egg
1¾ cups all-purpose flour
¾ teaspoon baking soda
¾ teaspoon salt

1. Heat oven to 375°F. Place sheets of foil on countertop for cooling cookies.

2. Place brown sugar, peanut butter, shortening, milk and vanilla in large bowl. Beat at medium speed of electric mixer until well blended. Add egg; beat just until blended.

3. Combine flour, baking soda and salt. Add to shortening mixture; beat at low speed just until blended.

4. Drop dough by rounded measuring tablespoonfuls 2 inches apart onto ungreased baking sheet. Flatten dough slightly in crisscross pattern with tines of fork.

5. Bake one baking sheet at a time at 375°F for 7 to 8 minutes or until cookies are set and just beginning to brown. *Do not overbake.* Cool 2 minutes on baking sheet. Remove cookies to foil to cool completely.

*Makes about 3 dozen cookies*

*Irresistible Peanut Butter Cookies*

## 8 CARAMEL–LAYERED BROWNIES

4 squares BAKER'S® Unsweetened
   Chocolate
¾ cup (1½ sticks) margarine or butter
2 cups sugar
3 eggs
1 teaspoon vanilla
1 cup all-purpose flour
1 cup BAKER'S® Semi-Sweet Real
   Chocolate Chips
1½ cups chopped nuts
1 package caramels (48)
⅓ cup evaporated milk

**HEAT** oven to 350°F.

**MICROWAVE** chocolate and margarine in large microwavable bowl on HIGH 2 minutes or until margarine is melted. Stir until chocolate is completely melted.

**STIR** sugar into melted chocolate mixture. Mix in eggs and vanilla until well blended. Stir in flour. Remove 1 cup of batter; set aside. Spread remaining batter into greased 13×9-inch pan. Sprinkle with chips and 1 cup of the nuts.

**MICROWAVE** caramels and milk in same bowl on HIGH 4 minutes, stirring after 2 minutes. Stir until caramels are completely melted and smooth. Spoon over chips and nuts, spreading to edges of pan. Gently spread reserved batter over caramel mixture. Sprinkle with the remaining ½ cup nuts.

**BAKE** for 40 minutes or until toothpick inserted into center comes out with fudgy crumbs. *Do not overbake.* Cool in pan; cut into squares.    *Makes about 24 brownies*

**Prep Time:** 20 minutes
**Bake Time:** 40 minutes

## 9 CHOCOLATE SUGAR DROPS

½ cup butter or margarine, softened
½ cup vegetable oil
½ cup powdered sugar
½ cup granulated sugar
1 egg
2 cups all-purpose flour
¼ cup unsweetened cocoa
½ teaspoon baking soda
½ teaspoon cream of tartar
¼ teaspoon salt
1 teaspoon vanilla
   Additional granulated sugar

Beat butter, oil, powdered sugar, ½ cup granulated sugar and egg in large bowl until light and fluffy. Combine flour, cocoa, baking soda, cream of tartar and salt in small bowl. Add to butter mixture with vanilla, stirring until dough is smooth. Cover; refrigerate 30 minutes or overnight, if desired.

Preheat oven to 350°F. Lightly grease cookie sheets or line with parchment paper. Shape dough into marble-sized balls. Place 2 inches apart on prepared cookie sheets. Flatten each cookie to about ⅓-inch thickness with bottom of greased glass dipped in additional granulated sugar.

Bake 10 minutes or until firm. Do not overbake. Remove to wire racks to cool.
   *Makes about 5 dozen cookies*

*Caramel-Layered Brownie*

## 10 CREAM CHEESE CUTOUT COOKIES

    1 cup butter, softened
    1 (8-ounce) package cream cheese, softened
1½ cups sugar
    1 egg
    1 teaspoon vanilla
    ½ teaspoon almond extract
3½ cups all-purpose flour
    1 teaspoon baking powder
      Almond Frosting (recipe follows)
      Assorted candies and colored sugars for decoration (optional)

In large bowl, beat butter and cream cheese until well combined. Add sugar; beat until fluffy. Add egg, vanilla and almond extract; beat well. In small bowl, combine flour and baking powder. Add dry ingredients to cream cheese mixture; beat until well mixed. Divide dough in half. Wrap each portion; refrigerate, about 1½ hours.

Preheat oven to 375°F. Roll out dough, half at a time, ⅛ inch thick on lightly floured surface. Cut out with desired cookie cutters. Place 2 inches apart on ungreased cookie sheet. Bake 8 to 10 minutes or until edges are lightly browned. Remove to wire racks; cool completely. Pipe or spread Almond Frosting onto cooled cookies. Garnish with assorted candies and colored sugars, if desired.        *Makes about 7 dozen cookies*

**ALMOND FROSTING:** In small bowl, beat 2 cups sifted confectioners' sugar, 2 tablespoons softened butter and ¼ teaspoon almond extract until smooth. For piping consistency, beat in 4 to 5 teaspoons milk. For spreading consistency, add a little more milk. If desired, tint with food coloring.

*Favorite recipe from **Wisconsin Milk Marketing Board***

## 11 LEMON NUT WHITE CHIP COOKIES

1½ cups all-purpose flour
    ¾ teaspoon baking soda
    ½ teaspoon salt
    ¾ cup (1½ sticks) butter or margarine, softened
    ½ cup packed brown sugar
    ¼ cup granulated sugar
    1 egg
    1 tablespoon lemon juice
    2 cups (12-ounce package) NESTLÉ® TOLL HOUSE® Premier White Morsels
    1 cup coarsely chopped walnuts or cashew nuts
    1 teaspoon grated lemon peel

**COMBINE** flour, baking soda and salt in small bowl. Beat butter, brown sugar and granulated sugar in large mixer bowl until creamy. Beat in egg and lemon juice; gradually beat in flour mixture. Stir in morsels, nuts and lemon peel. Drop by rounded tablespoon onto ungreased baking sheets.

**BAKE** in preheated 375°F. oven for 7 to 10 minutes or until edges are lightly browned. Cool for 3 minutes on baking sheets; remove to wire racks to cool completely.

        *Makes about 3 dozen cookies*

## 12 THE ORIGINAL KELLOGG'S® RICE KRISPIES TREATS® RECIPE

3 tablespoons margarine
1 package (10 ounces) regular
    marshmallows (about 40) or 4 cups
    miniature marshmallows
6 cups KELLOGG'S® RICE KRISPIES®
    Cereal
    Vegetable cooking spray

**1.** Melt margarine in large saucepan over low heat. Add marshmallows and stir until completely melted. Remove from heat.

**2.** Add KELLOGG'S® RICE KRISPIES® cereal. Stir until well coated.

**3.** Using buttered spatula or waxed paper, press mixture evenly into 13×9×2-inch pan coated with cooking spray. Cut into 2×2-inch squares when cool.

*Makes 24 treats*

**NOTE:** Use fresh marshmallows for best results. Do not use diet or reduced fat margarine.

**Microwave Directions:** Microwave margarine and marshmallows at HIGH 2 minutes in microwave-safe mixing bowl. Stir to combine. Microwave at HIGH 1 minute longer. Stir until smooth. Add cereal. Stir until well coated. Press into pan as directed in Step 3.

## 13 LUSCIOUS FRESH LEMON BARS

**CRUST:**
  ½ cup butter or margarine, softened
  ½ cup granulated sugar
    Grated peel of ½ SUNKIST® Lemon
1¼ cups all-purpose flour

**LEMON LAYER:**
  4 eggs
1⅔ cups granulated sugar
  3 tablespoons all-purpose flour
  ½ teaspoon baking powder
    Grated peel of ½ SUNKIST® Lemon
    Juice of 2 SUNKIST® Lemons
      (6 tablespoons)
  1 teaspoon vanilla extract
    Confectioners' sugar

To make crust, in bowl blend together butter, granulated sugar and lemon peel. Gradually stir in flour to form a soft crumbly dough. Press evenly into bottom of aluminum foil-lined 13×9×2-inch baking pan. Bake at 350°F for 15 minutes. Meanwhile to prepare lemon layer, in large bowl whisk or beat eggs well. Stir together granulated sugar, flour and baking powder. Gradually whisk sugar mixture into beaten eggs. Stir or whisk in lemon peel, lemon juice and vanilla. Pour over hot baked crust. Return to oven and bake for 20 to 25 minutes, or until top and sides are lightly browned. Cool. Using foil on two sides, lift out the cookie base and gently loosen foil along all sides. With a long wet knife, cut into bars or squares. Sprinkle tops with confectioners' sugar.

*Makes about 3 dozen cookies*

## 14 OATMEAL SCOTCHIES

1¼ cups all-purpose flour
 1 teaspoon baking soda
½ teaspoon salt
½ teaspoon ground cinnamon
 1 cup (2 sticks) butter or margarine,
   softened
¾ cup granulated sugar
¾ cup packed brown sugar
 2 eggs
 1 teaspoon vanilla extract or grated peel
   of 1 orange
 3 cups quick or old-fashioned oats
1⅔ cups (11-ounce package) NESTLÉ® TOLL
   HOUSE® Butterscotch Flavored
   Morsels

COMBINE flour, baking soda, salt and cinnamon in small bowl. Beat butter, granulated sugar, brown sugar, eggs and vanilla in large mixer bowl. Gradually beat in flour mixture. Stir in oats and morsels. Drop by rounded tablespoon onto ungreased baking sheets.

BAKE in preheated 375°F. oven for 7 to 8 minutes for chewy cookies; 9 to 10 minutes for crisp cookies. Cool on baking sheets for 2 minutes; remove to wire racks to cool completely.

*Makes about 4 dozen cookies*

PAN COOKIE VARIATION: Prepare dough as above. Spread dough into greased 15½×10½-inch jelly-roll pan. Bake in preheated 375°F. oven for 18 to 22 minutes or until very lightly browned. Cool completely on wire rack. Makes 4 dozen bars.

## 15 MOM'S BEST OATMEAL COOKIES

¾ BUTTER FLAVOR* CRISCO® Stick or
   ¾ cup BUTTER FLAVOR CRISCO
   all-vegetable shortening
1¼ cups firmly packed light brown sugar
 1 egg
⅓ cup milk
1½ teaspoons vanilla
 3 cups quick oats, uncooked
 1 cup all-purpose flour
½ teaspoon baking soda
½ teaspoon salt
¼ teaspoon ground cinnamon
 1 cup chopped pecans
⅔ cup flake coconut
⅔ cup sesame seeds

*Butter Flavor Crisco is artificially flavored.*

1. Heat oven to 350°F. Grease baking sheets with shortening. Place sheets of foil on countertop for cooling cookies.

2. Combine shortening, brown sugar, egg, milk and vanilla in large mixer bowl. Beat at medium speed of electric mixer until well blended.

3. Combine oats, flour, baking soda, salt and cinnamon. Mix into shortening mixture at low speed just until blended. Stir in pecans, coconut and sesame seeds.

4. Drop by rounded measuring tablespoonfuls of dough 2 inches apart onto prepared baking sheets.

5. Bake one baking sheet at a time at 375°F for 10 to 12 minutes or until lightly browned. *Do not overbake.* Cool 2 minutes on baking sheets. Remove cookies to foil to cool completely.

*Makes about 2½ dozen cookies*

*Oatmeal Scotchies*

## 16 MISSISSIPPI MUD BARS

½ cup butter or margarine, softened
¾ cup packed brown sugar
1 egg
1 teaspoon vanilla
½ teaspoon baking soda
¼ teaspoon salt
1 cup plus 2 tablespoons all-purpose flour
1 cup (6 ounces) semisweet chocolate chips, divided
1 cup (6 ounces) white chocolate chips, divided
½ cup chopped walnuts or pecans

Preheat oven to 375°F. Line 9-inch square baking pan with foil; grease foil.

Beat butter and sugar in large bowl until blended and smooth. Beat in egg and vanilla until light. Blend in baking soda and salt. Add flour, mixing until well blended. Stir in ¾ cup semisweet chocolate chips, ¾ cup white chocolate chips and nuts. Spread dough in prepared pan.

Bake 23 to 25 minutes or until center feels firm. Do not overbake. Remove from oven; sprinkle remaining ¼ cup each semisweet and white chocolate chips over the top. Let stand a few minutes until chips melt; spread evenly over bars. Cool in pan on wire rack until chocolate is set. Cut into bars.

*Makes about 3 dozen bars*

## 17 BUTTERSCOTCH BLONDIES

¾ cup (1½ sticks) butter or margarine, softened
¾ cup packed light brown sugar
½ cup granulated sugar
2 eggs
2 cups all-purpose flour
1 teaspoon baking soda
½ teaspoon salt
1⅔ cups (10-ounce package) HERSHEY'S Butterscotch Chips
1 cup chopped nuts (optional)

**1.** Heat oven to 350°F. Grease 13×9×2-inch baking pan.

**2.** In large bowl, beat butter, brown sugar and granulated sugar until light and fluffy. Add eggs; beat until well blended. Stir together flour, baking soda and salt; gradually add to butter mixture, mixing well. Stir in butterscotch chips and nuts, if desired. Spread into prepared pan.

**3.** Bake 30 to 35 minutes or until golden brown and center is set. Cool completely in pan on wire rack. Cut into bars.

*Makes about 36 bars*

*Butterscotch Blondies*

## 18 SOFT MOLASSES SPICE COOKIES

2¼ cups all-purpose flour
1 teaspoon baking soda
1 teaspoon ground cinnamon
½ teaspoon ground ginger
¼ teaspoon ground nutmeg
⅛ teaspoon ground cloves
⅛ teaspoon salt
½ cup plus 2 tablespoons butter, softened, divided
½ cup packed dark brown sugar
1 egg
½ cup molasses
1¼ teaspoons vanilla, divided
¼ cup plus 2 to 3 tablespoons milk, divided
¾ cup raisins (optional)
2 cups powdered sugar

**PREHEAT** oven to 350°F. Grease cookie sheets. Combine flour, baking soda, cinnamon, ginger, nutmeg, cloves and salt in medium bowl.

**BEAT** ½ cup butter in large bowl with electric mixer at medium speed until smooth and creamy. Gradually beat in brown sugar until blended; increase speed to high and beat until light and fluffy. Beat in egg until fluffy. Beat in molasses and 1 teaspoon vanilla until smooth. Beat in flour mixture at low speed alternately with ¼ cup milk until blended. Stir in raisins.

**DROP** rounded tablespoonfuls of dough about 1½ inches apart onto prepared cookie sheets. Bake 12 minutes or until set. Let cookies stand on cookie sheets 5 minutes; transfer to wire racks to cool completely.

For icing, **MELT** remaining 2 tablespoons butter in small saucepan over medium-low heat. Remove from heat; add powdered sugar and stir until blended. Add remaining 2 tablespoons milk and ¼ teaspoon vanilla; stir until smooth. If icing is too thick, add milk, 1 teaspoon at a time, until desired consistency.

**SPREAD** icing over tops of cookies. Let stand 15 minutes or until icing is set. Store in airtight container.

*Makes about 36 cookies*

## 19 LEMON COOKIES

⅔ cup MIRACLE WHIP® Salad Dressing
1 two-layer yellow cake mix
2 eggs
2 teaspoons grated lemon peel
⅔ cup ready-to-spread vanilla frosting
4 teaspoons lemon juice

• Preheat oven to 375°F.

• Blend salad dressing, cake mix and eggs at low speed with electric mixer until moistened. Add peel. Beat on medium speed 2 minutes. (Dough will be stiff.)

• Drop rounded teaspoonfuls of dough, 2 inches apart, onto greased cookie sheet.

• Bake 9 to 11 minutes or until lightly browned. (Cookies will still appear soft.) Cool 1 minute; remove from cookie sheet. Cool completely on wire rack.

• Stir together frosting and juice until well blended. Spread on cookies.

*Makes about 4 dozen cookies*

## 20 BAKER'S® CHOCOLATE CHIP COOKIES

1 cup (2 sticks) margarine or butter, softened
¾ cup firmly packed brown sugar
¾ cup granulated sugar
1 teaspoon vanilla
2 eggs
2¼ cups all-purpose flour
1 teaspoon baking soda
¼ teaspoon salt
1 package (12 ounces) BAKER'S® Semi-Sweet Real Chocolate Chips
1 cup chopped nuts (optional)

**HEAT** oven to 375°F.

**BEAT** margarine, brown sugar, granulated sugar, vanilla and eggs until light and fluffy. Mix in flour, baking soda and salt. Stir in chips and nuts. Drop by rounded teaspoonfuls, 2 inches apart, onto ungreased cookie sheets.

**BAKE** for 8 to 10 minutes or until golden brown. Remove from cookie sheets to cool on wire racks.

*Makes about 6 dozen cookies*

**Prep Time:** 15 minutes
**Bake Time:** 8 to 10 minutes

*Lemon Cookies*

## 21 SPICE COOKIES

½ cup butter, softened
1¼ cups all-purpose flour, divided
¼ cup milk, divided
1 cup packed brown sugar
1 egg
1 teaspoon ground cinnamon
½ teaspoon baking powder
¼ teaspoon ground cloves
½ cup chopped walnuts
1½ cups coarsely chopped OCEAN SPRAY®
    Fresh or Frozen Cranberries

Preheat oven to 375°F.

Beat butter, ¾ cup flour, ⅛ cup milk, brown sugar, egg, cinnamon, baking powder, cloves and walnuts in medium bowl with electric mixer at medium-high speed until thoroughly combined. Add remaining ¾ cup flour, ⅛ cup milk and cranberries. Beat at low speed until thoroughly combined.

Drop by rounded teaspoonfuls onto ungreased cookie sheets. Bake 10 minutes or until golden brown.

*Makes 2½ dozen cookies*

## 22 HERSHEY'S "PERFECTLY CHOCOLATE" CHOCOLATE CHIP COOKIES

2¼ cups all-purpose flour
⅓ cup HERSHEY'S Cocoa
1 teaspoon baking soda
½ teaspoon salt
1 cup (2 sticks) butter or margarine,
    softened
¾ cup granulated sugar
¾ cup packed light brown sugar
1 teaspoon vanilla extract
2 eggs
2 cups (12-ounce package) HERSHEY'S
    Semi-Sweet Chocolate Chips
1 cup chopped nuts (optional)

**1.** Heat oven to 375°F.

**2.** Stir together flour, cocoa, baking soda and salt. In large bowl, beat butter, granulated sugar, brown sugar and vanilla on medium speed of electric mixer until creamy. Add eggs; beat well. Gradually add flour mixture, beating until well blended. Stir in chocolate chips and nuts, if desired. Drop by rounded teaspoons onto ungreased cookie sheet.

**3.** Bake 8 to 10 minutes or until set. Cool slightly; remove from cookie sheet to wire rack. *Makes about 5 dozen cookies*

*Hershey's "Perfectly Chocolate"*
*Chocolate Chip Cookies*

## 23 FABULOUS BLONDE BROWNIES

1¾ cups all-purpose flour
1 teaspoon baking powder
¼ teaspoon salt
1 cup (6 ounces) white chocolate chips
1 cup (4 ounces) blanched whole
   almonds, coarsely chopped
1 cup English toffee bits
⅔ cup margarine or butter, softened
1½ cups packed light brown sugar
2 eggs
2 teaspoons vanilla

**PREHEAT** oven to 350°F. Lightly grease 13×9-inch baking pan.

**COMBINE** flour, baking powder and salt in small bowl; mix well.

**COMBINE** white chocolate, almonds and toffee in medium bowl; mix well.

**BEAT** margarine and brown sugar in large bowl with electric mixer at medium speed until light and fluffy. Beat in eggs and vanilla. Add flour mixture; beat at low speed until well blended. Stir in ¾ cup of white chocolate mixture. Spread evenly into prepared pan.

**BAKE** 20 minutes. Immediately after removing brownies from oven, sprinkle remaining white chocolate mixture evenly over brownies. Press down lightly. Return pan to oven; bake 15 to 20 minutes or until wooden pick inserted into center comes out clean. Cool brownies completely in pan on wire rack. Cut into 2×1½-inch bars.

**STORE** tightly covered at room temperature or freeze up to 3 months.

*Makes 3 dozen brownies*

## 24 HERSHEY'S PREMIUM DOUBLE CHOCOLATE BROWNIES

¾ cup HERSHEY'S Cocoa
½ teaspoon baking soda
⅔ cup butter or margarine, melted and
   divided
½ cup boiling water
2 cups sugar
2 eggs
1 teaspoon vanilla extract
1⅓ cups all-purpose flour
¼ teaspoon salt
2 cups (12-ounce package) HERSHEY'S
   Semi-Sweet Chocolate Chips
½ cup coarsely chopped nuts (optional)

**1.** Heat oven to 350°F. Grease 13×9×2-inch baking pan.

**2.** In large bowl, stir together cocoa and baking soda; stir in ⅓ cup butter. Add boiling water; stir until mixture thickens. Stir in sugar, eggs, remaining ⅓ cup butter and vanilla; stir until smooth. Gradually add flour and salt to cocoa mixture, beating until well blended. Stir in chocolate chips and nuts, if desired; pour batter into prepared pan.

**3.** Bake 35 to 40 minutes or until brownies begin to pull away from sides of pan. Cool completely in pan on wire rack. Cut into bars.          *Makes about 36 brownies*

*Fabulous Blonde Brownies*

## 25 CUT–OUT SUGAR COOKIES

⅔ **BUTTER FLAVOR\* CRISCO®** Stick or
   ⅔ cup **BUTTER FLAVOR CRISCO**
   all-vegetable shortening
¾ cup sugar
 1 tablespoon plus 1 teaspoon milk
 1 teaspoon vanilla
 1 egg
 2 cups all-purpose flour
1½ teaspoons baking powder
¼ teaspoon salt
   Colored sugars and decors (optional)

*\*Butter Flavor Crisco is artificially flavored.*

**1.** Combine shortening, sugar, milk and vanilla in large bowl. Beat at medium speed of electric mixer until well blended and creamy. Beat in egg.

**2.** Combine flour, baking powder and salt. Mix into creamed mixture at low speed until well blended. Cover and refrigerate several hours or overnight.

**3.** Preheat oven to 375°F. Roll out dough, half at a time, to about ⅛-inch thickness on floured surface. Cut dough out with cookie cutters. Place 2 inches apart on ungreased cookie sheet. Sprinkle with colored sugars and decors or leave plain and frost when cooled.

**4.** Bake 7 to 9 minutes, or until set. Remove immediately to wire rack.
*Makes about 3 dozen cookies*

**LEMON OR ORANGE CUT–OUT SUGAR COOKIES:** Add 1 teaspoon grated lemon or orange peel and 1 teaspoon lemon or orange extract to dough in Step 1.

**CREAMY VANILLA FROSTING:** Combine ½ Butter Flavor Crisco Stick or ½ cup Butter Flavor Crisco all-vegetable shortening, 1 pound (4 cups) powdered sugar, ⅓ cup milk and 1 teaspoon vanilla in medium bowl. Beat at low speed of electric mixer until well blended. Scrape bowl. Beat at high speed for 2 minutes, or until smooth and creamy. One or two drops food color can be used to tint each cup of frosting, if desired. Frost cooled cookies. (This frosting works well in decorating tube.)

**LEMON OR ORANGE CREAMY FROSTING:** Prepare Creamy Vanilla Frosting, adding ⅓ cup lemon or orange juice in place of milk. Add 1 teaspoon orange peel with orange juice.

**EASY CHOCOLATE FROSTING:** Place ⅓ Butter Flavor Crisco Stick or ⅓ cup Butter Flavor Crisco all-vegetable shortening in medium microwave-safe bowl. Cover with waxed paper. Microwave at HIGH (100% power) until melted (or melt on rangetop in small saucepan on low heat). Add ¾ cup unsweetened cocoa and ¼ teaspoon salt. Beat at low speed of electric mixer until blended. Add ½ cup milk and 2 teaspoons vanilla. Beat at low speed. Add 1 pound (4 cups) powdered sugar, 1 cup at a time. Beat at low speed after each addition until smooth and creamy. Add more sugar to thicken or milk to thin until of good spreading consistency.

**CHOCOLATE DIPPED CUT–OUT SUGAR COOKIES:** Combine 1 cup semi-sweet chocolate chips and 1 teaspoon Butter Flavor Crisco all-vegetable shortening in microwave-safe measuring cup. Microwave at MEDIUM (50% power). Stir after 1 minute. Repeat until smooth (or melt on rangetop in small saucepan on very low heat.) Dip one end of cooled cookie halfway up in chocolate. Place on waxed paper until chocolate is firm.

**CHOCOLATE NUT CUT–OUT SUGAR COOKIES:** Dip cookie in melted chocolate as directed for Chocolate Dipped Cut-Out Sugar Cookies. Sprinkle with finely chopped nuts before chocolate hardens.

## 26 EASY PEANUTTY SNICKERDOODLES

2 tablespoons sugar
2 teaspoons ground cinnamon
1 package (15 ounces) golden sugar cookie mix
1 egg
1 tablespoon water
1 cup REESE'S® Peanut Butter Chips

Heat oven to 375°F. In small bowl combine sugar and cinnamon. In medium bowl combine cookie mix (and enclosed flavor packet), egg and water; mix with spoon or fork until thoroughly blended. Stir in peanut butter chips. Shape dough into 1-inch balls. (If dough is too soft, cover and chill about 1 hour.) Roll balls in cinnamon-sugar. Place on ungreased cookie sheet.

Bake 8 to 10 minutes or until very lightly browned. Cool slightly; remove from cookie sheet to wire rack. Cool completely.

*Makes about 2 dozen cookies*

## 27 CHOCOLATE PECAN PIE BARS

1⅓ cups all-purpose flour
2 tablespoons plus ½ cup packed light brown sugar, divided
½ cup (1 stick) cold butter or margarine
2 eggs
½ cup light corn syrup
¼ cup HERSHEY'S Cocoa
2 tablespoons butter or margarine, melted
1 teaspoon vanilla extract
⅛ teaspoon salt
1 cup coarsely chopped pecans

Heat oven to 350°F. In large bowl, stir together flour and 2 tablespoons brown sugar. With pastry blender, cut in ½ cup butter until mixture resembles coarse crumbs; press onto bottom and about 1 inch up sides of ungreased 9-inch square baking pan. Bake 10 to 12 minutes or until set. Remove from oven. With back of spoon, lightly press crust into corners and against sides of pan. In small bowl, lightly beat eggs, corn syrup, remaining ½ cup brown sugar, cocoa, butter, vanilla and salt until well blended. Stir in pecans. Pour mixture over warm crust. Continue baking 25 minutes or until pecan filling is set. Cool completely in pan on wire rack. Cut into bars.

*Makes about 16 bars*

## 28 ULTIMATE CHOCOLATE CHIP COOKIES

1¼ cups firmly packed brown sugar
¾ BUTTER FLAVOR* CRISCO® Stick or
   ¾ cup BUTTER FLAVOR CRISCO
   all-vegetable shortening
2 tablespoons milk
1 tablespoon vanilla
1 egg
1¾ cups all-purpose flour
1 teaspoon salt
¾ teaspoon baking soda
1 cup semisweet chocolate chips
1 cup coarsely chopped pecans
   (optional)**

*Butter Flavor Crisco is artificially flavored.*

**If nuts are omitted, add an additional ½ cup semisweet chocolate chips.*

**1. Heat** oven to 375°F. **Place** sheets of foil on countertop for cooling cookies.

**2. Combine** brown sugar, shortening, milk and vanilla in large bowl. **Beat** at medium speed of electric mixer until well blended. **Beat** in egg.

**3. Combine** flour, salt and baking soda. **Mix** into shortening mixture just until blended. **Stir** in chocolate chips and pecan pieces.

**4. Drop** by rounded measuring tablespoonfuls 3 inches apart onto ungreased baking sheets.

**5. Bake** one baking sheet at a time at 375°F for 8 to 10 minutes for chewy cookies, or 11 to 13 minutes for crisp cookies. *Do not overbake.* **Cool** 2 minutes on baking sheets. **Remove** cookies to foil to cool completely.
*Makes about 3 dozen cookies*

## 29 FIVE LAYER BARS

¾ cup (1½ sticks) butter or margarine
1¾ cups graham cracker crumbs
¼ cup HERSHEY'S Cocoa
2 tablespoons sugar
1 can (14 ounces) sweetened condensed
   milk (not evaporated milk)
1 cup HERSHEY'S Semi-Sweet Chocolate
   Chips
1 cup raisins, chopped dried apricots or
   miniature marshmallows
1 cup chopped nuts

**1.** Heat oven to 350°F. Place butter in 13×9×2-inch baking pan. Heat in oven until melted. Remove pan from oven.

**2.** Stir together graham cracker crumbs, cocoa and sugar; sprinkle evenly over butter. Pour sweetened condensed milk evenly over crumb mixture. Sprinkle with chocolate chips and raisins. Sprinkle nuts on top; press down firmly.

**3.** Bake 25 to 30 minutes or until lightly browned. Cool completely in pan on wire rack. Cover with foil; let stand at room temperature 6 to 8 hours. Cut into bars.
*Makes about 36 bars*

**VARIATION:** Substitute 1 cup REESE'S® Peanut Butter Chips for chocolate chips. Sprinkle 1 cup golden raisins or chopped dried apricots over chips. Proceed as above.

*Ultimate Chocolate Chip Cookies*

## 30 PEANUT BUTTER CUT-OUT COOKIES

½ cup (1 stick) butter or margarine
1 cup REESE'S® Peanut Butter Chips
⅔ cup packed light brown sugar
1 egg
¾ teaspoon vanilla extract
1⅓ cups all-purpose flour
¾ teaspoon baking soda
½ cup finely chopped pecans
  CHOCOLATE CHIP GLAZE or PEANUT
  BUTTER CHIP GLAZE (recipes follow)

**1.** In medium saucepan, combine butter and peanut butter chips; cook over low heat, stirring constantly, until melted. Pour into large bowl; add brown sugar, egg and vanilla, beating until well blended. Stir in flour, baking soda and pecans; blend well. Refrigerate 15 to 20 minutes or until firm enough to roll.

**2.** Heat oven to 350°F.

**3.** Roll out dough, a small portion at a time, on lightly floured surface or between 2 pieces of wax paper, to ¼-inch thickness. (Keep remaining dough in refrigerator.) With cookie cutters, cut into desired shapes; place on ungreased cookie sheet.

**4.** Bake 7 to 8 minutes or until almost set (do not overbake). Cool 1 minute; remove from cookie sheet to wire rack. Cool completely. Drizzle CHOCOLATE CHIP GLAZE or PEANUT BUTTER CHIP GLAZE onto each cookie.

*Makes about 3 dozen cookies*

**CHOCOLATE CHIP GLAZE:** In small microwave-safe bowl, place 1 cup HERSHEY'S® Semi-Sweet Chocolate Chips and 1 tablespoon shortening (do not use butter, margarine or oil). Microwave at HIGH (100%) 1 minute; stir. If necessary, microwave at HIGH an additional 15 seconds at a time, stirring after each heating, just until chips are melted when stirred. Makes about ⅔ cup glaze.

**PEANUT BUTTER CHIP GLAZE:** In small microwave-safe bowl, place ⅔ cup REESE'S® Peanut Butter Chips and 1 tablespoon shortening (do not use butter, margarine or oil). Microwave at HIGH (100%) 30 seconds; stir. Microwave at HIGH an additional 15 seconds at a time, stirring after each heating, just until chips are melted when stirred.

**VARIATION:** Prepare dough as directed. Refrigerate 15 to 20 minutes or until firm enough to handle. Shape dough into two 6-inch rolls. Wrap rolls in wax paper or plastic wrap; freeze 1 to 2 hours or until firm enough to cut. Cut dough into ¼-inch thick slices. Proceed as directed for baking and cooling.

*Peanut Butter Cut-Out Cookies*

## 31 BROWNIE CARAMEL PECAN BARS

½ cup sugar
2 tablespoons butter or margarine
2 tablespoons water
2 cups (12-ounce package) HERSHEY'S Semi-Sweet Chocolate Chips, divided
2 eggs
1 teaspoon vanilla extract
⅔ cup all-purpose flour
¼ teaspoon baking soda
¼ teaspoon salt
CARAMEL TOPPING (recipe follows)
1 cup pecan pieces

**1.** Heat oven to 350°F. Line 9-inch square baking pan with foil, extending foil over edges of pan. Grease and flour foil.

**2.** In medium saucepan, combine sugar, butter and water; cook over low heat, stirring constantly, until mixture boils. Remove from heat. Immediately add 1 cup chocolate chips; stir until melted. Beat in eggs and vanilla until well blended. Stir together flour, baking soda and salt; stir into chocolate mixture. Spread batter into prepared pan.

**3.** Bake 15 to 20 minutes or until brownies begin to pull away from sides of pan. Meanwhile, prepare CARAMEL TOPPING. Remove brownies from oven; immediately and carefully spread with prepared topping. Sprinkle remaining 1 cup chips and pecans over topping. Cool completely in pan on wire rack, being careful not to disturb chips while soft. Lift out of pan. Cut into bars.

*Makes about 16 bars*

**CARAMEL TOPPING:** Remove wrappers from 25 caramels. In medium microwave-safe bowl, place ¼ cup (½ stick) butter or margarine, caramels and 2 tablespoons milk. Microwave at HIGH (100%) 1 minute; stir. Microwave an additional 1 to 2 minutes, stirring every 30 seconds, or until caramels are melted and mixture is smooth when stirred. Use immediately.

## 32 SMUCKER'S® GRANDMOTHER'S JELLY COOKIES

1 cup butter or margarine, softened
1½ cups sugar
1 egg
1½ teaspoons vanilla extract
3½ cups all-purpose flour
1 teaspoon salt
¾ cup SMUCKER'S® Red Raspberry, Strawberry or Peach Preserves

In a large bowl, cream together butter and sugar until light and fluffy. Add egg and vanilla; beat well. Stir in flour and salt; mix well. Stir to make a smooth dough. (If batter gets too hard to handle, mix with hands.)

Refrigerate about two hours.

Preheat oven to 375°. Lightly grease baking sheets. On a lightly floured board, roll out half of dough to about a ⅛-inch thickness. Cut with a 2½-inch cookie cutter. Roll out remaining dough; cut with a 2½-inch cutter with a hole in the middle. Place on baking sheets. Bake 8 to 10 minutes, or until lightly browned. Cool about 30 minutes.

To serve, spread preserves on plain cookie; top with a cookie with a hole.

*Makes approximately 3 dozen cookies*

*Brownie Caramel Pecan Bars*

## 33 DROP SUGAR COOKIES

2½ cups sifted all-purpose flour
¾ teaspoon salt
½ teaspoon ARM & HAMMER® Pure Baking
   Soda
½ cup butter or margarine, softened
½ cup vegetable shortening
1 cup sugar
1 egg
1 teaspoon vanilla extract
2 tablespoons milk

Preheat oven to 400°F. Sift together flour, salt and baking soda. Set aside. Beat butter and shortening in large bowl with electric mixer on medium speed until blended; add sugar gradually and continue beating until light and fluffy. Beat in egg and vanilla. Add flour mixture and beat until smooth; blend in milk. Drop dough by teaspoonfuls about 3 inches apart onto greased cookie sheets. Flatten with bottom of greased glass that has been dipped in sugar.

Bake 12 minutes or until edges are lightly browned. Cool on wire racks.

*Makes about 5½ dozen cookies*

## 34 OATMEAL APPLE COOKIES

1¼ cups firmly packed brown sugar
¾ BUTTER FLAVOR* CRISCO® Stick or
   ¾ cup BUTTER FLAVOR CRISCO
   all-vegetable shortening
¼ cup milk
1 egg
1½ teaspoons vanilla
1 cup all-purpose flour
1¼ teaspoons ground cinnamon
½ teaspoon salt
¼ teaspoon baking soda
¼ teaspoon ground nutmeg
3 cups quick-cooking oats (not instant or
   old-fashioned), uncooked
1 cup diced, peeled apples
¾ cup raisins (optional)
¾ cup coarsely chopped walnuts (optional)

*Butter Flavor Crisco is artificially flavored.*

**1.** Preheat oven to 375°F. Grease cookie sheet with shortening.

**2.** Combine brown sugar, shortening, milk, egg and vanilla in large bowl. Beat at medium speed of electric mixer until well blended and creamy.

**3.** Combine flour, cinnamon, salt, baking soda and nutmeg. Add gradually to creamed mixture at low speed. Mix just until blended. Stir in, one at a time, oats, apples, raisins and nuts with spoon. Drop by rounded tablespoonfuls 2 inches apart onto greased cookie sheet.

**4.** Bake at 375°F for 13 minutes or until set. Cool 2 minutes on cookie sheet before removing to wire rack.

*Makes about 2½ dozen cookies*

*Oatmeal Apple Cookies*

## 35 CRISPY NUT SHORTBREAD

6 tablespoons margarine, softened
⅓ cup sugar
1 egg
1 teaspoon vanilla
½ cup QUAKER® or AUNT JEMIMA®
    Enriched Corn Meal
½ cup all-purpose flour
½ cup finely chopped, husked, toasted
    hazelnuts or walnuts
½ cup semi-sweet chocolate pieces
1 tablespoon vegetable shortening
    Coarsely chopped nuts (optional)

Preheat oven to 300°F. Grease 13×9-inch baking pan. Beat margarine and sugar until fluffy. Blend in egg and vanilla. Add combined corn meal, flour and nuts; mix well. Spread onto bottom of prepared pan. Bake 40 to 45 minutes or until edges are golden brown.

In saucepan over low heat, melt chocolate pieces and shortening, stirring until smooth.* Spread over shortbread. Sprinkle with coarsely chopped nuts, if desired. Cool completely. Cut into 48 squares; cut diagonally into triangles. Store tightly covered.      *Makes 4 dozen cookies*

*Microwave directions: Place chocolate pieces and shortening in microwaveable bowl. Microwave at HIGH 1 to 2 minutes, stirring after 1 minute and then every 30 seconds until smooth.*

## 36 PEANUT BUTTER CHOCOLATE CHIPPERS

1 cup creamy or chunky peanut butter
1 cup packed light brown sugar
1 large egg
¾ cup milk chocolate chips
    Granulated sugar

**1.** Preheat oven to 350°F. Combine peanut butter, sugar and egg in medium bowl; mix with mixing spoon until well blended. Add chips; mix well.

**2.** Roll heaping tablespoonfuls of dough into 1½-inch balls. Place 2 inches apart on ungreased cookie sheets. Dip table fork into granulated sugar; press criss-cross fashion onto each ball, flattening to ½-inch thickness.

**3.** Bake 12 minutes or until set. Let cookies stand on cookie sheets 2 minutes. Remove cookies to wire racks; cool completely. Store tightly covered at room temperature or freeze up to 3 months.
      *Makes about 2 dozen cookies*

*Peanut Butter Chocolate Chippers*

# Chipperific Chips

## 37 CHOCOLATE CHIP 'N OATMEAL COOKIES

1 package (about 18 ounces) yellow cake mix
1 cup quick-cooking rolled oats
¾ cup (1½ sticks) butter or margarine, softened
2 eggs
1 cup HERSHEY'S Semi-Sweet Chocolate Chips

**1.** Heat oven to 350°F.

**2.** In large bowl, stir together cake mix, oats, butter and eggs; beat until well blended. Stir in chocolate chips. Drop by rounded teaspoons onto ungreased cookie sheet.

**3.** Bake 10 to 12 minutes or until very lightly browned. Cool slightly; remove from cookie sheet to wire rack. Cool completely.
*Makes about 4 dozen cookies*

## 38 CHOCOLATE CHIP WAFER COOKIES

½ cup butter or margarine, softened
½ cup sugar
1 egg
1 teaspoon vanilla
½ cup all-purpose flour
Dash salt
1 cup (6 ounces) semisweet chocolate chips
⅓ cup chopped pecans or walnuts

Preheat oven to 350°F. Line cookie sheets with foil; lightly grease foil.

Beat butter and sugar in large bowl until light and fluffy. Add egg; beat until creamy. Stir in vanilla, flour and salt. Add chocolate chips and nuts; mix until well blended. Drop dough by teaspoonfuls 3 inches apart onto prepared cookie sheets.

Bake 7 to 10 minutes or until edges are golden and centers are set. (Cookies are soft when hot, but become crispy as they cool.) Cool completely on foil, then peel foil from cookies.      *Makes about 2 dozen cookies*

*Chocolate Chip 'n Oatmeal Cookies*

## 39 SPICY RUM CORN CRISPS

1 cup (2 sticks) butter or margarine, softened
¾ cup firmly packed light brown sugar
1 teaspoon vanilla extract
½ teaspoon rum extract
1½ cups all-purpose flour
¾ cup yellow cornmeal
1 teaspoon ground ginger
1 teaspoon ground nutmeg
¼ teaspoon ground allspice
¼ teaspoon ground black pepper
1¾ cups "M&M's"® Chocolate Mini Baking Bits, divided

Preheat oven to 350°F. In large bowl cream butter and sugar until light and fluffy. Blend in vanilla and rum extracts. In medium bowl combine flour, cornmeal, ginger, nutmeg, allspice and pepper; stir into creamed mixture just until blended. Stir in *1 cup "M&M's"® Chocolate Mini Baking Bits.* On lightly floured surface, carefully roll dough into 12×8-inch rectangle. Press remaining ¾ *cup "M&M's"® Chocolate Mini Baking Bits* into top before cutting into 48 pieces. Transfer to ungreased cookie sheets. Bake 12 to 14 minutes or until lightly browned. Cool completely on wire racks. Store in tightly covered container.

*Makes about 4 dozen cookies*

## 40 LOW FAT CHOCOLATE CHIP COOKIES

1 cup Prune Purée (recipe follows) or prepared prune butter
¾ cup granulated sugar
¾ cup packed brown sugar
3 egg whites
1 teaspoon vanilla
2¼ cups all-purpose flour
1 teaspoon baking soda
1 teaspoon salt
2 cups (12 ounces) semisweet chocolate chips

Preheat oven to 375°F. Coat baking sheets with vegetable cooking spray. In large bowl, beat prune purée, sugars, egg whites and vanilla until well blended. In small bowl, combine flour, baking soda and salt; mix into prune purée mixture until well blended. Stir in chocolate chips. Drop tablespoonfuls of dough onto prepared baking sheets, spacing 2 inches apart; flatten slightly. Bake in center of oven about 10 minutes until lightly browned around edges. Remove from baking sheets to wire racks to cool completely.

*Makes about 60 (2¼-inch) cookies*

**PRUNE PURÉE:** Combine 1⅓ cups (8 ounces) pitted prunes and 6 tablespoons hot water in container of food processor or blender. Pulse on and off until prunes are finely chopped and smooth. Store leftovers in a covered container in the refrigerator for up to two months.

*Favorite recipe from* **California Prune Board**

*Spicy Rum Corn Crisps*

## CHIPPERIFIC CHIPS

### 41 CARAMEL NUT CHOCOLATE COOKIES

1½ cups firmly packed light brown sugar
⅔ CRISCO® Stick or ⅔ cup CRISCO all-vegetable shortening
1 tablespoon water
1 teaspoon vanilla
2 eggs
1¾ cups all-purpose flour
⅓ cup unsweetened cocoa powder
½ teaspoon salt
¼ teaspoon baking soda
2 cups (12 ounces) miniature semisweet chocolate chips
1 cup chopped pecans
20 to 25 caramels, unwrapped and halved

1. Heat oven to 375°F. Place sheets of foil on countertop for cooling cookies.

2. Place brown sugar, shortening, water and vanilla in large bowl. Beat at medium speed of electric mixer until well blended. Add eggs; beat well.

3. Combine flour, cocoa, salt and baking soda. Add to shortening mixture; beat at low speed just until blended. Stir in small chocolate chips.

4. Shape dough into 1¼-inch balls. Dip tops in chopped pecans. Place 2 inches apart on ungreased baking sheet. Press caramel half in center of each ball.

5. Bake one baking sheet at a time at 375°F for 7 to 9 minutes or until cookies are set. *Do not overbake.* Cool 2 minutes on baking sheet. Remove cookies to foil to cool completely.

*Makes about 4 dozen cookies*

### 42 CHOCOLATE CHIP RUGALACH

1 cup (2 sticks) butter or margarine, slightly softened
2 cups all-purpose flour
1 cup vanilla ice cream, softened
½ cup strawberry jam
1 cup BAKER'S® Semi-Sweet Real Chocolate Chips
1 cup finely chopped nuts
   Powdered sugar

**BEAT** butter and flour. Beat in ice cream until well blended. Divide dough into 4 balls; wrap each in waxed paper. Refrigerate until firm, about 1 hour.

**HEAT** oven to 350°F. Roll dough, one ball at a time, on floured surface into 11×6-inch rectangle, about ⅛ inch thick. Spread with 2 tablespoons of the jam; sprinkle with ¼ cup of the chips and ¼ cup of the nuts. Roll up lengthwise as for jelly roll. Place on ungreased cookie sheet. Cut 12 diagonal slits in roll, being careful not to cut all the way through. Repeat with the remaining dough.

**BAKE** for 35 minutes or until golden brown. Cool 5 minutes on cookie sheet. Cut through each roll; separate pieces. Finish cooling on wire racks. Sprinkle with powdered sugar, if desired. *Makes 4 dozen pieces*

**Prep Time:** 30 minutes
**Chill Time:** 1 hour
**Bake Time:** 35 minutes

*Caramel Nut Chocolate Cookies*

## CHIPPERIFIC CHIPS

### 43 CANNED PEANUT BUTTER CANDY COOKIES

¾ **cup chunky peanut butter**
½ **cup butter or margarine, softened**
1 **cup packed light brown sugar**
½ **teaspoon baking powder**
½ **teaspoon baking soda**
1 **egg**
1½ **teaspoons vanilla**
1¼ **cups all-purpose flour**
2 **cups quartered miniature peanut butter cups**
⅓ **cup milk chocolate chips or chopped milk chocolate bar**

**EQUIPMENT:**
   **Decorative container**

**1.** Beat peanut butter and butter in large bowl with electric mixer at medium speed until well blended. Beat in sugar, baking powder and baking soda until well blended. Beat in egg and vanilla until well blended. Beat in flour at low speed just until combined. Stir in peanut butter cups with wooden spoon. Cover with plastic wrap. Refrigerate 1 hour or until firm.

**2.** Preheat oven to 375°F. For test cookie, measure inside diameter of container. Form ⅓ cup dough into ¼-inch-thick disc, about 2 inches in diameter less than the diameter of container. One-third cup dough patted into 4-inch disc yields 5-inch cookie. (Measure amount of dough used and diameter of cookie before and after baking. Make adjustments before making remaining cookies.)

**3.** Place cookies on *ungreased* baking sheet. Bake 10 minutes or until lightly browned. Remove with spatula to wire racks; cool completely.

**4.** Place chocolate in small resealable plastic freezer bag; seal bag. Microwave at MEDIUM (50% power) 1 minute. Turn bag over; microwave at MEDIUM 1 minute or until melted. Knead bag until chocolate is smooth. Cut off very tiny corner of bag; pipe chocolate decoratively onto cookies. Let stand until chocolate is set.

**5.** Stack cookies between layers of waxed paper in container. Store loosely covered at room temperature up to 1 week.
*Makes 9 (5-inch) cookies*

### 44 WHITE CHIP APRICOT OATMEAL COOKIES

¾ **cup (1½ sticks) butter or margarine, softened**
½ **cup granulated sugar**
½ **cup packed light brown sugar**
1 **egg**
1 **cup all-purpose flour**
1 **teaspoon baking soda**
2½ **cups rolled oats**
1⅔ **cups (10-ounce package) HERSHEY®S Premier White Chips**
½ **cup chopped dried apricots**

**1.** Heat oven to 375°F.

**2.** In large bowl, beat butter, granulated sugar and brown sugar until light and fluffy. Add egg; beat well. Add flour and baking soda; beat until well blended. Stir in oats, white chips and apricots. Loosely form rounded teaspoonfuls batter into balls; place on ungreased cookie sheet.

**3.** Bake 7 to 9 minutes or just until lightly browned; do not overbake. Cool slightly; remove from cookie sheet to wire rack. Cool completely.
*Makes about 3½ dozen cookies*

*Canned Peanut Butter Candy Cookies*

## 45 CHOCOLATE RASPBERRY THUMBPRINTS

½ cup (1 stick) butter or margarine, softened
½ cup granulated sugar
½ cup firmly packed light brown sugar
1 large egg
1 teaspoon vanilla extract
2 cups all-purpose flour
½ teaspoon baking powder
1¾ cups "M&M's"® Chocolate Mini Baking Bits, divided
Powdered sugar
½ cup raspberry jam

In large microwave-safe bowl melt butter in microwave; add sugars and mix well. Stir in egg and vanilla. In medium bowl combine flour and baking powder; blend into butter mixture. Stir in *1¼ cups "M&M's"®* *Chocolate Mini Baking Bits;* refrigerate dough 1 hour. Preheat oven to 350°F. Lightly grease cookie sheets. Roll dough into 1-inch balls and place about 2 inches apart onto prepared cookie sheets. Make an indentation in center of each ball with thumb. Bake 8 to 10 minutes. Remove from oven and reindent, if necessary; transfer to wire racks. Lightly dust warm cookies with powdered sugar; fill each indentation with ½ teaspoon raspberry jam. Sprinkle with remaining *½ cup "M&M's"®* *Chocolate Mini Baking Bits.* Cool completely. Dust with additional powdered sugar, if desired. Store in tightly covered container.

*Makes about 4 dozen cookies*

## 46 CHERRY CASHEW COOKIES

1 cup butter or margarine, softened
¾ cup granulated sugar
¾ cup firmly packed brown sugar
2 eggs
1 teaspoon vanilla extract
2¼ cups all-purpose flour
1 teaspoon baking soda
1 package (10 ounces) vanilla milk chips or 1⅔ cups coarsely chopped white chocolate
1½ cups dried tart cherries
1 cup lightly salted cashews

In a large mixing bowl, combine butter, granulated sugar, brown sugar, eggs and vanilla. Mix with electric mixer on medium speed until thoroughly mixed. Combine flour and baking soda; gradually add flour mixture to butter mixture. Stir in vanilla milk chips, dried cherries and cashews. Drop by rounded tablespoonfuls onto ungreased baking sheets.

Bake in a preheated 375°F oven 12 to 15 minutes, or until golden brown. Let cool on wire racks; store in a tightly covered container. *Makes 4½ dozen cookies.*

*Favorite recipe from* **Cherry Marketing Institute, Inc.**

*Chocolate Raspberry Thumbprints*

## 47 BRIAN'S BUFFALO COOKIES

1 BUTTER FLAVOR* CRISCO® Stick or
   1 cup BUTTER FLAVOR CRISCO
   all-vegetable shortening, melted
1 cup granulated sugar
1 cup firmly packed brown sugar
2 tablespoons milk
1 teaspoon vanilla
2 eggs
2 cups all-purpose flour
1 teaspoon baking powder
1 teaspoon baking soda
½ teaspoon salt
1 cup rolled oats (quick or old fashioned),
   uncooked
1 cup cornflakes cereal, crushed to about
   ½ cup
1 cup semisweet chocolate chips
½ cup chopped pecans
½ cup flake coconut

*Butter Flavor Crisco is artificially flavored.

**1. Heat** oven to 350°F. **Grease** baking sheets with shortening. **Place** sheets of foil on countertop for cooling cookies.

**2. Combine** shortening, granulated sugar, brown sugar, milk and vanilla in large bowl. **Beat** at low speed of electric mixer until well blended. **Add** eggs; beat at medium speed until well blended.

**3. Combine** flour, baking powder, baking soda and salt. **Add** gradually to shortening mixture at low speed. **Stir** in oats, cereal, chocolate chips, nuts and coconut. **Scoop** out about ¼ cupful of dough for each cookie. **Level** with knife. **Drop** 3 inches apart onto prepared baking sheets.

**4. Bake** one baking sheet at a time at 350°F for 13 to 15 minutes or until lightly browned around edges but still slightly soft in center.

*Do not overbake.* **Cool** 3 minutes on baking sheets. **Remove** cookies to foil with wide, thin spatula.

*Makes 2 to 2½ dozen cookies*

## 48 CHOCO–SCUTTERBOTCH

⅔ BUTTER FLAVOR* CRISCO® Stick or
   ⅔ cup BUTTER FLAVOR CRISCO
   all-vegetable shortening
½ cup firmly packed brown sugar
2 eggs
1 package DUNCAN HINES® Moist
   Deluxe Yellow Cake Mix
1 cup crispy rice cereal
½ cup milk chocolate chunks
½ cup butterscotch chips
½ cup semisweet chocolate chips
½ cup coarsely chopped walnuts or pecans

*Butter Flavor Crisco is artificially flavored.

**1.** Preheat oven to 375°F.

**2.** Combine shortening and brown sugar in large bowl. Beat at medium speed of electric mixer until well blended. Beat in eggs. Add cake mix gradually at low speed. Mix until well blended. Stir in cereal, chocolate chunks, butterscotch chips, chocolate chips and nuts with spoon. Stir until well blended. Shape dough into 1¼-inch balls. Place 2 inches apart on ungreased baking sheets. Flatten slightly to form circles. Bake at 375°F for 7 to 9 minutes or until lightly browned around edges. Cool 2 minutes before removing to cooling racks. Cool completely. Store in airtight container.

*Makes about 3 dozen cookies*

*Choco-Scutterbotch*

## 49 JUMBO CHUNKY COOKIES

1 cup (2 sticks) margarine or butter, softened
¾ cup packed brown sugar
¾ cup granulated sugar
2 eggs
1 teaspoon vanilla
1¾ cups all-purpose flour
½ cup quick oats
1 teaspoon baking soda
½ teaspoon cinnamon
¼ teaspoon salt
1 (8-ounce) package BAKER'S® Semi-Sweet Chocolate, cut into chunks, or 1 (12-ounce) package BAKER'S® Semi-Sweet Real Chocolate Chips
1 cup BAKER'S® ANGEL FLAKE® Coconut
⅔ cup chopped nuts
½ cup raisins (optional)

**Heat** oven to 375°F.

**Beat** margarine, sugars, eggs and vanilla until light and fluffy. Mix in flour, oats, baking soda, cinnamon and salt.

**Stir** in chocolate, coconut, nuts and raisins, if desired. Drop by rounded tablespoonfuls, 2½ inches apart, onto ungreased cookie sheets.

**Bake** for 15 minutes or until golden brown. Remove from cookie sheets to cool on wire racks.          *Makes about 2½ dozen cookies*

**Prep Time:** 20 minutes
**Bake Time:** 15 minutes

## 50 CRUNCHY CHOCOLATE CHIPSTERS

1¼ cups packed light brown sugar
¾ BUTTER FLAVOR* CRISCO® Stick or ¾ cup BUTTER FLAVOR CRISCO all-vegetable shortening
2 tablespoons milk
1 tablespoon vanilla
1 egg
1½ cups flour
1 teaspoon salt
¾ teaspoon baking soda
2 cups crispy rice cereal
1 cup semisweet miniature chocolate chips

*Butter Flavor Crisco is artificially flavored.*

**1. Heat** oven to 375°F. **Place** sheets of foil on countertop for cooling cookies.

**2. Combine** brown sugar, shortening, milk and vanilla in large bowl. **Beat** at medium speed of electric mixer until well blended. **Beat** egg into shortening mixture.

**3. Combine** flour, salt and baking soda. **Mix** into shortening mixture just until blended. **Stir** in cereal and chocolate chips.

**4. Drop** by rounded tablespoonfuls 2 inches apart onto ungreased baking sheets.

**5. Bake** one baking sheet at a time at 375°F for 10 to 12 minutes. *Do not overbake.* **Cool** 2 minutes on baking sheets. **Remove** cookies to foil to cool completely.
          *Makes about 3 dozen cookies*

*Top to bottom: Jumbo Chunky Cookies and Microwave Chewy Granola Squares (page 156)*

## 51 IVORY CHIP STRAWBERRY FUDGE DROPS

²/₃ **BUTTER FLAVOR* CRISCO®** Stick or
    ²/₃ cup **BUTTER FLAVOR CRISCO**
    all-vegetable shortening
 1 cup sugar
 1 egg
 ½ teaspoon strawberry extract
 ½ cup buttermilk**
 6 tablespoons puréed frozen sweetened
    strawberries
1¾ cups all-purpose flour
 6 tablespoons unsweetened cocoa powder
 ¾ teaspoon baking soda
 ½ teaspoon salt
1½ cups white chocolate baking chips or
    white chocolate bar, cut into pieces

*Butter Flavor Crisco is artificially flavored.*

**You may substitute 1½ teaspoons lemon juice or
vinegar plus enough milk to make ½ cup for the
buttermilk. Stir. Wait 5 minutes before using.*

**1. Heat** oven to 350°F. **Grease** baking
sheets with shortening. **Place** sheets of foil
on countertop for cooling cookies.

**2. Combine** shortening, sugar, egg and
strawberry extract in large bowl. **Beat** at
medium speed of electric mixer until well
blended. **Beat** in buttermilk and strawberry
purée.

**3. Combine** flour, cocoa, baking soda and
salt. **Mix** into shortening mixture at low
speed of electric mixer until blended. **Stir** in
white chocolate chips.

**4. Drop** by rounded tablespoonfuls 2 inches
apart onto prepared baking sheets.

**5. Bake** one baking sheet at a time at 350°F
for 11 to 12 minutes or until tops spring back
when pressed lightly. *Do not overbake.* **Cool**
2 minutes on baking sheets. **Remove**
cookies to foil to cool completely.
*Makes about 2½ dozen cookies*

## 52 DOUBLE NUT CHOCOLATE CHIP COOKIES

 1 package DUNCAN HINES® Moist
    Deluxe Yellow Cake Mix
 ½ cup butter or margarine, melted
 1 egg
 1 cup semi-sweet chocolate chips
 ½ cup finely chopped pecans
 1 cup sliced almonds, divided

**1.** Preheat oven to 375°F. Grease baking
sheet.

**2.** Combine cake mix, butter and egg in large
bowl. Mix at low speed with electric mixer
until just blended. Stir in chocolate chips,
pecans and ¼ cup of the almonds. Shape
rounded tablespoonfuls of dough into balls.
Place remaining ¾ cup almonds in shallow
bowl. Press tops of cookies in almonds.
Place 1 inch apart on greased baking sheet.
Bake at 375°F for 9 to 11 minutes or until
lightly browned. Cool 2 minutes on baking
sheet. Remove to cooling rack. Cool
completely. Store in airtight containers.
*Makes 3 to 3½ dozen cookies*

*Double Nut Chocolate Chip Cookies*

## 53 WHITE CHOCOLATE BIGGIES

1½ cups butter or margarine, softened
 1 cup granulated sugar
 ¾ cup packed light brown sugar
 2 teaspoons vanilla
 2 eggs
2½ cups all-purpose flour
 ⅔ cup unsweetened cocoa
 1 teaspoon baking soda
 ½ teaspoon salt
 1 package (10 ounces) large white chocolate chips
 ¾ cup pecan halves, coarsely chopped
 ½ cup golden raisins

Preheat oven to 350°F. Lightly grease cookie sheets or line with parchment paper. Cream butter, granulated sugar, brown sugar, vanilla and eggs in large bowl until light and fluffy. Combine flour, cocoa, baking soda and salt in medium bowl; blend into creamed mixture until smooth. Stir in white chocolate chips, pecans and raisins.

Scoop out about ⅓ cupful of dough for each cookie. Place on prepared cookie sheets, spacing about 4 inches apart. Press each cookie to flatten slightly.

Bake 12 to 14 minutes or until firm in center. Cool 5 minutes on cookie sheet, then remove to wire racks to cool completely.
*Makes about 2 dozen cookies*

## 54 HERSHEY'S MINT CHOCOLATE COOKIES

 ¾ cup (1½ sticks) butter or margarine, softened
 1 cup sugar
 1 egg
 1 teaspoon vanilla extract
1½ cups all-purpose flour
 ½ teaspoon baking soda
 ¼ teaspoon salt
1⅔ cups (10-ounce package) HERSHEY'S Mint Chocolate Chips

**1.** Heat oven to 350°F.

**2.** In large bowl, beat butter and sugar until light and fluffy. Add egg and vanilla; beat well. Stir together flour, baking soda and salt; gradually blend into butter mixture. Stir in chocolate chips. Drop by rounded teaspoonfuls onto ungreased cookie sheet.

**3.** Bake 8 to 9 minutes or just until lightly browned. Cool slightly; remove from cookie sheet to wire rack. Cool completely.
*Makes about 2½ dozen cookies*

*Peanut Butter Chip Orange Cookies*

## 55 PEANUT BUTTER CHIP ORANGE COOKIES

½ cup (1 stick) butter or margarine, softened
½ cup shortening
¾ cup granulated sugar
¾ cup packed light brown sugar
2 eggs
1 tablespoon freshly grated orange peel
1 teaspoon vanilla extract
2¼ cups all-purpose flour
1 teaspoon baking soda
1 teaspoon salt
¼ cup orange juice
1⅔ cups (10-ounce package) REESE'S® Peanut Butter Chips

**1.** Heat oven to 350°F.

**2.** In large bowl, beat butter, shortening, granulated sugar and brown sugar until light and fluffy. Add eggs, orange peel and vanilla; beat until blended. Stir together flour, baking soda and salt; add alternately with orange juice to butter mixture, beating until well blended. Stir in peanut butter chips. Drop by teaspoons onto ungreased cookie sheet.

**3.** Bake 8 to 10 minutes or until lightly browned. Cool slightly; remove from cookie sheet to wire rack. Cool completely.

*Makes about 6 dozen cookies*

## 56 COLORIFIC CHOCOLATE CHIP COOKIES

1 cup (2 sticks) butter or margarine, softened
⅔ cup granulated sugar
½ cup firmly packed light brown sugar
1 large egg
1 teaspoon vanilla extract
2 cups all-purpose flour
¾ teaspoon baking soda
¾ teaspoon salt
1¾ cups "M&M's"® Semi-Sweet Chocolate Mini Baking Bits
¾ cup chopped nuts, optional

Preheat oven to 375°F. In large bowl cream butter and sugars until light and fluffy; beat in egg and vanilla. In medium bowl combine flour, baking soda and salt; blend into creamed mixture. Stir in "M&M's"® Semi-Sweet Chocolate Mini Baking Bits and nuts, if using. Drop by heaping tablespoonfuls about 2 inches apart onto ungreased cookie sheets. Bake 9 to 12 minutes or until lightly browned. Cool 1 minute on cookie sheets; cool completely on wire racks. Store in tightly covered container.

*Makes about 3 dozen cookies*

**HINT:** For chewy cookies bake 9 to 10 minutes; for crispy cookies bake 11 to 12 minutes.

**PAN COOKIE VARIATION:** Prepare dough as directed; spread into lightly greased 15×10×1-inch jelly-roll pan. Bake at 375°F for 18 to 22 minutes. Cool completely before cutting into 35 (2-inch) squares. For a more festive look, reserve ½ cup baking bits to sprinkle on top of dough before baking.

## 57 DOUBLE PEANUT BUTTER JOY

1 cup granulated sugar
1 cup firmly packed brown sugar
1 cup JIF® Creamy Peanut Butter
½ BUTTER FLAVOR* CRISCO® Stick or ½ cup BUTTER FLAVOR CRISCO all-vegetable shortening
2 eggs
1½ cups all-purpose flour
½ teaspoon baking soda
¼ teaspoon salt
2 cups peanut butter chips

*Butter Flavor Crisco is artificially flavored.*

**1.** Preheat oven to 350°F.

**2.** Combine granulated sugar, brown sugar, peanut butter and shortening in large bowl. Beat at medium speed of electric mixer until well blended and creamy. Add eggs, one at a time, beating after each addition.

**3.** Combine flour, baking soda and salt. Add gradually to creamed mixture at low speed. Mix just until well blended. Stir in peanut butter chips with spoon. (Dough will be stiff.) Shape into 1½-inch balls. Place 2 inches apart on ungreased cookie sheet. Make crisscross marks on top with floured forked tines, smoothing edges of cookies, if necessary.

**4.** Bake at 350°F for 8 to 10 minutes or until edges are set and tops are moist. Cool about 8 minutes on cookie sheet before removing to wire rack.

*Makes about 3 dozen cookies*

*Colorific Chocolate Chip Cookies*

## 58 DREAMY CHOCOLATE CHIP COOKIES

1¼ cups firmly packed brown sugar
¾ BUTTER FLAVOR* CRISCO® Stick or
    ¾ cup BUTTER FLAVOR CRISCO
    all-vegetable shortening
3 eggs, lightly beaten
2 teaspoons vanilla
1 (4-ounce) package German sweet
    chocolate, melted, cooled
3 cups all-purpose flour
1 teaspoon baking soda
½ teaspoon salt
1 (11½-ounce) package milk chocolate
    chips
1 (10-ounce) package premium semisweet
    chocolate pieces
1 cup coarsely chopped macadamia nuts

*Butter Flavor Crisco is artificially flavored.*

1. **Heat** oven to 375°F. **Place** sheets of foil on countertop for cooling cookies.

2. **Combine** brown sugar, shortening, eggs and vanilla in large bowl. **Beat** at low speed of electric mixer until blended. **Increase** speed to high. **Beat** 2 minutes. **Add** melted chocolate. **Mix** until well blended.

3. **Combine** flour, baking soda and salt. **Add** gradually to shortening mixture at low speed.

4. **Stir** in chocolate chips, chocolate pieces and nuts with spoon. **Drop** by rounded tablespoonfuls 3 inches apart onto ungreased baking sheets.

5. **Bake** one baking sheet at a time at 375°F for 9 to 11 minutes or until set. *Do not overbake.* **Cool** 2 minutes on baking sheets. **Remove** cookies to foil to cool completely.
*Makes about 3 dozen cookies*

## 59 MARBLED MOCHA DROPS

1 cup (2 sticks) butter or margarine,
    softened
⅔ cup granulated sugar
⅔ cup firmly packed light brown sugar
1 large egg
2 tablespoons instant coffee granules,
    dissolved in 1 tablespoon water
1 teaspoon vanilla extract
2¼ cups all-purpose flour
1 teaspoon baking soda
½ teaspoon salt
¾ cup coarsely chopped nuts
¼ cup unsweetened cocoa powder
1¾ cups "M&M's"® Semi-Sweet Chocolate
    Mini Baking Bits

Preheat oven to 350°F. In large bowl cream butter and sugars until light and fluffy; add egg, dissolved coffee granules and vanilla. In medium bowl combine flour, baking soda and salt. Blend flour mixture and nuts into creamed mixture. Remove half of the dough to small bowl; set aside. Blend cocoa powder into remaining dough. Stir "M&M's"® Semi-Sweet Chocolate Mini Baking Bits into the two doughs, using half for each. Combine two doughs by folding together just enough to marble, about 4 strokes. Drop by heaping tablespoonfuls about 2 inches apart onto ungreased cookie sheets. Bake 10 to 12 minutes or just until set. *Do not overbake.* Cool 1 minute on cookie sheets; cool completely on wire racks. Store in tightly covered container.
*Makes about 2½ dozen cookies*

## CHIPPERIFIC CHIPS

### 60 WALNUT–ORANGE CHOCOLATE CHIPPERS

1½ cups all-purpose flour
½ cup packed brown sugar
½ cup granulated sugar
1½ teaspoons baking powder
½ teaspoon salt
⅓ cup butter, softened
2 eggs, slightly beaten
2 cups (12 ounces) semisweet chocolate chips
1 cup coarsely chopped California walnuts
2 tablespoons grated orange peel

Combine flour, brown sugar, granulated sugar, baking powder and salt in large bowl; mix in butter and eggs. Add remaining ingredients and mix thoroughly (batter will be stiff). Spread dough evenly into greased and floured 9-inch square pan (use wet hands to smooth). Bake at 350°F 25 minutes or until golden brown. Cool; cut into squares.          *Makes 36 squares*

*Favorite recipe from* **Walnut Marketing Board**

### 61 PINEAPPLE OATMEAL "SCOTCHIES"

2 cans (8 ounces each) DOLE® Crushed Pineapple
1½ cups margarine
1½ cups packed brown sugar
1 egg
3 cups rolled oats
2 cups all-purpose flour
1 teaspoon baking powder
1 teaspoon ground cinnamon
½ teaspoon salt
6 ounces butterscotch chips

• Drain pineapple well; save juice for a beverage.

• Beat margarine and sugar until light and fluffy. Beat in egg and pineapple.

• Combine oats, flour, baking powder, cinnamon and salt; blend into pineapple mixture. Stir in chips.

• Drop by two tablespoonsful onto cookie sheets coated with cooking spray; flatten top with back of spoon. Bake in 375°F oven 20 minutes or until brown.
*Makes 3½ dozen cookies*

**Prep Time:** 20 minutes
**Bake Time:** 20 minutes/batch

## 62 PUMPKIN WHITE CHOCOLATE DROPS

2 cups butter or margarine, softened
2 cups granulated sugar
1 can (16 ounces) solid pack pumpkin
2 eggs
4 cups all-purpose flour
2 tablespoons pumpkin pie spice
1 teaspoon baking powder
½ teaspoon baking soda
1 bag (12 ounces) vanilla baking chips
1 container (16 ounces) ready-to-spread cream cheese frosting
¼ cup packed brown sugar

1. Preheat oven to 375°F. Beat butter and sugar in large bowl until light and fluffy. Add pumpkin and eggs; beat until smooth. Add flour, pumpkin pie spice, baking powder and baking soda; beat just until well blended. Stir in baking chips.

2. Drop dough by teaspoonfuls 2 inches apart onto ungreased baking sheets. Bake 10 to 14 minutes or until set and bottoms are brown. Cool 1 minute on baking sheets. Remove from baking sheets to wire rack to cool.

3. Combine frosting and brown sugar in small bowl. Spread on warm cookies.
*Makes about 6 dozen cookies*

**TIP:** These cookies work great if you want to make the dough ahead and bake the cookies later. Simply prepare the cookie dough and drop by 2 teaspoonfuls onto wax-paper lined baking sheets. Freeze about 1½ hours or until firm. Transfer cookie dough to resealable plastic food storage bags; freeze

up to 2 months. Place frozen cookies about 2 inches apart onto ungreased baking sheets; bake 12 to 16 minutes or until set and bottoms are brown. Cool 1 minute on baking sheets. Remove from baking sheets to wire rack to cool.

## 63 OATMEAL CRANBERRY WHITE CHOCOLATE CHUNK COOKIES

⅔ cup butter or margarine, softened
⅔ cup brown sugar
2 eggs
1½ cups oats
1½ cups flour
1 teaspoon baking soda
½ teaspoon salt
1 (6-ounce) package CRAISINS® Sweetened Dried Cranberries
⅔ cup white chocolate chunks or chips

Preheat oven to 375°.

Using an electric mixer, beat butter or margarine and sugar together in a medium mixing bowl until light and fluffy. Add eggs, mixing well. Combine oats, flour, baking soda and salt in a separate mixing bowl. Add to butter mixture in several additions, mixing well after each addition. Stir in dried cranberries and white chocolate chunks.

Drop by rounded teaspoonfuls onto ungreased cookie sheets. Bake for 10 to 12 minutes or until golden brown.
*Makes 2½ dozen cookies*

*Pumpkin White Chocolate Drops*

## CHIPPERIFIC CHIPS

### 64 SOUR CREAM CHOCOLATE CHIP COOKIES

1 BUTTER FLAVOR* CRISCO® Stick or
   1 cup BUTTER FLAVOR CRISCO
   all-vegetable shortening
1 cup packed brown sugar
½ cup granulated sugar
1 egg
½ cup sour cream
¼ cup warm honey
2 teaspoons vanilla
2½ cups all-purpose flour
1½ teaspoons baking powder
½ teaspoon salt
2 cups semisweet or milk chocolate chips
1 cup coarsely chopped walnuts

*Butter Flavor Crisco is artificially flavored.*

1. **Heat** oven to 375°F. **Grease** baking sheets with shortening. **Place** sheets of foil on countertop for cooling cookies.

2. **Combine** shortening, brown sugar and granulated sugar in large bowl. **Beat** at medium speed of electric mixer until well blended. **Beat** in egg, sour cream, honey and vanilla. **Beat** until just blended.

3. **Combine** flour, baking powder and salt. **Mix** into shortening mixture at low speed until just blended. **Stir** in chocolate chips and nuts.

4. **Drop** slightly rounded measuring tablespoonfuls of dough 2 inches apart onto prepared baking sheets.

5. **Bake** one baking sheet at a time at 375°F for 10 to 12 minutes or until set. *Do not overbake.* **Cool** 2 minutes on baking sheets. **Remove** cookies to foil to cool completely.
*Makes about 5 dozen cookies*

### 65 PUDDING CHIP COOKIES

1 cup PARKAY® Margarine, softened
¾ cup firmly packed light brown sugar
¼ cup granulated sugar
1 package (4-serving size) JELL-O® Instant
   Pudding and Pie Filling, Butter Pecan,
   Butterscotch, Chocolate, Milk
   Chocolate, Chocolate Fudge, French
   Vanilla or Vanilla Flavor
1 teaspoon vanilla
2 eggs
2¼ cups all-purpose flour
1 teaspoon baking soda
1 package (12 ounces) BAKER'S®
   Semi-Sweet Real Chocolate Chips
1 cup chopped nuts (optional)

Preheat oven to 375°F. Beat margarine, sugars, pudding mix and vanilla in large bowl until smooth and creamy. Beat in eggs. Gradually add flour and baking soda. Stir in chips and nuts. (Dough will be stiff.) Drop by teaspoonfuls 2 inches apart onto ungreased cookie sheets.

Bake 8 to 10 minutes or until lightly browned. Remove from cookie sheets; cool on racks.     *Makes about 7 dozen cookies*

**Prep Time:** 30 minutes
**Bake Time:** 30 minutes

*Sour Cream Chocolate Chip Cookies*

## 66 OATMEAL CANDIED CHIPPERS

¾ cup all-purpose flour
¾ teaspoon salt
½ teaspoon baking soda
¾ cup butter or margarine, softened
¾ cup granulated sugar
¾ cup packed light brown sugar
3 tablespoons milk
1 large egg
2 teaspoons vanilla
3 cups uncooked quick-cooking or
   old-fashioned oats
1⅓ cups (10-ounce package) candy-coated
   semisweet chocolate chips*

*Or, substitute 1 cup (8-ounce package) candy coated milk chocolate chips.*

**1.** Preheat oven to 375°F. Grease cookie sheets; set aside.

**2.** Place flour, salt and baking soda in small bowl; stir to combine.

**3.** Beat butter, granulated sugar and brown sugar in large bowl with electric mixer at medium speed until light and fluffy. Add milk, egg and vanilla; beat well. Add flour mixture. Beat at low speed. Stir in oats and chips.

**4.** Drop dough by tablespoonfuls 2 inches apart on prepared cookie sheets.** Bake 10 to 11 minutes or until edges are golden brown. Let cookies stand 2 minutes on cookie sheets. Remove cookies to wire racks; cool completely.

**5.** Store tightly covered at room temperature or freeze up to 3 months.

*Makes about 4 dozen cookies*

***Or, use a small ice cream scoop, #80, filled with dough and pressed against the side of the bowl to level.*

## 67 SOFT BANANA CHIP COOKIES

1 cup shortening
1½ cups sugar
2 eggs
1 teaspoon vanilla extract
2¾ cups all-purpose flour
1½ teaspoons baking soda
½ teaspoon salt
½ cup buttermilk or sour milk*
1 cup mashed ripe bananas (3 medium)
1 cup chopped nuts
2 cups (12-ounce package) HERSHEY'S
   Semi-Sweet Chocolate Chips OR
   2 cups (11.5-ounce package)
   HERSHEY'S Milk Chocolate Chips

*To sour milk: Use 1½ teaspoons white vinegar plus enough milk to equal ½ cup.*

**1.** Heat oven to 375°F. Lightly grease cookie sheet.

**2.** In large bowl, beat shortening and sugar until well blended. Add eggs and vanilla; beat well. Stir together flour, baking soda and salt; add alternately with buttermilk and bananas to shortening mixture, beating until well blended. Stir in nuts and chocolate chips. (Dough will be soft.) Drop by teaspoons onto prepared cookie sheet.

**3.** Bake 8 to 10 minutes or until lightly browned. Cool slightly; remove from cookie sheet to wire rack. Cool completely.

*Makes about 7 dozen cookies*

*Oatmeal Candied Chippers*

## CHIPPERIFIC CHIPS

### 68 PEANUT BUTTER CHIP TASSIES

1 package (3 ounces) cream cheese, softened
½ cup (1 stick) butter, softened
1 cup all-purpose flour
1 egg, slightly beaten
½ cup sugar
2 tablespoons butter, melted
¼ teaspoon lemon juice
¼ teaspoon vanilla extract
1 cup REESE'S® Peanut Butter Chips, chopped*
6 red candied cherries, quartered (optional)

*Do not chop peanut butter chips in food processor or blender.*

**1.** In medium bowl, beat cream cheese and ½ cup butter; stir in flour. Cover; refrigerate about one hour or until dough is firm. Shape into 24 one-inch balls; place each ball into ungreased, small muffin cups (1¾ inches in diameter). Press dough evenly against bottom and sides of each cup.

**2.** Heat oven to 350°F.

**3.** In medium bowl, combine egg, sugar, melted butter, lemon juice and vanilla; stir until smooth. Add chopped peanut butter chips. Fill muffin cups ¾ full with mixture.

**4.** Bake 20 to 25 minutes or until filling is set and lightly browned. Cool completely; remove from pan to wire rack. Garnish with candied cherries, if desired.

*Makes about 2 dozen*

### 69 CHOCOLATE CHIP CINNAMON CRINKLES

½ cup butter or margarine, softened
½ cup firmly packed brown sugar
¼ cup plus 2 tablespoons granulated sugar, divided
1 egg
1 teaspoon vanilla
1 teaspoon cream of tartar
½ teaspoon baking soda
⅛ teaspoon salt
1⅓ cups all-purpose flour
1 cup (6 ounces) semisweet chocolate chips
2 teaspoons unsweetened cocoa
1 teaspoon ground cinnamon

Preheat oven to 400°F. Line cookie sheets with parchment paper or leave ungreased.

Beat butter, brown sugar, ¼ cup granulated sugar, egg and vanilla in large bowl until light and fluffy. Beat in cream of tartar, baking soda and salt. Add flour; mix until dough is blended and stiff. Stir in chocolate chips. Combine remaining 2 tablespoons granulated sugar, cocoa and cinnamon in small bowl. Shape rounded teaspoonfuls of dough into balls about 1¼ inches in diameter. Roll balls in cinnamon mixture until coated on all sides. Place 2 inches apart on cookie sheets.

Bake 8 to 10 minutes or until firm. Do not overbake. Remove to wire racks to cool.

*Makes about 3½ dozen cookies*

*Peanut Butter Chip Tassies*

## 70 RASPBERRY FRECKLES

### COOKIES

1 cup sugar
½ BUTTER FLAVOR* CRISCO® Stick or ½ cup BUTTER FLAVOR CRISCO all-vegetable shortening
1 egg
1 tablespoon raspberry-flavored liqueur
2⅔ cups all-purpose flour
1 teaspoon baking powder
½ teaspoon baking soda
½ teaspoon salt
½ cup sour cream
1 cup cubed (⅛- to ¼-inch) white confectionery coating
¾ cup mini semisweet chocolate chips
½ cup (2¼-ounce bag) crushed, sliced almonds

### TOPPING

¼ cup seedless red raspberry jam
1 teaspoon raspberry-flavored liqueur
⅓ cup chopped white confectionery coating
2 teaspoons BUTTER FLAVOR CRISCO Stick or 2 teaspoons BUTTER FLAVOR CRISCO all-vegetable shortening

*Butter Flavor Crisco is artificially flavored.*

1. **Heat** oven to 375°F. **Grease** baking sheets with shortening. **Place** sheets of foil on countertop for cooling cookies.

2. For cookies, **combine** sugar and shortening in large bowl. **Stir** with spoon until well blended. **Stir** in egg and 1 tablespoon liqueur.

3. **Combine** flour, baking powder, baking soda and salt. **Add** alternately with sour cream to shortening mixture. **Stir** in cubed confectionery coating, chocolate chips and almonds.

4. **Roll** dough to ¼-inch thickness on floured surface. **Cut** with 3-inch scalloped round cutter. **Place** 2 inches apart on prepared baking sheets.

5. **Bake** one baking sheet at a time at 375°F for 7 minutes or just until beginning to brown. *Do not overbake.* **Cool** 2 minutes on baking sheets. **Remove** cookies to foil to cool completely.

6. For topping, **combine** raspberry jam and 1 teaspoon liqueur in microwave-safe measuring cup or bowl. **Microwave** at MEDIUM (50%) until jam melts (or melt on rangetop in small saucepan on very low heat). **Drop** mixture in 10 to 12 dots to resemble freckles on top of each cookie.

7. **Combine** chopped confectionery coating and 2 teaspoons shortening in heavy resealable plastic food storage bag. **Seal.** **Microwave** at MEDIUM (50%). **Knead** bag after 1 minute. **Repeat** until smooth (or melt by placing in bowl of hot water). **Cut** pinpoint hole in corner of bag. **Squeeze** out and drizzle over cookies.

*Makes about 3 dozen cookies*

*Raspberry Freckles*

## 71 BANANA CHOCOLATE CHIP SOFTIES

    1 ripe, medium banana
1¼ cups all-purpose flour
    1 teaspoon baking powder
    ½ teaspoon salt
    ⅓ cup butter or margarine, softened
    ⅓ cup granulated sugar
    ⅓ cup packed light brown sugar
    1 large egg
    1 teaspoon vanilla
    1 cup milk chocolate chips
    ½ cup coarsely chopped walnuts (optional)

**1.** Preheat oven to 375°F. Lightly grease cookie sheets.

**2.** Mash enough banana with fork to measure ½ cup; set aside.

**3.** Place flour, baking powder and salt in small bowl; stir to combine.

**4.** Beat butter, granulated sugar and brown sugar in large bowl with electric mixer at medium speed until light and fluffy. Beat in banana, egg and vanilla. Add flour mixture. Beat at low speed until well blended. Stir in chips and walnuts. (Dough will be soft.)

**5.** Drop rounded teaspoonfuls of dough 2 inches apart onto prepared cookie sheets. Bake 9 to 11 minutes or until edges are golden brown. Let cookies stand on cookie sheets 2 minutes. Remove cookies with spatula to wire racks; cool completely.

**6.** Store tightly covered at room temperature. These cookies do not freeze well.          *Makes about 3 dozen cookies*

## 72 CHEWY MILK CHOCOLATE OATMEAL COOKIES

1¼ cups (2½ sticks) butter or margarine, softened
    ¾ cup firmly packed light brown sugar
    ½ cup granulated sugar
    1 large egg
1½ teaspoons vanilla extract
    3 cups quick-cooking or old-fashioned oats, uncooked
1½ cups all-purpose flour
    1 teaspoon baking soda
    1 teaspoon salt
1¾ cups "M&M's"® Milk Chocolate Mini Baking Bits

Preheat oven to 375°F. In large bowl cream butter and sugars until light and fluffy; beat in egg and vanilla. In medium bowl combine oats, flour, baking soda and salt; blend into creamed mixture. Stir in "M&M's"® Milk Chocolate Mini Baking Bits. Drop by rounded tablespoonfuls about 2 inches apart onto ungreased cookie sheets. Bake 8 to 9 minutes or until set. *Do not overbake.* Cool 1 minute on cookie sheets; cool completely on wire racks. Store in tightly covered container.          *Makes about 4 dozen cookies*

*Banana Chocolate Chip Softies*

## CHIPPERIFIC CHIPS

### 73 DOUBLE CHOCOLATE WALNUT DROPS

¾ cup (1½ sticks) butter or margarine, softened
¾ cup granulated sugar
¾ cup firmly packed light brown sugar
1 large egg
1 teaspoon vanilla extract
2¼ cups all-purpose flour
⅓ cup unsweetened cocoa powder
1 teaspoon baking soda
½ teaspoon salt
1¾ cups "M&M's"® Chocolate Mini Baking Bits
1 cup coarsely chopped English or black walnuts

Preheat oven to 350°F. Lightly grease cookie sheets; set aside. In large bowl cream butter and sugars until light and fluffy; beat in egg and vanilla. In medium bowl combine flour, cocoa powder, baking soda and salt; add to creamed mixture. Stir in "M&M's"® Chocolate Mini Baking Bits and nuts. Drop by heaping tablespoonfuls about 2 inches apart onto prepared cookie sheets. Bake 12 to 14 minutes for chewy cookies or 14 to 16 minutes for crispy cookies. Cool completely on wire racks. Store in tightly covered container.

*Makes about 4 dozen cookies*

**VARIATION:** Shape dough into 2-inch-thick roll. Cover with plastic wrap; refrigerate. When ready to bake, slice dough into ¼-inch-thick slices and bake as directed.

### 74 PEANUT BUTTER SUNSHINE COOKIES

½ BUTTER FLAVOR* CRISCO® Stick or ½ cup BUTTER FLAVOR CRISCO all-vegetable shortening
¾ cup JIF® Extra Crunchy Peanut Butter
1 cup sugar
½ cup orange marmalade
2 eggs
1 teaspoon vanilla
2 cups all-purpose flour
1 tablespoon baking powder
½ teaspoon salt
1 cup butterscotch-flavored chips

*Butter Flavor Crisco is artificially flavored.*

**1.** Preheat oven to 350°F. Grease cookie sheet with shortening.

**2.** Combine shortening, peanut butter and sugar in large bowl. Beat at medium speed of electric mixer until well blended. Beat in marmalade, eggs and vanilla.

**3.** Combine flour, baking powder and salt. Mix into creamed mixture at low speed until just blended. Stir in butterscotch chips.

**4.** Drop rounded teaspoonfuls of dough 2 inches apart onto cookie sheet.

**5.** Bake 10 to 12 minutes or until lightly browned. Cool 2 minutes on cookie sheet. Remove to cooling rack.

*Makes about 4 dozen cookies*

*Double Chocolate Walnut Drops*

# Cookie
# Bonanza

## 75 BANANA CRESCENTS

½ cup DOLE® Chopped Almonds, toasted
6 tablespoons sugar
½ cup margarine, cut in pieces
1½ cups plus 2 tablespoons all-purpose flour
⅛ teaspoon salt
1 extra-ripe, medium DOLE® Banana, peeled
2 to 3 ounces semisweet chocolate chips

• Pulverize almonds with 2 tablespoons sugar.

• Beat margarine, almonds, remaining sugar, flour and salt.

• Purée banana (½ cup); add to batter and mix until well blended.

• Using 1 tablespoon batter, roll into log then shape into crescent. Place on ungreased cookie sheet. Bake in 375°F oven 25 minutes or until golden. Cool on rack.

• Melt chocolate in microwave dish at MEDIUM (50%) 1½ to 2 minutes, stirring once. Dip ends of cookies in chocolate. Refrigerate until chocolate hardens.

*Makes 2 dozen cookies*

**Prep Time:** 20 minutes
**Bake Time:** 25 minutes

## 76 CHUNKY FRUIT CHEWS

4 cups QUAKER® Oats (quick or old-fashioned, uncooked)
1¼ teaspoons ground cinnamon
¾ cup non-fat dry milk
½ cup KRETSCHMER® Wheat Germ, any flavor or QUAKER® Unprocessed Bran
¾ cup (1½ sticks) margarine or butter, softened
2 eggs
⅔ cup honey
1 cup mixed dried fruit, chopped
½ cup semi-sweet chocolate pieces

Preheat oven to 325°F. In small bowl, combine oats, cinnamon, non-fat dry milk and wheat germ; set aside.

In large mixer bowl, beat margarine, eggs and honey until creamy. Gradually add flour mixture. Stir in fruit and chocolate pieces. Drop by rounded teaspoonfuls onto ungreased cookie sheets.

Bake 10 to 12 minutes or until edges are firm. Cool 2 minutes on cookie sheets; remove to wire racks. Cool completely. Store tightly covered.

*Makes about 5½ dozen cookies*

*Banana Crescents*

## COOKIE BONANZA

## 77 OATMEAL SHAGGIES COOKIES

### COOKIES

2 cups quick oats, uncooked
1 cup finely shredded carrots
1 cup firmly packed brown sugar
1 cup raisins
1 cup all-purpose flour
1 teaspoon baking powder
1 teaspoon baking soda
1 teaspoon salt
1/2 teaspoon ground cinnamon
1/2 teaspoon crushed cloves
2 eggs, beaten
1/2 BUTTER FLAVOR* CRISCO® Stick or 1/2 cup BUTTER FLAVOR CRISCO all-vegetable shortening, melted and cooled
1/3 cup milk
1 cup shredded coconut
1/2 cup finely chopped walnuts

### FROSTING

1 cup confectioners' sugar
2 tablespoons butter or margarine, softened
2 teaspoons grated orange peel
1 tablespoon plus 1 teaspoon orange juice

*Butter Flavor Crisco is artificially flavored.*

1. **Heat** oven to 350°F. Grease baking sheets with shortening. **Place** sheets of foil on countertop for cooling cookies.

2. For cookies, **combine** oats, carrots, brown sugar and raisins in large bowl.

3. **Combine** flour, baking powder, baking soda, salt, cinnamon and cloves. **Stir** into oat mixture with spoon.

4. **Combine** eggs, shortening and milk. **Stir** into oat mixture. **Stir** in coconut and nuts. **Drop** by rounded tablespoonfuls 2½ inches apart onto greased baking sheets.

5. **Bake** one baking sheet at a time at 350°F for 10 to 12 minutes or until lightly browned. *Do not overbake.* **Cool** on baking sheets 2 minutes. **Remove** cookies to foil to cool completely.

6. For frosting, **combine** confectioners' sugar, butter, orange peel and orange juice in small bowl. **Stir** until smooth and of desired spreading consistency. **Frost** cookies.

*Makes 2½ to 3 dozen cookies*

## 78 ROMAN MEAL® CHEWY DROP COOKIES

3½ cups flour
1/2 teaspoon baking soda
1/2 teaspoon salt
1 cup packed brown sugar
1 cup shortening
2 eggs
1/2 cup skim milk
2 teaspoons vanilla
2½ cups ROMAN MEAL® Honey Nut Granola

Heat oven to 350°F. In medium bowl, stir together flour, soda and salt. In large bowl, beat together sugar and shortening until light and fluffy. Blend in eggs, milk and vanilla. Stir in flour mixture and cereal. Drop by rounded teaspoons onto lightly greased baking sheet. Bake 10 to 12 minutes or until lightly browned.

*Makes about 4 dozen cookies*

*Oatmeal Shaggies Cookies*

## COOKIE BONANZA

## 79 CINNAMON FLATS

1¾ cups all-purpose flour
½ cup sugar
1½ teaspoons ground cinnamon
¼ teaspoon ground nutmeg
¼ teaspoon salt
8 tablespoons cold margarine
3 egg whites, divided
1 teaspoon vanilla
1 teaspoon water
Sugar Glaze (recipe follows)

1. Preheat oven to 350°F. Combine flour, sugar, cinnamon, nutmeg and salt in medium bowl. Cut in margarine with pastry blender or two knives until mixture forms coarse crumbs. Beat in 2 egg whites and vanilla, forming crumbly mixture; mix with hands to form soft dough.

2. Divide dough into 6 equal pieces and place, evenly spaced, on greased 15×10-inch jelly-roll pan. Spread dough evenly to edges of pan using hands; smooth top of dough with metal spatula or palms of hands. Mix remaining egg white and water in small cup; brush over top of dough. Lightly score dough into 2×1½-inch squares.

3. Bake 20 to 25 minutes or until lightly browned and firm when lightly touched with fingertip. While still warm, cut into squares; drizzle or spread Sugar Glaze over squares. Let stand 15 minutes or until glaze is firm before removing from pan.

*Makes 50 cookies*

### SUGAR GLAZE
1½ cups powdered sugar
2 to 3 tablespoons skim milk
1 teaspoon vanilla

1. Combine powdered sugar, 2 tablespoons milk and vanilla in small bowl. If glaze is too thick, add remaining 1 tablespoon milk.

*Makes about 1¾ cup*

## 80 OAT PECAN PRALINE COOKIES

1 cup (2 sticks) margarine or butter, softened
1¼ cups firmly packed brown sugar
2 eggs
2 tablespoons molasses
1 teaspoon maple flavoring
1¼ cups all-purpose flour
1 teaspoon baking soda
2½ cups QUAKER® Oats (quick or old-fashioned, uncooked)
1 cup pecans, coarsely chopped
¾ cup pecan halves (about 48 halves)

Beat together margarine and sugar until creamy. Add eggs, molasses and maple flavoring; beat well. Add combined flour and baking soda; mix well. Stir in oats and chopped nuts; mix well. Cover dough; chill at least 1 hour.

Heat oven to 350°F. Lightly grease cookie sheet. Shape dough into 1-inch balls. Place 3 inches apart on prepared cookie sheet. Flatten each ball by pressing a pecan half in center. Bake 10 to 12 minutes or until deep golden brown. Immediately remove to wire rack; cool completely. Store in tightly covered container.

*Makes about 4 dozen cookies*

*Cinnamon Flats*

## COOKIE BONANZA

## 81 KENTUCKY OATMEAL–JAM COOKIES

½ BUTTER FLAVOR* CRISCO®Stick or
   ½ cup BUTTER FLAVOR CRISCO
   all-vegetable shortening
¾ cup sugar
 1 egg
¼ cup buttermilk**
½ cup strawberry jam
 1 teaspoon vanilla
 1 cup all-purpose flour
½ cup unsweetened cocoa powder
 1 teaspoon cinnamon
½ teaspoon baking soda
¼ teaspoon nutmeg
¼ teaspoon ground cloves
1½ cups quick oats (not instant or old
   fashioned), uncooked
½ cup raisins
½ cup chopped pecans (optional)
   About 24 pecan halves (optional)

*Butter Flavored Crisco is artificially flavored.*

**You may substitute ¾ teaspoon lemon juice or vinegar plus enough milk to make ¼ cup for buttermilk. Stir. Wait 5 minutes before using.*

**1.** Preheat oven to 350°F. Grease cookie sheet with shortening.

**2.** Combine shortening, sugar, egg, buttermilk, jam and vanilla in large bowl. Beat at medium speed of electric mixer until well blended.

**3.** Combine flour, cocoa, cinnamon, baking soda, nutmeg and cloves. Mix into creamed mixture at low speed until blended. Stir in oats, raisins and chopped nuts with spoon.

**4.** Drop 2 tablespoonfuls of dough in a mound 3 inches apart onto cookie sheet. Repeat for each cookie. Top each with pecan half.

**5.** Bake 10 to 12 minutes or until set. Cool 2 minutes on cookie sheet. Remove to cooling rack.

*Makes about 2 dozen cookies*

## 82 BANANA PEANUT JUMBLES

 2 extra-ripe, medium DOLE® Bananas,
   peeled
½ cup packed brown sugar
½ cup peanut butter
½ cup roasted peanuts
1⅓ cups buttermilk baking mix
 1 tablespoon water

• **Mash** bananas; measure 1 cup.

• **Combine** banana, brown sugar, peanut butter and peanuts. Add baking mix and water. Stir until well blended.

• **Drop** batter by heaping tablespoonsful onto cookie sheets coated with cooking spray.

• **Bake** in 350°F oven 20 to 25 minutes or until golden. Cool on rack.

*Makes 18 cookies*

**Prep Time:** 15 minutes
**Bake Time:** 25 minutes

*Kentucky Oatmeal-Jam Cookies*

## 83 YUMMY CHOCOLATE COOKIES WITH ORANGE FROSTING

**COOKIES**
1 cup granulated sugar
¾ BUTTER FLAVOR* CRISCO® Stick or
    ¾ cup BUTTER FLAVOR CRISCO
    all-vegetable shortening
1 egg
½ teaspoon vanilla
1¾ cups all-purpose flour
½ cup unsweetened cocoa
1 teaspoon baking soda
½ teaspoon salt
1 cup mashed ripe bananas (2 to
    3 medium bananas)
1 cup raisins
½ teaspoon grated orange peel
2 teaspoons orange juice

**FROSTING**
1 package (3 ounces) cream cheese,
    softened
¼ BUTTER FLAVOR CRISCO Stick or
    ¼ cup BUTTER FLAVOR CRISCO
    all-vegetable shortening
3 cups confectioners sugar
2 tablespoons orange juice
⅛ teaspoon grated orange peel (optional)
    Yellow and red food color (optional)

*Butter Flavor Crisco is artificially flavored.*

**1.** Preheat oven to 350°F. Grease cookie sheet with shortening.

**2.** For Cookies, combine granulated sugar, ¾ cup shortening, egg and vanilla in large bowl. Beat at medium speed of electric mixer until well blended and creamy.

**3.** Combine flour, cocoa, baking soda and salt in medium bowl. Stir well. Add alternately with bananas to creamed mixture, beating at low speed until well blended. Stir in raisins, ½ teaspoon orange peel and 2 teaspoons orange juice with spoon. Drop by heaping teaspoonfuls 2 inches apart onto greased cookie sheet.

**4.** Bake at 350°F for 12 minutes or until set. Cool 2 minutes on cookie sheet before removing to wire rack. Cool completely.

**5.** For Frosting, combine cream cheese and ¼ cup shortening in medium bowl. Beat at medium speed until well blended. Gradually add confectioners sugar and 2 tablespoons orange juice; beat until creamy. Add ⅛ teaspoon orange peel and food color, if desired. Beat until blended. Frost cookies.

*Makes about 3 dozen cookies*

*Yummy Chocolate Cookies with
Orange Frosting*

## 84 BANANA ORANGE SOFTIES

### COOKIES

1²/₃ cups mashed, ripe bananas (about 3 large bananas)
³/₄ cup (1½ sticks) margarine or butter, softened
½ cup orange juice
2 eggs
2 teaspoons vanilla
1 teaspoon grated orange peel
2 cups QUAKER® Oats (quick or old fashioned, uncooked)
2 cups all-purpose flour
³/₄ teaspoon baking soda
½ teaspoon salt (optional)
³/₄ cup raisins

### ICING

³/₄ cup powdered sugar
2 to 3 teaspoons orange juice
1 teaspoon grated orange peel

Preheat oven to 350°F. For Cookies, in large bowl, beat bananas, margarine and orange juice until smooth. Blend in eggs, vanilla and orange peel. Add combined dry ingredients; mix well. Stir in raisins. Drop dough by rounded tablespoonfuls onto ungreased cookie sheet. Bake 20 to 22 minutes or until light golden brown. Cool 2 minutes on cookie sheet; remove to wire rack. Cool completely.

For Icing, in small bowl, combine powdered sugar, orange juice and orange peel; drizzle over cooled cookies. Store tightly covered.

*Makes about 2½ dozen cookies*

## 85 OATMEAL LEMON–CHEESE COOKIES

1 BUTTER FLAVOR* CRISCO® Stick or 1 cup BUTTER FLAVOR CRISCO all-vegetable shortening
1 package (3 ounces) cream cheese, softened
1¼ cups sugar
1 egg, separated
1 teaspoon lemon extract
2 teaspoons grated lemon peel
1¼ cups all-purpose flour
1¼ cups quick oats (not instant or old-fashioned), uncooked
½ teaspoon salt
1 egg
Sugar for sprinkling
½ cup sliced almonds

*Butter Flavor Crisco is artificially flavored.*

1. **Heat** oven to 350°F. **Place** sheets of foil on countertop for cooling cookies.

2. **Combine** shortening, cream cheese and sugar in large bowl. **Beat** at medium speed of electric mixer until well blended. **Beat** in egg yolk, lemon extract and lemon peel. **Combine** flour, oats and salt. **Stir** into shortening mixture with spoon until blended.

3. **Drop** rounded teaspoonfuls of dough 2 inches apart onto ungreased baking sheets. **Beat** whole egg with egg white. **Brush** over tops of cookies. **Sprinkle** lightly with sugar. **Press** almond slices lightly on top.

4. **Bake** one baking sheet at a time at 350°F for 10 to 12 minutes or until edges are lightly browned. *Do not overbake.* **Cool** 2 minutes on baking sheets. **Remove** cookies to foil to cool completely.

*Makes about 6 dozen cookies*

## 86 BUTTERSCOTCH COOKIES WITH BURNT BUTTER ICING

½ cup butter, softened
1½ cups packed brown sugar
2 eggs
1 teaspoon vanilla
2½ cups flour
1 teaspoon baking soda
½ teaspoon salt
1 cup dairy sour cream
1 cup finely chopped walnuts
    Burnt Butter Icing (recipe follows)

Beat butter and sugar until light and fluffy. Blend in eggs and vanilla; mix well. Add combined dry ingredients alternately with sour cream, mixing well after each addition. Stir in nuts. Chill 4 hours or over night. Drop rounded teaspoonfuls of dough, 3 inches apart, onto well buttered cookie sheet. Bake at 400°F for 8 to 10 minutes or until lightly browned. Cool. Frost with Burnt Butter Icing.

### BURNT BUTTER ICING

6 tablespoons butter
2 cups sifted powdered sugar
1 teaspoon vanilla
2 to 3 tablespoons hot water

Melt butter in small saucepan over medium heat; continue heating until golden brown. Cool. Blend in sugar and vanilla. Add enough water to reach spreading consistency.

*Makes 5 dozen*

*Favorite recipe from* **Wisconsin Milk Marketing Board**

## 87 HOT 'N NUTTY COOKIES

¾ cup unsalted butter, softened
1 cup granulated sugar
1 cup packed brown sugar
2 cups peanut butter, smooth or crunchy
½ cup macadamia nuts, chopped (optional)
2 eggs
1 teaspoon vanilla extract
1 teaspoon TABASCO® pepper sauce
3 cups all-purpose flour
1 teaspoon salt
1 teaspoon baking soda

Preheat oven to 350°F. Lightly butter and flour cookie sheet.

In large bowl, cream together butter, granulated sugar and brown sugar. Stir in peanut butter and macadamia nuts; mix until well blended. Add eggs, vanilla and TABASCO® sauce. Mix until well combined.

In another bowl, mix together flour, salt and baking soda. Add to nut mixture and stir until blended.

Spoon about 1 heaping tablespoon of batter on prepared cookie sheet. Coat tines of fork in flour and score each cookie in crisscross pattern. Bake 15 to 17 minute or until edges begin to turn golden. Set aside to cool on racks.

*Makes 2 dozen cookies*

## 88 ORANGE PECAN REFRIGERATOR COOKIES

2⅓ cups all-purpose flour
½ teaspoon baking soda
¼ teaspoon salt
½ cup butter or margarine, softened
½ cup packed brown sugar
½ cup granulated sugar
1 egg, lightly beaten
  Grated peel of 1 SUNKIST® Orange
3 tablespoons fresh squeezed orange juice
¾ cup pecan pieces

In bowl, stir together flour, baking soda and salt. In large bowl, blend together butter, brown sugar and granulated sugar. Add egg, orange peel and juice; beat well. Stir in pecans. Gradually beat in flour mixture. (Cookie dough will be stiff.) Divide mixture in half and shape each half (on a long piece of wax paper) into a roll about 1¼ inches in diameter and 12 inches long. Roll up tightly in the wax paper. Chill several hours or overnight.

Cut into ¼-inch slices and arrange on lightly greased cookie sheets. Bake at 350°F for 10 to 12 minutes, or until *lightly* browned. Remove and cool on wire racks.

*Makes about 6 dozen cookies*

**VARIATION:** Chocolate Filled Sandwich Cookies: Cut each roll into ⅛-inch slices and bake as above. When cool, to make each sandwich cookie, spread about 1 teaspoon canned chocolate fudge frosting on the bottom side of one cookie; cover with a second cookie of the same shape. Makes about 4 dozen double cookies.

## 89 LITTLE RAISIN LOGS

1 cup butter or margarine, softened
⅓ cup sugar
2 teaspoons brandy (optional)
2 teaspoons vanilla
½ teaspoon salt
1 cup SUN-MAID® Raisins, finely chopped
1 cup DIAMOND® Walnuts, finely chopped
2 cups all-purpose flour
1 package (6 ounces) real semisweet chocolate pieces
3 tablespoons vegetable shortening

Preheat oven to 350°F. In large bowl, cream butter and sugar. Beat in brandy, vanilla and salt. Stir in raisins, walnuts and flour. Pinch off dough and roll with hands on lightly floured board into logs about ½ inch in diameter and 2½ inches long.

Bake on ungreased cookie sheet 15 to 20 minutes. (Cookies do not brown.) Remove to wire rack to cool.

Meanwhile, in top of double boiler, melt chocolate and shortening over simmering water, blending thoroughly. When cookies have cooled, dip one end into melted chocolate. Place on wire rack to set.

*Makes about 6 dozen cookies*

*Top to bottom: Orange Pecan Refrigerator Cookies and Luscious Fresh Lemon Bars (page 15)*

## COOKIE BONANZA

### 90 CANDIED PEEL CITRUS DROPS

¼ cup minced lemon peel
¾ cup granulated sugar, divided
¼ cup water
1¼ cups all-purpose flour
½ teaspoon baking soda
½ teaspoon salt
½ cup butter or margarine, softened
¼ cup packed light brown sugar
1 egg
½ cup chopped pecans or walnuts
Citrus Glaze (recipe follows)

In a small saucepan, combine the lemon peel, ¼ cup of the granulated sugar and water; bring to a boil, stirring to dissolve the sugar. Reduce heat and simmer briskly for 10 minutes, or until liquid is syrupy; cool slightly. Meanwhile, sift together the flour, baking soda and salt. In a large bowl, cream together the butter, remaining ½ cup of granulated sugar and brown sugar. Beat in the egg. Stir in nuts and peel with syrup. Gradually blend in dry ingredients; cover and chill for 1 hour or longer. Drop dough by teaspoons onto lightly greased cookie sheets. Bake at 375°F for 10 to 12 minutes. Remove and cool on wire racks. Spread cookies with Citrus Glaze.

*Makes about 3 dozen*

### CITRUS GLAZE
1 cup confectioners' sugar
1 teaspoon fresh grated lemon peel
1 tablespoon fresh squeezed lemon juice
1 tablespoon water
1 tablespoon butter or margarine, softened

In a small bowl, combine all the ingredients.
*Makes about ½ cup*

*Favorite recipe from **Sunkist Growers***

### 91 PEANUT BUTTER CHOCOLATE STARS

1 cup peanut butter
1 cup packed light brown sugar
1 egg
48 milk chocolate candy stars or other solid milk chocolate candy

**PREHEAT** oven to 350°F. Line cookie sheets with parchment paper or leave ungreased.

**COMBINE** peanut butter, sugar and egg in medium bowl until blended and smooth.

**SHAPE** dough into 48 balls about 1½ inches in diameter. Place 2 inches apart on cookie sheets. Press one chocolate star on top of each cookie.

**BAKE** 10 to 12 minutes or until set. Transfer to wire racks to cool completely.
*Makes 48 cookies*

*Peanut Butter Chocolate Stars*

## 92 SLICE 'N' BAKE GINGER WAFERS

½ cup butter or margarine, softened
1 cup packed brown sugar
¼ cup light molasses
1 egg
2 teaspoons ground ginger
1 teaspoon grated orange peel
¼ teaspoon salt
¼ teaspoon ground cinnamon
¼ teaspoon ground cloves
2 cups all-purpose flour

**1.** Beat butter, sugar and molasses in large bowl until light and fluffy. Add egg, ginger, orange peel, salt, cinnamon and cloves; beat until well blended. Stir in flour until well blended (dough will be very stiff).

**2.** Divide dough in half. Roll each half into 8×1½-inch log. Wrap logs in wax paper or plastic wrap; refrigerate at least 5 hours or up to 5 days.

**3.** Preheat oven to 350°F. Cut dough into ¼-inch-thick slices. Place about 2 inches apart onto ungreased baking sheets. Bake 12 to 14 minutes or until set. Remove from baking sheet to wire rack to cool.

*Makes about 4½ dozen cookies*

## 93 DEEP FRIED SOUR CREAM COOKIES

1⅔ cups all-purpose flour
1 tablespoon granulated sugar
½ teaspoon salt
½ cup sour cream
3 egg yolks, slightly beaten
2 tablespoons CRISCO® Oil
1 teaspoon vanilla
CRISCO® Oil for frying
Confectioners' sugar

**1.** Combine flour, granulated sugar and salt in medium mixing bowl. Make well in center of mixture.

**2.** Blend sour cream, egg yolks, CRISCO® Oil and vanilla in small mixing bowl. Pour into well in dry ingredients. Mix with fork.

**3.** Transfer mixture to lightly floured surface. Knead until blended. Roll dough to ⅛-inch thickness. Cut into diamond shapes, 3 inches long and 2 inches wide.

**4.** Heat 2 to 3 inches CRISCO® Oil in deep-fryer or large saucepan to 375°F. Fry a few cookies at a time, about 1½ minutes, or until light golden brown, turning over once. Drain on paper towels. Sprinkle with confectioners' sugar.

*Makes about 2 dozen cookies*

*Coconut Clouds*

## 94 COCONUT CLOUDS

2⅔ cups flaked coconut, divided
1 package DUNCAN HINES® Moist
    Deluxe Yellow Cake Mix
½ cup CRISCO® Oil or CRISCO® Puritan®
    Canola Oil
¼ cup water
1 egg
1 teaspoon almond extract

**1.** Preheat oven to 350°F. Place 1⅓ cups coconut in medium bowl; set aside.

**2.** Combine cake mix, oil, water, egg and almond extract in large bowl. Stir until thoroughly blended. Stir in remaining 1⅓ cups coconut. Drop rounded teaspoonful dough into coconut. Roll to cover lightly. Place on ungreased baking sheet. Repeat with remaining dough placing balls 2 inches apart. Bake at 350°F for 10 to 12 minutes or until light golden brown. Cool 1 minute on baking sheets. Remove to cooling racks. Cool completely. Store in airtight container.

*Makes 3½ dozen cookies*

**TIP:** To save time when forming dough into balls, use a 1-inch spring-operated cookie scoop. Spring-operated cookie scoops are available at kitchen specialty shops.

## 95 BUTTER–FLAVORED BRICKLE DRIZZLES

**COOKIES**
1 BUTTER FLAVOR* CRISCO Stick or
　1 cup BUTTER FLAVOR CRISCO
　all-vegetable shortening
1 cup granulated sugar
1 cup firmly packed brown sugar
1 can (14 ounces) sweetened condensed
　milk (not evaporated milk)
1 teaspoon vanilla
1¾ cups all-purpose flour
1 teaspoon salt
½ teaspoon baking soda
3 cups quick-cooking oats (not instant or
　old-fashioned), uncooked
1 cup almond brickle chips

**DRIZZLE**
1 cup milk chocolate chips

*Butter Flavor Crisco is artificially flavored.*

1. Preheat oven to 350°F. Grease cookie sheet with shortening.

2. For Cookies, combine shortening, granulated sugar and brown sugar in large bowl. Stir with spoon until well blended and creamy. Stir in condensed milk and vanilla. Mix well.

3. Combine flour, salt and baking soda. Stir into creamed mixture. Stir in oats.

4. Shape dough into 1-inch balls. Press tops into brickle chips. Place, brickle side up, 2 inches apart on greased cookie sheet.

5. Bake at 350°F for 9 to 10 minutes or until set but not browned. Remove to wire rack. Cool completely.

6. For Drizzle, place chocolate chips in heavy resealable sandwich bag. Seal. Microwave at MEDIUM (50% power). Knead bag after 1 minute. Repeat until smooth (or melt by placing in bowl of hot water). Cut tiny tip off corner of bag. Squeeze out and drizzle over cookies.

*Makes about 6 dozen cookies*

## 96 MOCHA COOKIES

2½ tablespoons instant coffee
1½ tablespoons skim milk
⅓ cup light brown sugar
¼ cup granulated sugar
¼ cup margarine
1 egg
½ teaspoon almond extract
2 cups all-purpose flour, sifted
¼ cup wheat flakes cereal
½ teaspoon ground cinnamon
¼ teaspoon baking powder

Preheat oven to 350°F. Spray cookie sheets with non-stick cooking spray. In small cup, dissolve coffee in milk. In large bowl, cream together brown sugar, granulated sugar and margarine. Beat in egg, almond extract and coffee mixture. Stir together flour, wheat flakes, cinnamon and baking powder; beat into sugar mixture gradually. Drop by teaspoonfuls, 2 inches apart, onto cookie sheets. Flatten with back of fork. Bake 8 to 10 minutes or until set. Remove from cookie sheets. Cool completely.

*Makes 40 cookies*

*Favorite recipe from **The Sugar Association, Inc.***

*Butter-Flavored Brickle Drizzles*

## COOKIE BONANZA

## 97 SPICY SOUR CREAM COOKIES

1 package DUNCAN HINES® Moist Deluxe Spice Cake Mix
1 cup dairy sour cream
1 cup chopped pecans or walnuts
¼ cup butter or margarine, softened
1 egg

**1.** Preheat oven to 350°F. Grease baking sheets.

**2.** Combine cake mix, sour cream, pecans, butter and egg in large bowl. Mix at low speed with electric mixer until blended. Drop by rounded teaspoonfuls onto baking sheet. Bake at 350°F for 9 to 11 minutes or until lightly browned. Cool 2 minutes on baking sheets. Remove to cooling rack. Cool completely. Store in airtight container.

*Makes about 4½ dozen cookies*

**TIP:** Sprinkle cooled cookies with confectioners sugar.

## 98 KOLACKY

½ cup margarine or butter, softened
3 ounces cream cheese, softened
1 teaspoon vanilla
1 cup all-purpose flour
⅛ teaspoon salt
¼ cup all-fruit spread, assorted flavors
1 egg
1 teaspoon cold water

**COMBINE** margarine and cream cheese in large bowl; beat with electric mixer at medium speed until smooth and creamy. Beat in vanilla. Combine flour and salt in small bowl; gradually add to margarine mixture, beating until mixture forms soft dough. Divide dough in half; wrap each half in plastic wrap. Refrigerate until firm.

**PREHEAT** oven to 375°F.

**ROLL** out half of dough on lightly floured pastry cloth or board to ⅛-inch thickness. Cut with top of glass or biscuit cutter into 3-inch rounds. Spoon ½ teaspoon fruit spread onto center of each dough circle. Beat egg with water in small bowl; lightly brush onto edges of dough circles. Bring three edges of dough up over fruit spread; pinch edges together to seal. Place on *ungreased* cookie sheets; brush with egg mixture. Repeat with remaining dough and fruit spread.

**BAKE** 12 minutes or until golden brown. Let stand on cookie sheets 1 minute. Transfer kolackys to wire rack; cool completely. Store in tightly covered container.

*Makes 2 dozen kolacky*

*Kolacky*

## COOKIE BONANZA

## 99 DOUBLE CHOCOLATE TREASURES

1 package (12 ounces) semi-sweet
    chocolate (2 cups), divided
1/2 cup (1 stick) margarine, softened
3/4 cup granulated sugar
2 eggs
1 teaspoon vanilla
2 cups QUAKER® Oats (quick or
    old-fashioned, uncooked)
1 1/2 cups all-purpose flour
2 teaspoons baking powder
1/4 teaspoon salt (optional)
1/2 cup powdered sugar

Preheat oven to 350°F. In small saucepan over low heat, melt 1 cup chocolate pieces, stirring constantly until smooth; cool slightly.* Beat margarine and sugar in large bowl until light and fluffy. Blend in eggs, vanilla and melted chocolate. Combine oats, flour, baking powder and salt. Stir into chocolate mixture; mix well. Stir in remaining 1 cup chocolate pieces. Shape into 1-inch balls. Roll in powdered sugar, coating heavily. Place on ungreased cookie sheet.

Bake 10 to 12 minutes. Cool 1 minute on cookie sheet; remove to wire rack. Cool completely. Store tightly covered.

*Makes about 5 dozen cookies*

*\*To Microwave: Place chocolate pieces in microwaveable bowl. Microwave at HIGH (100% power) 1 to 2 minutes, stirring every 30 seconds until smooth.*

## 100 BANANA SPICE LEMON DROPS

2 cups all-purpose flour
1 teaspoon baking soda
1/4 teaspoon ground cinnamon
1/8 teaspoon ground cloves
6 tablespoons margarine, divided
1 cup packed brown sugar
1 egg
1 large, ripe DOLE® Banana, mashed
    (about 2/3 cup)
    Vegetable cooking spray
2 cups powdered sugar
2 to 3 tablespoons lemon juice

• **Combine** flour, baking soda, cinnamon and cloves in small bowl; set aside.

• **Beat** 4 tablespoons margarine, brown sugar and egg in large bowl until blended. Stir in banana. Add flour mixture; stir until well blended.

• **Drop** dough by rounded teaspoonfuls onto baking sheets sprayed with vegetable cooking spray, 1 inch apart.

• **Bake** at 375°F 10 to 12 minutes or until edges are light brown. Remove to wire rack; let cool completely.

• **Beat** remaining margarine, powdered sugar and 2 tablespoons lemon juice in small bowl until smooth, adding additional lemon juice, if needed. Spread frosting over cooled cookies. *Makes 3 dozen cookies*

## 101 OATMEAL–RAISIN SPICE COOKIES

½ cup granulated sugar
½ cup packed light brown sugar
⅓ cup Prune Purée (recipe follows) or prepared prune butter or 1 jar (2½ ounces) first-stage baby food prunes
¼ cup water
2 tablespoons nonfat milk
2 teaspoons vanilla
1 cup all-purpose flour
1½ teaspoons pumpkin pie spice
1 teaspoon baking soda
½ teaspoon salt
1½ cups rolled oats
½ cup golden or dark raisins

Preheat oven to 350°F. Coat baking sheets with vegetable cooking spray. In large bowl, whisk together sugars, prune purée, water, milk and vanilla until mixture is creamy, about 1 minute. In medium bowl, combine flour, spice, baking soda and salt; stir into sugar mixture until well blended. Stir in oats and raisins. Spoon twelve mounds of dough onto prepared baking sheets, spacing 2 inches apart. Bake in center of oven 18 to 20 minutes or until set and golden brown. Remove from baking sheets to wire rack to cool completely.     *Makes 12 large cookies*

**PRUNE PURÉE:** Combine 1⅓ cups (8 ounces) pitted prunes and 6 tablespoons hot water in container of food processor or blender. Pulse on and off until prunes are finely chopped and smooth. Store leftovers in a covered container in the refrigerator for up to two months. Makes 1 cup.

*Favorite recipe from* **California Prune Board**

## 102 CHOCOLATE– COCONUT COOKIES

2 squares (1 ounce each) unsweetened chocolate
½ cup butter or margarine, softened
1 cup packed light brown sugar
1 egg
1¼ cups all-purpose flour
¼ teaspoon baking powder
⅛ teaspoon baking soda
Dash salt
2 cups chopped walnuts or pecans
½ cup flaked coconut
Pecan halves or red candied cherry halves

Preheat oven to 350°F. Lightly grease cookie sheet or line with parchment paper.

Melt chocolate in top of double boiler over hot, not boiling, water. Remove from heat; cool. Beat butter and sugar in large bowl until blended. Add egg and melted chocolate; beat until light. Combine flour, baking powder, baking soda and salt in small bowl. Stir into butter mixture until blended. Mix in nuts and coconut. Drop dough by teaspoonfuls 2 inches apart onto prepared cookie sheets. Press a pecan or cherry half into center of each cookie.

Bake 10 to 12 minutes or until firm. Remove to wire racks to cool.

*Makes about 4 dozen cookies*

**COOKIE BONANZA**

## 103 WHOLE WHEAT OATMEAL COOKIES

¾ BUTTER FLAVOR* CRISCO® Stick or
   ¾ cup BUTTER FLAVOR CRISCO
   all-vegetable shortening
¾ cup firmly packed brown sugar
⅓ cup apple juice
¼ cup molasses
¼ cup honey
 1 egg
 1 teaspoon vanilla
 1 cup whole wheat flour
 1 teaspoon ground cinnamon
½ teaspoon baking soda
¼ teaspoon salt
⅛ teaspoon ground nutmeg
 3 cups quick-cooking oats (not instant or
   old-fashioned), uncooked
¾ cup raisins
¾ cup chopped walnuts

*Butter Flavor Crisco is artificially flavored.*

**1.** Preheat oven to 350°F. Grease cookie sheet with shortening.

**2.** Combine shortening, sugar, juice, molasses, honey, egg and vanilla in large bowl. Beat at medium speed of electric mixer until blended and creamy.

**3.** Combine flour, cinnamon, baking soda, salt and nutmeg. Mix into creamed mixture at low speed until just blended. Stir in oats, raisins and nuts with spoon. Drop rounded tablespoonfuls of dough 2 inches apart onto greased cookie sheet.

**4.** Bake at 350°F for 13 to 14 minutes or until set. Cool 5 minutes on cookie sheet. Remove to wire rack.

*Makes about 3 dozen cookies*

## 104 PINEAPPLE OATMEAL CRUNCHIES

 2 cans (8 ounces each) DOLE® Crushed
   Pineapple
1½ cups margarine
1½ cups packed brown sugar
 2 eggs
 3 cups all-purpose flour
 3 cups old-fashioned rolled oats
 1 teaspoon ground cinnamon
 1 teaspoon baking powder
½ teaspoon salt
 5 bags (1.4 ounces each) chocolate
   covered toffee nuggets

• Drain pineapple well, reserve ½ cup juice.

• Beat margarine and sugar until light and fluffy. Beat in eggs. Stir in pineapple and reserved juice.

• Combine flour, oats, cinnamon, baking powder and salt. Add to pineapple mixture and mix well. Stir in candy.

• Drop by ¼ cup scoopfuls 1 inch apart onto cookie sheets coated with cooking spray. Flatten slightly. Bake in 375°F oven 30 minutes. *Makes 24 large cookies*

**Prep Time:** 20 minutes
**Bake Time:** 30 minutes/batch

*Whole Wheat Oatmeal Cookies*

## 105 PEANUT GEMS

2½ cups all-purpose flour
1 teaspoon baking powder
⅛ teaspoon salt
1 cup butter, softened
1 cup packed light brown sugar
2 eggs
2 teaspoons vanilla
1½ cups cocktail peanuts, finely chopped
Powdered sugar (optional)

**PREHEAT** oven to 350°F. Combine flour, baking powder and salt in small bowl.

**BEAT** butter in large bowl with electric mixer at medium speed until smooth. Gradually beat in brown sugar; increase speed to medium-high and beat until light and fluffy. Beat in eggs, 1 at a time, until fluffy. Beat in vanilla. Gradually stir in flour mixture until blended. Stir in peanuts until blended.

**DROP** heaping tablespoonfuls of dough about 1 inch apart onto *ungreased* cookie sheets; flatten slightly with hands.

**BAKE** 12 minutes or until set. Let cookies stand on cookie sheets 5 minutes; transfer to wire racks to cool completely. Dust cookies with powdered sugar, if desired. Store in airtight container.    *Makes 30 cookies*

## 106 DATE–OATMEAL COOKIES

1 cup all-purpose flour
¾ cup quick-cooking oats
1 cup DOLE® Pitted Dates or Pitted Prunes, chopped
1 teaspoon ground cinnamon
¾ teaspoon baking powder
¼ cup light margarine, softened
⅔ cup packed brown sugar
1 egg
1 medium, ripe DOLE® Banana, mashed (about ½ cup)
1 teaspoon vanilla extract
Vegetable cooking spray

• **Combine** flour, oats, dates, cinnamon and baking powder in medium bowl; set aside.

• **Beat** margarine and sugar in large bowl until well blended. Add egg, banana and vanilla; beat until blended. Stir in flour mixture until just moistened.

• **Drop** dough by rounded teaspoonfuls, 2 inches apart, onto baking sheets sprayed with vegetable cooking spray.

• **Bake** at 375°F 10 to 12 minutes or until cookies are firm and bottoms are browned. Remove cookies to wire rack; cool. Store in airtight container.    *Makes 32 servings*

*Peanut Gems*

## 107 NUTTY CLUSTERS

4 squares (1 ounce each) unsweetened
  chocolate, divided
½ cup plus 2 tablespoons butter or
  margarine, softened, divided
1 cup granulated sugar
1 egg
⅓ cup buttermilk
1 teaspoon vanilla
1¾ cups all-purpose flour
½ teaspoon baking soda
1 cup mixed salted nuts, coarsely chopped
2 cups powdered sugar
2 to 3 tablespoons water

For cookies, preheat oven to 400°F. Line
cookie sheets with parchment paper or leave
ungreased. Melt 2 squares chocolate in
heavy small saucepan over very low heat.
Remove from heat; let cool.

Beat ½ cup butter and granulated sugar in
large bowl with electric mixer until smooth.
Beat in melted chocolate, egg, buttermilk
and vanilla until light. Stir in flour and
baking soda just until blended. Stir in nuts.

Drop teaspoonfuls of dough 2 inches apart
onto prepared cookie sheets.

Bake 8 to 10 minutes or until almost no
imprint remains when touched. Immediately
transfer cookies to wire rack.

Meanwhile, for icing, melt remaining
2 squares chocolate and 2 tablespoons
butter in small heavy saucepan over low
heat, stirring until completely melted. Add
powdered sugar and water, mixing until
smooth. Frost cookies while still warm.

*Makes about 48 cookies*

## 108 GRANOLA APPLE COOKIES

1 cup firmly packed brown sugar
¾ cup margarine or butter, softened
1 egg
¾ cup MOTT'S® Natural Apple Sauce
1 teaspoon vanilla
3 cups granola with dates and raisins
1½ cups all-purpose flour
1 teaspoon baking powder
½ teaspoon baking soda
1 teaspoon cinnamon
½ teaspoon allspice
½ teaspoon salt
1 cup flaked coconut
1 cup unsalted sunflower nuts

In large bowl, combine brown sugar,
margarine, egg, apple sauce and vanilla; beat
well. Stir in remaining ingredients; mix well.
Refrigerate 1 to 2 hours for ease in handling.

Preheat oven to 375°F. Grease cookie sheets.
Drop dough by teaspoonfuls 2 inches apart
onto prepared cookie sheets. Bake 11 to
13 minutes or until edges are light golden
brown. Immediately remove from cookie
sheets. Cool on wire racks. Store cookies in
airtight container to retain their soft, chewy
texture.     *Makes about 5 dozen cookies*

**VARIATION:** For larger cookies, press ¼ cup
dough onto greased cookie sheet. Bake at
375°F for 13 to 15 minutes.

*Nutty Clusters*

## 109 CINNAMON–APRICOT TART OATMEAL COOKIES

$\frac{1}{3}$ cup water
1 package (6 ounces) dried apricot halves, diced
$\frac{3}{4}$ BUTTER FLAVOR* CRISCO® Stick or $\frac{3}{4}$ cup BUTTER FLAVOR CRISCO all-vegetable shortening
$1\frac{1}{4}$ cups firmly packed light brown sugar
1 egg
$\frac{1}{3}$ cup milk
$1\frac{1}{2}$ teaspoons vanilla
3 cups quick oats, uncooked
1 cup all-purpose flour
$\frac{1}{2}$ teaspoon baking soda
$\frac{1}{2}$ teaspoon salt
$\frac{1}{4}$ teaspoon cinnamon
1 cup plus 2 tablespoons chopped pecans

*Butter Flavor Crisco is artificially flavored.*

**1. Place** $\frac{1}{3}$ cup water in small saucepan. Heat to boiling over high heat. Place diced apricots in strainer over boiling water. Reduce heat to low. Cover; steam 15 minutes. Set aside.

**2. Heat** oven to 375°F. Grease baking sheets with shortening. Place sheets of foil on countertop for cooling cookies.

**3. Combine** shortening, brown sugar, egg, milk and vanilla in large bowl. Beat at medium speed of electric mixer until well blended.

**4. Combine** oats, flour, baking soda, salt and cinnamon. Mix into shortening mixture at low speed until just blended. Stir in pecans, apricots and liquid from apricots.

**5. Drop** by rounded measuring tablespoonfuls of dough 2 inches apart onto prepared baking sheets.

**6. Bake** one baking sheet at a time at 375°F for 10 to 12 minutes or until lightly browned. *Do not overbake.* Cool 2 minutes on baking sheet. Remove cookies to foil to cool completely.

*Makes 3½ to 4 dozen cookies*

## 110 DOUBLE ALMOND BUTTER COOKIES

2 cups softened butter
$2\frac{1}{2}$ cups powdered sugar, sifted and divided
4 cups flour
$2\frac{1}{4}$ teaspoons vanilla, divided
$\frac{2}{3}$ cup BLUE DIAMOND® Blanched Almond Paste
$\frac{1}{4}$ cup firmly packed, light brown sugar
$\frac{1}{2}$ cup BLUE DIAMOND® Chopped Natural Almonds, toasted

Cream butter with 1 cup powdered sugar. Gradually beat in flour. Beat in 2 teaspoons vanilla. Chill $\frac{1}{2}$ hour. Combine almond paste, brown sugar, almonds and remaining $\frac{1}{4}$ teaspoon vanilla. Shape small amount of dough around $\frac{1}{2}$ teaspoon almond paste mixture; form into 1-inch balls. Place on ungreased baking pans. Bake at 350°F for 15 minutes. Cool. Roll in remaining $1\frac{1}{2}$ cups powdered sugar or sift powdered sugar over cookies. *Makes 8 dozen cookies*

*Cinnamon-Apricot Tart Oatmeal Cookies*

## 111 NUTTY TOPPERS

**PEANUT BUTTER LAYER**
   ¾ **BUTTER FLAVOR\* CRISCO® Stick or**
      ¾ **cup BUTTER FLAVOR CRISCO**
      **all-vegetable shortening**
   1 cup JIF® Creamy Peanut Butter
   1 cup sugar
   2 eggs
   1 teaspoon vanilla
   1 teaspoon water
   2 cups all-purpose flour
   1 teaspoon baking soda
   ¼ teaspoon salt

**CHOCOLATE LAYER**
   ½ cup dough from Peanut Butter Layer
   1 egg
   1 tablespoon unsweetened cocoa
   48 pecans or walnut halves

*\*Butter Flavor Crisco is artificially flavored.*

**1.** Preheat oven to 375°F.

**2.** For Peanut Butter Layer, combine shortening, peanut butter, sugar, 2 eggs, vanilla and water in large bowl. Beat at medium speed of electric mixer until well blended and creamy.

**3.** Combine flour, baking soda and salt. Mix into creamed mixture at low speed until blended.

**4.** For Chocolate Layer, combine ½ cup of dough from Peanut Butter Layer, 1 egg and cocoa. Beat at low speed until blended.

**5.** Form Peanut Butter Layer dough into 1-inch balls. Place 2 inches apart on ungreased cookie sheets. Flatten slightly with bottom of greased and sugared glass. Place leveled ½ teaspoonful of Chocolate Layer on flattened dough. Press nut into each center. Repeat with remaining dough.

**6.** Bake at 375°F for 10 minutes or until edges are lightly browned. Cool 2 minutes on cookie sheets. Remove to wire rack.
*Makes about 4 dozen cookies*

## 112 SPICY LEMON CRESCENTS

   1 cup (2 sticks) butter or margarine, softened
   1½ cups powdered sugar, divided
   ½ teaspoon lemon extract
   ½ teaspoon grated lemon zest
   2 cups cake flour
   ½ cup finely chopped almonds, walnuts or pecans
   1 teaspoon ground cinnamon
   ½ teaspoon ground cardamom
   ½ teaspoon ground nutmeg
   1¾ cups "M&M's"® Chocolate Mini Baking Bits

Preheat oven to 375°F. Lightly grease cookie sheets; set aside. In large bowl cream butter and ½ **cup sugar;** add lemon extract and zest until well blended. In medium bowl combine flour, nuts, cinnamon, cardamom and nutmeg; add to creamed mixture until well blended. Stir in "M&M's"® Chocolate Mini Baking Bits. Using 1 tablespoon of dough at a time, form into crescent shapes; place about 2 inches apart onto prepared cookie sheets. Bake 12 to 14 minutes or until edges are golden. Cool 2 minutes on cookie sheets. Gently roll warm crescents in remaining **1 cup sugar.** Cool completely on wire racks. Store in tightly covered container.    *Makes about 2 dozen cookies*

*Nutty Toppers*

# Bountiful Bar Cookies

## 113 ROCKY ROAD BARS

2 cups (12-ounce package) NESTLÉ® TOLL HOUSE® Semi-Sweet Chocolate Morsels, *divided*
1½ cups all-purpose flour
1½ teaspoons baking powder
1 cup granulated sugar
6 tablespoons (¾ stick) butter or margarine, softened
1½ teaspoons vanilla extract
2 eggs
2 cups (4 ounces) miniature marshmallows
1½ cups coarsely chopped walnuts

**MICROWAVE** *1 cup* morsels in medium, microwave-safe bowl on HIGH (100%) power for 1 minute; stir. Microwave at additional 10- to 20-second intervals; stir until smooth. Cool to room temperature. Combine flour and baking powder in small bowl.

**BEAT** sugar, butter and vanilla in large mixer bowl until crumbly. Beat in eggs. Add melted chocolate; beat until smooth. Gradually beat in flour mixture. Spread batter into greased 13×9-inch baking pan.

**BAKE** in preheated 375°F. oven for 16 to 20 minutes or until wooden pick inserted in center comes out still slightly sticky.

**REMOVE** from oven; sprinkle immediately with marshmallows, nuts and *remaining* morsels. Return to oven for 2 minutes. Remove from oven; cool in pan on wire rack.
*Makes 2½ dozen bars*

*Rocky Road Bars*

## 114 MINTY SHORTBREAD SQUARES

1½ cups (3 sticks) butter, softened
1½ cups powdered sugar
  2 teaspoons mint extract, divided
  3 cups all-purpose flour
  ½ cup unsweetened cocoa powder
1¾ cups "M&M's"® Chocolate Mini Baking
      Bits, divided
  1 16-ounce container prepared white
      frosting
      Several drops green food coloring

Preheat oven to 325°F. Lightly grease
15×10×1-inch baking pan; set aside. In large
bowl cream butter and sugar until light and
fluffy; add **1 teaspoon mint extract.** In
medium bowl combine flour and cocoa
powder; blend into creamed mixture. Stir in
**1 cup "M&M's"® Chocolate Mini Baking
Bits.** *Dough will be stiff.* Press dough into
prepared baking pan with lightly floured
fingers. Bake 16 to 18 minutes. Cool
completely. Combine frosting, remaining
**1 teaspoon mint extract** and green food
coloring. Spread frosting over shortbread;
sprinkle with remaining ¾ *cup "M&M's"®
Chocolate Mini Baking Bits.* Cut into
squares. Store in tightly covered container.

*Makes 36 squares*

**VARIATION:** Use 1 (19- to 21-ounce)
package fudge brownie mix, prepared
according to package directions for chewy
brownies, adding 1 teaspoon mint extract to
liquid ingredients. Stir in 1 cup "M&M's"®
Chocolate Mini Baking Bits. Spread dough in
lightly greased 13×9×2-inch baking pan.
Bake in preheated oven according to
package directions. Cool completely.
Prepare frosting and decorate as directed
above. Store in tightly covered container.
Makes 24 squares.

## 115 EASY APRICOT OATMEAL BARS

1½ cups all-purpose flour
  ¾ cup firmly packed brown sugar
  1 teaspoon baking powder
  1 cup cold butter or margarine
1½ cups quick-cooking oats, uncooked
  ½ cup flaked coconut
  ½ cup coarsely chopped walnuts
  1 can SOLO® or 1 jar BAKER® Apricot,
      Raspberry or Strawberry Filling

Preheat oven to 350°F. Grease 13×9-inch
baking pan; set aside.

Combine flour, brown sugar and baking
powder in medium bowl. Cut in butter until
mixture resembles coarse crumbs. Add oats,
coconut and walnuts; mix until crumbly.
Press half of mixture into bottom of
prepared pan. Spoon apricot filling over
crumb mixture. Sprinkle remaining crumb
mixture over apricot layer.

Bake 25 to 30 minutes or until lightly
browned. (Center may seem soft but will set
when cool.) Cool completely in pan on wire
rack. Cut into bars.

*Makes about 3 dozen bars*

*Minty Shortbread Squares*

## 116 ORANGE PUMPKIN BARS

**BARS**
1½ cups all-purpose flour
1 teaspoon baking powder
1 teaspoon pumpkin pie spice
½ teaspoon baking soda
½ teaspoon salt
1 cup solid pack canned pumpkin (not pumpkin pie filling)
¾ cup granulated sugar
⅔ cup CRISCO® Oil
2 eggs
¼ cup firmly packed light brown sugar
2 tablespoons orange juice
½ cup chopped nuts
½ cup raisins

**ICING**
1½ cups confectioners' sugar
2 tablespoons orange juice
2 tablespoons butter or margarine, softened
½ teaspoon grated orange peel

**1.** Preheat oven to 350°F. Grease and flour 12×8-inch baking dish; set aside.

**2.** For Bars, combine flour, baking powder, pumpkin pie spice, baking soda and salt in medium mixing bowl; set aside.

**3.** Combine pumpkin, granulated sugar, CRISCO® Oil, eggs, brown sugar and orange juice in large mixing bowl. Beat at low speed of electric mixer until blended, scraping bowl constantly. Add flour mixture. Beat at medium speed until smooth, scraping bowl frequently. Stir in nuts and raisins. Pour into prepared pan.

**4.** Bake 35 minutes or until center springs back when touched lightly. Cool bars completely in pan on wire rack.

**5.** For Icing, combine all ingredients. Beat at medium speed of electric mixer until smooth. Spread over cooled base. Cut into bars. *Makes about 24 bars*

## 117 CHERRY BARS

¾ cup butter or margarine
2 cups firmly packed brown sugar
2 cups all-purpose flour
2 cups old-fashioned or quick-cooking oats, uncooked
2 teaspoons baking soda
1 can (21 ounces) cherry filling and topping
2 tablespoons granulated sugar
1 tablespoon cornstarch
½ teaspoon almond extract

Beat butter and brown sugar in medium bowl with electric mixer at medium speed until light and fluffy. Combine flour, oats and baking soda. Add flour mixture to sugar mixture; mix on low speed until crumbly.

Spread two-thirds of the oat mixture into bottom of ungreased 13×9×2-inch baking pan. Press down to make crust.

Process cherry filling in food processor or blender until smooth. Pour into medium saucepan. Combine granulated sugar and cornstarch; stir into cherry filling. Cook, stirring constantly, over low heat until mixture is thick and bubbly. Stir in almond extract. Pour cherry mixture over oat layer; spread evenly. Top with remaining oat mixture.

Bake in preheated 325°F oven 45 minutes or until golden brown. Cool before cutting.
*Makes 32 (2-inch) bars*

*Favorite recipe from* **Cherry Marketing Institute, Inc.**

## BOUNTIFUL BAR COOKIES

### 118 HEATH® BARS

1 cup butter, softened
1 cup firmly packed brown sugar
1 egg yolk
1 teaspoon vanilla
2 cups flour
2 (6-ounce) bags HEATH® Bits, divided
½ cup finely chopped pecans

Preheat oven to 350°F. In large bowl, with electric mixer, cream butter well; blend in brown sugar, egg yolk and vanilla. By hand, mix in flour, 1½ bags HEATH® Bits and nuts. Press into ungreased 15½×10½-inch jelly-roll pan.

Bake 18 to 20 minutes, or until browned. Remove from oven and immediately sprinkle remaining ½ bag HEATH® Bits over top. Cool slightly; cut into bars while warm.

*Makes about 4 dozen bars*

**Heath® Bars**

### 119 CHEWY BAR COOKIES

½ cup margarine, softened
1 cup firmly packed light brown sugar
2 eggs
3 (1¼-ounce) packages Mix 'n Eat CREAM OF WHEAT® Cereal Apple 'n Cinnamon Flavor
⅔ cup all-purpose flour
2 teaspoons baking powder
1 cup PLANTERS® Walnuts, finely chopped

Preheat oven to 350°F. In large bowl, with electric mixer at medium speed, beat margarine and brown sugar until creamy. Beat in eggs until light and fluffy. Stir in cereal, flour and baking powder. Mix in walnuts. Spread batter in greased 15½×10½×1-inch baking pan.

Bake 20 to 25 minutes or until golden brown. Cool completely in pan on wire rack. Cut into bars. *Makes about 48 bars*

## 120 LAYERED CHOCOLATE CHEESE BARS

¼ cup (½ stick) margarine or butter
1½ cups graham cracker crumbs
¾ cup sugar
1 package (4 ounces) BAKER'S®
    GERMAN'S® Sweet Chocolate
1 package (8 ounces) PHILADELPHIA
    BRAND® Cream Cheese, softened
1 egg
1 cup BAKER'S® ANGEL FLAKE® Coconut
1 cup chopped nuts

**HEAT** oven to 350°F.

**MELT** margarine in oven in 13×9-inch pan. Add graham cracker crumbs and ¼ cup of the sugar; mix well. Press into pan. Bake for 10 minutes.

**MELT** chocolate. Stir in remaining ½ cup sugar, cream cheese and egg. Spread over crust. Sprinkle with coconut and nuts; press lightly.

**BAKE** for 30 minutes. Cool; cut into bars.

*Makes about 24 bars*

**Prep Time:** 20 minutes
**Bake Time:** 40 minutes

## 121 BLUEBERRY CHEESECAKE BARS

1 package DUNCAN HINES® Bakery Style
    Blueberry Muffin Mix
¼ cup butter or margarine, softened
⅓ cup finely chopped pecans
1 package (8 ounces) cream cheese,
    softened
½ cup sugar
1 egg
3 tablespoons lemon juice
1 teaspoon grated lemon peel

**1.** Preheat oven to 350°F. Grease 9-inch square pan.

**2.** Rinse blueberries from Mix with cold water and drain.

**3.** Place muffin mix in medium bowl. Cut in butter with pastry blender or two knives. Stir in pecans. Press into bottom of pan. Bake at 350°F for 15 minutes or until set.

**4.** Combine cream cheese and sugar in medium bowl. Beat until smooth. Add egg, lemon juice and lemon peel. Beat well. Spread over baked crust. Sprinkle with blueberries. Sprinkle topping packet from Mix over blueberries. Return to oven. Bake at 350°F for 35 to 40 minutes or until filling is set. Cool completely. Refrigerate until ready to serve. Cut into bars.   *Makes 16 bars*

**TIP:** Lower oven temperature by 25°F when using glass baking dishes. Glass heats more quickly and retains heat longer.

*Blueberry Cheesecake Bars*

## 122 BLUEBERRY BRAN BARS

1 3/4 cups QUAKER® Oats (quick or
    old-fashioned, uncooked)
1 cup QUAKER® Oat Bran hot cereal,
    uncooked
1/2 cup all-purpose flour
1/2 cup firmly packed brown sugar
1/2 teaspoon baking powder
1/4 teaspoon salt (optional)
1/3 cup liquid vegetable oil margarine
1/3 cup light corn syrup
2 cups fresh or frozen blueberries
1/2 cup granulated sugar
3 tablespoons water, divided
2 tablespoons cornstarch
2 teaspoons lemon juice

Preheat oven to 350°F. Lightly spray
11×7-inch baking dish with nonstick
cooking spray or oil lightly.

Combine oats, oat bran cereal, flour, brown
sugar, baking powder and salt. Add
margarine and corn syrup, mixing until
mixture resembles coarse crumbs; reserve
1 cup. Press remaining mixture onto bottom
of prepared dish.

Bake 10 minutes. Meanwhile, combine
blueberries, granulated sugar and
2 tablespoons water in small saucepan.
Bring to a boil; simmer 2 minutes,
uncovered, stirring occasionally. Combine
remaining 1 tablespoon water, cornstarch
and lemon juice; mix well. Gradually stir
into blueberry mixture; cook and stir about
30 seconds or until thickened and clear.
Spread over partially baked base to within
1/4 inch of edge; sprinkle with reserved oat
mixture.

Bake 18 to 20 minutes or until topping is
lightly browned. Cool in pan on wire rack.
Cut into bars. Store loosely covered.

*Makes about 15 bars*

## 123 APPLE LEMON BARS

Cookie Crust (recipe follows)
1 cup diced, peeled Golden Delicious
    apples
1/3 cup sugar
1 egg, beaten
2 tablespoons butter or margarine, melted
2 teaspoons grated lemon peel
3/4 cup flour
1/4 teaspoon ground cinnamon
1/4 teaspoon baking powder
1/4 teaspoon salt
Lemon Glaze (recipe follows)

Preheat oven to 350°F. Prepare Cookie
Crust. Combine apples, sugar, egg, butter
and lemon peel in large bowl; mix
thoroughly. Combine flour, cinnamon,
baking powder and salt in medium bowl;
mix well. Stir flour mixture into apple
mixture. Spread evenly over crust. Bake
25 minutes or until apples are tender. Cool in
pan on wire rack. Brush with Lemon Glaze.

*Makes 16 bars*

**COOKIE CRUST:** Beat 1/2 cup butter or
margarine, 1/4 cup powdered sugar and
2 teaspoons grated lemon peel until creamy;
blend in 1 cup flour. Press into bottom of
ungreased 8-inch square baking pan. Bake at
350°F 15 to 18 minutes or until lightly
browned.

**LEMON GLAZE:** Combine 3/4 cup powdered
sugar and 1 tablespoon lemon juice; mix
thoroughly. *Makes about 1/3 cup*

*Favorite recipe from **Washington Apple
Commission***

## BOUNTIFUL BAR COOKIES

### 124 CHOCOLATE WALNUT PIE BARS

**CRUST**
1½ cups all-purpose flour
½ cup (1 stick) butter or margarine, softened
¼ cup packed brown sugar

**FILLING**
3 eggs
¾ cup light corn syrup
¾ cup granulated sugar
2 tablespoons butter or margarine, melted
1 teaspoon vanilla extract
2 cups (12-ounce package) NESTLÉ® TOLL HOUSE® Semi-Sweet Chocolate Morsels
1½ cups coarsely chopped walnuts

*Chocolate Walnut Pie Bars*

*FOR CRUST:*
**BEAT** flour, butter and brown sugar in small mixer bowl until crumbly. Press into bottom of greased 13×9-inch baking pan.

**BAKE** in preheated 350°F. oven for 12 to 15 minutes or until lightly browned.

*FOR FILLING:*
**BEAT** eggs, corn syrup, granulated sugar, butter and vanilla in large mixer bowl. Stir in morsels and nuts; pour over hot crust.

**BAKE** at 350°F. for 25 to 30 minutes or until set. Cool completely in pan on wire rack.
*Makes about 3 dozen bars*

## 125 MOLASSES APPLESAUCE BARS

½ cup butter or margarine, softened
1 cup granulated sugar
¼ cup dark molasses
2 eggs
2⅓ cups sifted flour
1 teaspoon baking soda
1 teaspoon ground cinnamon
½ teaspoon salt
½ teaspoon ground nutmeg
½ teaspoon ground ginger
1 cup applesauce
1 cup DEL MONTE® Seedless Raisins, chopped
1 tablespoon grated orange peel
Powdered sugar

Preheat oven to 350°F. In large bowl, cream butter and granulated sugar until light and fluffy. Add molasses and eggs; mix well. In medium bowl, sift together flour, baking soda, cinnamon, salt, nutmeg and ginger. Add flour mixture alternately with applesauce to creamed mixture, mixing well after each addition. Stir in raisins and orange peel. Spread into greased and floured 13×9-inch baking pan. Bake 25 to 30 minutes or until wooden toothpick inserted in center comes out clean. Cool completely in pan on wire rack. Sprinkle with powdered sugar. Cut into bars.     *Makes about 3 dozen bars*

## 126 CHOCOLATE ORANGE GEMS

⅔ cup butter-flavored solid vegetable shortening
¾ cup firmly packed light brown sugar
1 large egg
¼ cup orange juice
1 tablespoon grated orange zest
2¼ cups all-purpose flour
½ teaspoon baking powder
½ teaspoon baking soda
½ teaspoon salt
1¾ cups "M&M's"® Chocolate Mini Baking Bits
1 cup coarsely chopped pecans
⅓ cup orange marmalade
Vanilla Glaze (recipe follows)

Preheat oven to 350°F. In large bowl cream shortening and sugar until light and fluffy; beat in egg, orange juice and orange zest. In medium bowl combine flour, baking powder, baking soda and salt; blend into creamed mixture. Stir in "M&M's"® Chocolate Mini Baking Bits and nuts. Reserve 1 cup dough; spread remaining dough into ungreased 13×9×2-inch baking pan. Spread marmalade evenly over top of dough to within ½ inch of edges. Drop reserved dough by teaspoonfuls randomly over marmalade. Bake 25 to 30 minutes or until light golden brown. *Do not overbake.* Cool completely; drizzle with **Vanilla Glaze.** Cut into bars. Store in tightly covered container.     *Makes 24 bars*

**VANILLA GLAZE:** Combine 1 cup powdered sugar and 1 to 1½ tablespoons warm water until desired consistency. Place glaze in resealable plastic sandwich bag; seal bag. Cut a tiny piece off one corner of the bag (not more than ⅛ inch). Drizzle glaze over cookies.

*Chocolate Orange Gems*

## BOUNTIFUL BAR COOKIES

## 127 DOUBLE CHOCOLATE CRISPY BARS

6 cups crispy rice cereal
½ cup peanut butter
⅓ cup butter or margarine
2 squares (1 ounce each) unsweetened chocolate
1 package (8 ounces) marshmallows
1 cup (6 ounces) semisweet chocolate chips or 6 ounces bittersweet chocolate, chopped
6 ounces white chocolate, chopped
2 teaspoons shortening, divided

Preheat oven to 350°F. Spread cereal on cookie sheet; toast in oven 10 minutes or until light brown. Place in large bowl. Line 13×9-inch pan with waxed paper.

Meanwhile, combine peanut butter, butter and unsweetened chocolate in large heavy saucepan. Stir over low heat until chocolate is melted. Add marshmallows; stir until melted and smooth. Pour chocolate mixture over cereal; mix until evenly coated. Press firmly into prepared pan.

Place semisweet chocolate and white chocolate into separate bowls. Add 1 teaspoon shortening to each bowl. Place bowls over very warm water; stir until chocolates are melted and mixtures are smooth. Spread top of cereal mixture with melted semisweet chocolate; cool until chocolate is set. Turn cereal mixture out of pan onto sheet of waxed paper, chocolate-side-down. Remove waxed paper from cereal mixture; spread white chocolate over surface. Cool until white chocolate is set. Cut into bars using sharp, thin knife.

*Makes about 3 dozen bars*

## 128 BUTTERY OATMEAL TURTLE BARS

1 cup all-purpose flour
1 cup rolled oats
¾ cup packed brown sugar
½ cup (1 stick) butter, softened
1½ cup whole pecans
2 bars (4 ounces each) sweet baking chocolate

**CARAMEL TOPPING**
½ cup (1 stick) butter
⅔ cup packed brown sugar
½ teaspoon vanilla

Combine flour, rolled oats, brown sugar and butter. Mix until well blended. Pat firmly into ungreased 13×9×2-inch baking pan. Sprinkle with pecans. To prepare Caramel Topping, combine butter and sugar in heavy saucepan. Cook over medium heat, stirring constantly until entire surface of mixture is boiling. Boil 1 minute. Remove from heat; add vanilla. Pour evenly over pecans and crust. Bake at 350°F 15 to 18 minutes or until caramel is bubbly. Break chocolate into 1-inch chunks. Sprinkle evenly over caramel layer. Bake 1 minute longer to allow chocolate to melt. Swirl chocolate for a marbled effect. Cool slightly, then chill to set chocolate. Cut into bars.

*Makes 4 to 5 dozen bars*

*White Chip Lemon Bars*

## 129 WHITE CHIP LEMON BARS

1¼ cups all-purpose flour, divided
1 cup granulated sugar, divided
⅓ cup butter or margarine, softened
¾ cup HERSHEY'S Premier White Chips
2 eggs, slightly beaten
¼ cup lemon juice
2 teaspoons freshly grated lemon peel
Powdered sugar

**1.** Heat oven to 350°F.

**2.** In medium bowl, stir together 1 cup flour and ¼ cup granulated sugar. Cut in butter with pastry blender until mixture resembles coarse crumbs. Press mixture onto bottom of 9-inch square baking pan.

**3.** Bake 15 minutes or until lightly browned. Remove from oven; sprinkle white chips over crust.

**4.** In medium bowl, stir together eggs, lemon juice, lemon peel, remaining ¼ cup flour and remaining ¾ cup sugar; carefully pour over chips and crust.

**5.** Bake 15 minutes or until set. Cool slightly in pan on wire rack; sift with powdered sugar. Cool completely in pan on wire rack; cut into bars.          *Makes about 36 bars*

## 130 TRI–LAYER CHOCOLATE OATMEAL BARS

### CRUST
1 cup uncooked rolled oats
½ cup all-purpose flour
½ cup firmly packed light brown sugar
¼ cup MOTT'S® Natural Apple Sauce
1 tablespoon margarine, melted
¼ teaspoon baking soda

### FILLING
⅔ cup all-purpose flour
½ teaspoon baking powder
¼ teaspoon salt
¾ cup granulated sugar
¼ cup MOTT'S® Natural Apple Sauce
1 whole egg
1 egg white
2 tablespoons unsweetened cocoa powder
1 tablespoon margarine, melted
½ teaspoon vanilla extract
¼ cup low fat buttermilk

### ICING
1 cup powdered sugar
1 tablespoon unsweetened cocoa powder
1 tablespoon skim milk
1 teaspoon instant coffee powder

1. Preheat oven to 350°F. Spray 8-inch square baking pan with nonstick cooking spray.

2. **To prepare Crust,** in medium bowl, combine oats, ½ cup flour, brown sugar, ¼ cup apple sauce, 1 tablespoon margarine and baking soda. Stir with fork until mixture resembles coarse crumbs. Press evenly into bottom of prepared pan. Bake 10 minutes.

3. **To prepare Filling,** in small bowl, combine ⅔ cup flour, baking powder and salt.

4. In large bowl, combine granulated sugar, ¼ cup apple sauce, whole egg, egg white, 2 tablespoons cocoa, 1 tablespoon margarine and vanilla.

5. Add flour mixture to apple sauce mixture alternately with buttermilk; stir until well blended. Spread filling over baked crust.

6. Bake 25 minutes or until toothpick inserted in center comes out clean. Cool completely on wire rack.

7. **To prepare Icing,** in small bowl, combine powdered sugar, 1 tablespoon cocoa, milk and coffee powder until smooth. Spread evenly over bars. Let stand until set. Run tip of knife through icing to score. Cut into 14 bars. *Makes 14 servings*

## 131 CHOCOLATE PEANUTTY CRUMBLE BARS

½ cup butter or margarine
1 cup all-purpose flour
¾ cup instant oats, uncooked
⅓ cup firmly packed brown sugar
½ teaspoon baking soda
½ teaspoon vanilla extract
4 SNICKERS® Bars (2.07 ounces each), cut into 8 slices each

Preheat oven to 350°F. Grease bottom of an 8-inch square pan. Melt butter in large saucepan. Remove from heat and stir in flour, oats, brown sugar, baking soda and vanilla. Blend until crumbly. Press ⅔ of the mixture into prepared pan. Arrange SNICKERS® Bar slices in pan, about ½ inch from the edge of pan. Finely crumble the remaining mixture over the sliced SNICKERS® Bars. Bake for 25 minutes or until edges are golden brown. Cool in pan on cooling rack. Cut into bars or squares to serve. *Makes 24 bars*

*Tri-Layer Chocolate Oatmeal Bars*

## BOUNTIFUL BAR COOKIES

### 132 KAHLÚA® PUMPKIN SQUARES WITH PRALINE TOPPING

1 cup all-purpose flour
¼ cup powdered sugar
½ cup cold unsalted butter
1 cup LIBBY'S® Solid Pack Pumpkin
1 (8-ounce) package cream cheese, cut up and softened
2 eggs
¼ cup granulated sugar
¼ cup KAHLÚA®
1 cup chopped walnuts or pecans
¾ cup firmly packed brown sugar
¼ cup unsalted butter, melted

Preheat oven to 350°F. In medium bowl, combine flour and powdered sugar. Using 2 knives or pastry blender, cut in ½ cup butter until mixture forms fine crumbs. Press mixture into bottom of 8-inch square baking dish. Bake 15 to 18 minutes or until golden.

Meanwhile, in food processor or blender, purée pumpkin, cream cheese, eggs, granulated sugar and Kahlúa® until smooth. Pour pumpkin mixture over warm baked crust; return to oven and bake about 20 minutes or until set. Cool in dish on wire rack. Cover; refrigerate.

In small bowl, combine nuts, brown sugar and melted butter. Just before serving, sprinkle nut mixture over pumpkin filling.

*Makes about 16 squares*

### 133 TROPICAL SUN BARS

CRUST
1 cup all-purpose flour
¼ cup sugar
⅓ cup margarine, softened
1 tablespoon grated tangerine or orange peel

FILLING
½ cup sugar
½ cup flaked coconut
2 tablespoons all-purpose flour
½ teaspoon baking powder
⅛ teaspoon salt
1½ tablespoons grated tangerine or orange peel
2 eggs
1 tablespoon orange juice
1 tablespoon orange liqueur
Thin strips of orange peel (optional)

Preheat oven to 350°F. For crust, combine 1 cup flour, ¼ cup sugar, margarine and 1 tablespoon tangerine peel in small mixer bowl. Beat at low speed of electric mixer, scraping bowl often, until coarse crumbs form, 1 to 2 minutes. Press on bottom of 9-inch square baking pan. Bake 10 to 12 minutes or until edges are lightly browned.

For filling, combine ½ cup sugar, coconut, 2 tablespoons flour, baking powder, salt, 1½ tablespoons tangerine peel, eggs, orange juice and liqueur in small mixer bowl. Beat at medium speed, scraping bowl often, until well blended, 1 to 2 minutes. Pour over hot crust. Bake 20 to 25 minutes or until edges are lightly browned. Immediately sprinkle with orange peel, if desired. Cool completely. Cut into bars.

*Makes about 24 bars*

## BOUNTIFUL BAR COOKIES

### 134 BANANA CARAMEL BARS

2½ cups all-purpose flour
  1 cup sugar
  1 teaspoon baking powder
  1 cup margarine, cubed
  1 large egg, beaten
  2 extra-ripe, medium DOLE® Bananas,
    peeled
  ½ cup caramel topping

• Combine flour, sugar and baking powder in medium bowl. Cut in margarine with pastry blender until mixture resembles coarse meal. Slowly stir in egg, mixing with fork until crumbly. Pat half of mixture into 13×9-inch baking pan to form crust.

• For filling, mash bananas (1 cup). Blend bananas with caramel topping. Pour over crust; spread evenly.

• Sprinkle remaining crust mixture over filling. Pat gently. Bake in 375°F oven 35 minutes or until golden brown. Cool on wire rack. Cut into bars when cooled.

*Makes 24 bars*

**Prep Time:** 20 minutes
**Bake Time:** 35 minutes

*Banana Caramel Bars*

## 135 BANANA SPLIT BARS

⅓ cup margarine or butter, softened
1 cup sugar
1 egg
1 banana, mashed
½ teaspoon vanilla
1¼ cups all-purpose flour
1 teaspoon CALUMET® Baking Powder
¼ teaspoon salt
⅓ cup chopped nuts
2 cups KRAFT® Miniature Marshmallows
1 cup BAKER'S® Semi-Sweet Real Chocolate Chips
⅓ cup maraschino cherries, drained and quartered

**PREHEAT** oven to 350°F. Beat margarine and sugar until light and fluffy. Add egg, banana and vanilla; mix well. Mix in flour, baking powder and salt. Stir in nuts. Pour batter into greased 13×9-inch pan.

**BAKE** for 20 minutes. Remove from oven. Sprinkle with marshmallows, chips and cherries. Bake 10 to 15 minutes longer or until wooden toothpick inserted in center comes out clean. Cool in pan; cut into bars.

*Makes about 24 bars*

## 136 APPLE CRUMB SQUARES

2 cups QUAKER® Oats (quick or old fashioned, uncooked)
1½ cups all-purpose flour
1 cup packed brown sugar
1 teaspoon ground cinnamon
½ teaspoon salt (optional)
½ teaspoon baking soda
¼ teaspoon ground nutmeg
¾ cup butter or margarine, melted
1 cup commercially prepared applesauce
½ cup chopped nuts

Preheat oven to 350°F. In large bowl, combine all ingredients except applesauce and nuts; mix until crumbly. Reserve 1 cup oats mixture. Press remaining oats mixture onto bottom of greased 13×9-inch pan. Bake 13 to 15 minutes; cool. Spread applesauce over partially baked crust; sprinkle with nuts. Sprinkle reserved 1 cup oats mixture over top. Bake 13 to 15 minutes or until golden brown. Cool in pan on wire rack; cut into 2-inch squares.

*Makes about 24 squares*

*Apple Crumb Squares*

## 137 TOFFEE-BRAN BARS

¾ cup all-purpose flour
¾ cup 100% bran cereal, divided
1¼ cups firmly packed light brown sugar, divided
½ cup margarine, melted
2 eggs, slightly beaten
1 teaspoon DAVIS® Baking Powder
1 teaspoon vanilla extract
1 cup semisweet chocolate chips
½ cup flaked coconut, toasted
⅓ cup Planters® Walnuts, chopped

Preheat oven to 350°F. In small bowl, combine flour, ½ cup bran, ½ cup brown sugar and margarine. Press on bottom of 13×9×2-inch baking pan. Bake 10 minutes; set aside.

In medium bowl, with electric mixer at high speed, beat remaining ¼ cup bran, ¾ cup brown sugar, eggs, baking powder and vanilla until thick and foamy. Spread over prepared crust. Bake 25 minutes more or until set. Remove pan from oven. Sprinkle with chocolate chips; let stand 5 minutes. Spread softened chocolate evenly over baked layer. Immediately sprinkle coconut and chopped walnuts in alternating diagonal strips over chocolate. Cool completely in pan on wire rack. Cut into 3×1½-inch bars. Store in airtight container.

*Makes 24 bars*

## 138 BUTTERSCOTCH CAKE BARS

¼ cup Prune Purée (recipe, page 97) or prepared prune butter or 1 jar (2½ ounces) baby food prunes
2 tablespoons molasses
1 tablespoon vegetable oil
1 teaspoon instant espresso coffee powder
1 teaspoon vanilla
¼ teaspoon salt
4 egg whites
1 cup packed brown sugar
1 cup all-purpose flour
Cream Cheese Icing (recipe follows)
2 tablespoons finely chopped walnuts

Preheat oven to 350°F. Coat 13×9×2-inch pan with vegetable cooking spray. In small bowl, whisk together prune purée, molasses, oil, espresso powder, vanilla and salt. In mixer bowl, beat egg whites with sugar on medium speed 30 seconds; beat on high 2½ minutes until thick and fluffy. Add prune purée mixture to egg white mixture; beat until well blended. Fold in flour. Spread batter evenly in prepared pan. Bake in center of oven 20 to 25 minutes or until golden brown and springy to the touch. Cool completely in pan on wire rack. Meanwhile, make Cream Cheese Icing. Spread over cookies; sprinkle with walnuts. Let stand until icing is set before cutting into 3¼×2¼-inch bars. *Makes 16 bars*

**CREAM CHEESE ICING:** In small mixer bowl, beat together 1 cup powdered sugar, 4 ounces (½ of 8-ounce package) reduced fat cream cheese and 1 tablespoon lemon juice until very smooth.

*Favorite recipe from California Prune Board*

## 139 PEANUT BUTTER CHOCOLATE BARS

½ cup (1 stick) margarine, softened
⅓ cup sugar
½ cup QUAKER® or AUNT JEMIMA®
    Enriched Corn Meal
½ cup all-purpose flour
½ cup chopped almonds
½ cup peanut butter
¼ cup semi-sweet chocolate pieces
1 teaspoon shortening

Preheat oven to 375°F. Beat margarine and sugar until fluffy. Stir in combined corn meal, flour and almonds. Press onto bottom of ungreased 9-inch square baking pan.

Bake 25 to 30 minutes or until edges are light golden brown. Cool about 10 minutes; spread with peanut butter. In small saucepan over low heat, melt chocolate pieces and shortening, stirring until smooth.* Drizzle over peanut butter. Cool completely in pan on wire rack. Cut into bars. Store tightly covered. *Makes about 16 bars*

*To Microwave: Place chocolate pieces and shortening in small microwaveable bowl. Microwave at HIGH (100% power) 1 to 1½ minutes, stirring after 1 minute and then every 15 seconds until smooth.*

*Peanut Butter Chocolate Bars and Crispy Nut Shortbread (page 36)*

## BOUNTIFUL BAR COOKIES

### 140 HEAVENLY OAT BARS

½ cup (1 stick) MAZOLA® Margarine, softened
½ cup firmly packed brown sugar
½ cup KARO® Light or Dark Corn Syrup
1 teaspoon vanilla
3 cups uncooked quick or old-fashioned oats
1 cup (6 ounces) semi-sweet chocolate chips
½ cup SKIPPY® Creamy Peanut Butter

1. Preheat oven to 350°F. Lightly grease 9-inch square baking pan.

2. In large bowl with mixer at medium speed, beat margarine, brown sugar, corn syrup and vanilla until blended and smooth. Stir in oats. Spread in prepared pan.

3. Bake 25 minutes or until center is just firm. Cool slightly on wire rack.

4. In small heavy saucepan over low heat, stir chocolate chips until melted and smooth. Remove from heat; stir in peanut butter until smooth. Spread over warm bars. Cool completely in pan on wire rack before cutting. *Makes about 2 dozen bars*

TIP: To melt chocolate chips in microwave, place in dry microwavable bowl or glass measuring cup. Microwave on HIGH (100% power) 1 minute; stir. Microwave on HIGH 1 minute longer. Stir until chocolate is smooth.

### 141 CRANBERRY CHEESE BARS

2 cups all-purpose flour
1½ cups quick-cooking or old-fashioned oats, uncooked
¾ cup plus 1 tablespoon firmly packed light brown sugar, divided
1 cup (2 sticks) butter or margarine, softened
1¾ cups "M&M's"® Chocolate Mini Baking Bits, divided
1 8-ounce package cream cheese
1 14-ounce can sweetened condensed milk
¼ cup lemon juice
1 teaspoon vanilla extract
2 tablespoons cornstarch
1 16-ounce can whole berry cranberry sauce

Preheat oven to 350°F. Lightly grease 13×9×2-inch baking pan; set aside. In large bowl combine flour, oats, *¾ cup sugar* and butter; mix until crumbly. Reserve 1½ cups crumb mixture for topping. Stir *½ cup "M&M's"® Chocolate Mini Baking Bits* into remaining crumb mixture; press into prepared pan. Bake 15 minutes. Cool completely. In large bowl beat cream cheese until light and fluffy; gradually mix in condensed milk, lemon juice and vanilla until smooth. Pour evenly over crust. In small bowl combine remaining *1 tablespoon sugar,* cornstarch and cranberry sauce. Spoon over cream cheese mixture. Stir remaining *1¼ cups "M&M's"® Chocolate Mini Baking Bits* into reserved crumb mixture. Sprinkle over cranberry mixture. Bake 40 minutes. Cool at room temperature; refrigerate before cutting. Store in refrigerator in tightly covered container. *Makes 32 bars*

*Cranberry Cheese Bars*

## BOUNTIFUL BAR COOKIES

### 142 LEMON NUT BARS

1⅓ cups all-purpose flour
½ cup firmly packed brown sugar
¼ cup granulated sugar
¾ cup butter or margarine
1 cup old-fashioned or quick oats, uncooked
½ cup chopped nuts
1 (8-ounce) package PHILADELPHIA BRAND® Cream Cheese, softened
1 egg
1 tablespoon grated lemon peel
3 tablespoons lemon juice

• Preheat oven to 350°F.

• Stir together flour and sugars in medium bowl. Cut in butter until mixture resembles coarse crumbs. Stir in oats and nuts. Reserve 1 cup crumb mixture; press remaining crumb mixture onto bottom of greased 13×9-inch baking pan. Bake 15 minutes.

• Beat cream cheese, egg, lemon peel and juice in small mixing bowl at medium speed with electric mixer until well blended. Pour over crust; sprinkle with reserved crumb mixture.

• Bake 25 minutes. Cool in pan on wire rack. Cut into bars.

*Makes about 3 dozen bars*

**Prep Time:** 30 minutes
**Cook Time:** 25 minutes

### 143 CURRANT CHEESECAKE BARS

½ cup butter or margarine, softened
1 cup all-purpose flour
½ cup packed light brown sugar
½ cup finely chopped pecans
1 package (8 ounces) cream cheese, softened
¼ cup granulated sugar
1 egg
1 tablespoon milk
2 teaspoons grated lemon peel
⅓ cup currant jelly or seedless raspberry jam

**PREHEAT** oven to 350°F. Grease 9-inch square baking pan. Beat butter in medium bowl with electric mixer at medium speed until smooth. Add flour, brown sugar and pecans; beat at low speed until well blended. Press mixture into bottom and partially up sides of prepared pan.

**BAKE** about 15 minutes or until light brown. If sides of crust have shrunk down, press back up and reshape with spoon. Cool 5 minutes on wire rack.

*Meanwhile,* **BEAT** cream cheese in large bowl with electric mixer at medium speed until smooth. Add granulated sugar, egg, milk and lemon peel; beat until well blended.

**HEAT** jelly in small saucepan over low heat 2 to 3 minutes or until smooth.

**POUR** cream cheese mixture over crust. Drizzle jelly in 7 to 8 strips across filling with spoon. Swirl jam through filling with knife to create marbleized effect.

**RETURN** pan to oven; bake 20 to 25 minutes or until filling is set. Cool completely on wire rack before cutting into bars. Store in airtight container in refrigerator up to 1 week.

*Makes about 32 bars*

*Banana Cocoa Marbled Bars*

## 144 BANANA COCOA MARBLED BARS

½ cup uncooked rolled oats
1½ cups all-purpose flour
2 teaspoons baking powder
½ teaspoon baking soda
½ teaspoon salt
1 cup sugar
½ cup MOTT'S® Natural Apple Sauce
1 whole egg
1 egg white
2 tablespoons vegetable oil
⅓ cup low-fat buttermilk
2 tablespoons unsweetened cocoa powder
1 large ripe banana, mashed (⅔ cup)

**1.** Preheat oven to 350°F. Spray 9-inch square baking pan with nonstick cooking spray.

**2.** Place oats in food processor or blender; process until finely ground.

**3.** In medium bowl, combine oats, flour, baking powder, baking soda and salt.

**4.** In large bowl, combine sugar, apple sauce, whole egg, egg white and oil.

**5.** Add flour mixture to apple sauce mixture; stir until well blended. (Mixture will look dry.)

**6.** Remove 1 cup of batter to small bowl. Add buttermilk and cocoa; mix well.

**7.** Add banana to remaining batter. Mix well; spread into prepared pan.

**8.** Drop tablespoonfuls of cocoa batter over banana batter. Run knife through batters to marble.

**9.** Bake 35 minutes or until toothpick inserted in center comes out clean. Cool on wire rack 15 minutes; cut into 14 bars.

*Makes 14 servings*

## BOUNTIFUL BAR COOKIES

### 145 "CORDIALLY YOURS" CHOCOLATE CHIP BARS

¾ BUTTER FLAVOR* CRISCO® Stick or
    ¾ cup BUTTER FLAVOR CRISCO
    all-vegetable shortening
 2 eggs
½ cup granulated sugar
¼ cup firmly packed brown sugar
1½ teaspoons vanilla
 1 teaspoon almond extract
 2 cups all-purpose flour
 1 teaspoon baking soda
½ teaspoon cinnamon
 1 can (21 ounces) cherry pie filling
1½ cups milk chocolate chips
    Powdered sugar

*Butter Flavor Crisco is artificially flavored.*

1. Preheat oven to 350°F. Grease
15½×10½×1-inch pan with shortening.

2. Combine shortening, eggs, granulated
sugar, brown sugar, vanilla and almond
extract in large bowl. Beat at medium speed
of electric mixer until well blended.

3. Combine flour, baking soda and
cinnamon. Mix into creamed mixture at low
speed until just blended. Stir in pie filling
and chocolate chips. Spread in pan.

4. Bake 25 minutes or until lightly browned
and top springs back when lightly pressed.
Cool completely in pan on wire rack.
Sprinkle with powdered sugar. Cut into
2½×2-inch bars.          *Makes 30 bars*

### 146 CARAMEL OATMEAL CHEWIES

1¾ cups quick or old-fashioned oats
1¾ cups all-purpose flour, *divided*
 ¾ cup packed brown sugar
 ½ teaspoon baking soda
 ¼ teaspoon salt (optional)
 ¾ cup (1½ sticks) butter or margarine,
     melted
 1 cup chopped nuts
 2 cups (12-ounce package) NESTLÉ® TOLL
     HOUSE® Semi-Sweet Chocolate
     Morsels
 1 cup caramel ice-cream topping

**COMBINE** oats, *1½ cups* flour, brown
sugar, baking soda and salt in large bowl; stir
to break up brown sugar. Stir in butter,
mixing until well blended. Reserve *1 cup* oat
mixture; press *remaining* oat mixture onto
bottom of greased 13×9-inch baking pan.
**BAKE** in preheated 350°F. oven for 10 to
12 minutes or until light brown; cool on wire
rack for 10 minutes. Sprinkle with nuts and
morsels. Mix caramel topping with
*remaining* flour in small bowl; drizzle over
morsels to within ¼ inch of pan edges.
Sprinkle with *reserved* oat mixture. **BAKE**
at 350°F. for 18 to 22 minutes or until golden
brown. Cool in pan on wire rack; chill until
firm.          *Makes about 2½ dozen bars*

*Caramel Oatmeal Chewies*

## BOUNTIFUL BAR COOKIES

## 147 OATMEAL CARMELITA BARS

¾ BUTTER FLAVOR* CRISCO® Stick or
    ¾ cup BUTTER FLAVOR CRISCO
    all-vegetable shortening, melted
1½ cups quick oats (not instant or old
    fashioned), uncooked
¾ cup firmly packed brown sugar
½ cup plus 3 tablespoons all-purpose flour,
    divided
½ cup whole wheat flour
½ teaspoon baking soda
¼ teaspoon cinnamon
1⅓ cups milk chocolate chips
½ cup chopped walnuts
1 jar (12.5 ounces) or ¾ cup caramel ice
    cream topping

*Butter Flavor Crisco is artificially flavored.*

**1. Heat** oven to 350°F. **Grease** bottom and
sides of 9×9×2-inch baking pan with
shortening. **Place** rack on countertop.

**2. Combine** shortening, oats, sugar, ½ cup
all-purpose flour, whole wheat flour, baking
soda and cinnamon in large bowl. **Mix** at
low speed of electric mixer until crumbs
form. **Reserve** ½ cup for topping. **Press**
remaining crumbs into prepared pan.

**3. Bake** at 350°F for 10 minutes. *Do not
overbake.* **Sprinkle** chocolate chips and
nuts over crust.

**4. Combine** caramel topping and remaining
3 tablespoons all-purpose flour. **Stir** until
well blended. **Drizzle** over chocolate chips
and nuts. **Sprinkle** reserved ½ cup crumbs
over caramel topping.

**5. Return** to oven. **Bake** at 350°F for 20 to
25 minutes or until golden brown. *Do not
overbake.* **Run** spatula around edge of pan
before cooling. **Cool** completely in pan on
cooling rack. **Cut** into 1½×1½-inch squares.
                              *Makes 3 dozen squares*

## 148 CRISPY CHOCOLATE BARS

1 package (6 ounces, 1 cup) semi-sweet
    chocolate chips
1 package (6 ounces, 1 cup) butterscotch
    chips
½ cup peanut butter
5 cups KELLOGG'S CORN FLAKES® cereal
    Vegetable cooking spray

**1.** In large saucepan, combine chocolate and
butterscotch chips and peanut butter. Stir
over low heat until smooth. Remove from
heat.

**2.** Add KELLOGG'S CORN FLAKES® cereal.
Stir until well coated.

**3.** Using buttered spatula or waxed paper,
press mixture evenly into 9×9×2-inch pan
coated with cooking spray. Cut into bars
when cool.                    *Makes 16 bars*

## 149 NO–FUSS BAR COOKIES

24 graham cracker squares
 1 cup semisweet chocolate chips
 1 cup flaked coconut
¾ cup coarsely chopped walnuts
 1 can (14 ounces) sweetened condensed
    milk

**PREHEAT** oven to 350°F. Grease 13×9-inch
baking pan.

**PLACE** graham crackers in food processor.
Process until crackers form fine crumbs.
Measure 2 cups of crumbs.

**COMBINE** graham cracker crumbs, chips,
coconut and walnuts in medium bowl; stir to
blend. Add milk; stir until blended. Spread
batter evenly into prepared pan.

## BOUNTIFUL BAR COOKIES

**BAKE** 15 to 18 minutes or until edges are golden brown. Cool completely on wire rack before cutting. Cut into bars. Store tightly covered at room temperature or freeze up to 3 months.    *Makes 20 bars*

## 150 PUMPKIN SNACK BARS

**CAKE**
  1 package (2-layer size) spice cake mix
  1 can (16 ounces) pumpkin
  ¾ cup MIRACLE WHIP® or MIRACLE
    WHIP® LIGHT Dressing
  3 eggs

**FROSTING**
3½ cups powdered sugar
  ½ cup (1 stick) PARKAY® Spread Sticks,
    softened
  2 tablespoons milk
  1 teaspoon vanilla

• *Cake:* Heat oven to 350°F.

• Blend cake mix, pumpkin, dressing and eggs with electric mixer on medium speed until well blended. Pour into greased 15×10×1-inch baking pan.

• Bake 18 to 20 minutes or until toothpick inserted in center comes out clean. Cool completely on wire rack.

• *Frosting:* Blend all ingredients with electric mixer on low speed until moistened. Beat on high speed until light and fluffy. Spread over cake. Cut into bars.
    *Makes about 3 dozen*

**Prep Time:** 20 minutes
**Cook Time:** 20 minutes

## 151 FUDGY CHOCOLATE MINT OATMEAL SQUARES

1¼ cups all-purpose flour
  ½ teaspoon baking soda
  1 cup packed brown sugar
  ½ cup (1 stick) butter or margarine,
    softened
  1 egg
1½ cups quick or old fashioned oats
  1 cup chopped nuts
1½ cups (10-ounce package) NESTLÉ® TOLL
    HOUSE® Mint-Chocolate Morsels
1¼ cups (14-ounce can) CARNATION®
    Sweetened Condensed Milk
  2 tablespoons butter or margarine

**COMBINE** flour and baking soda in small bowl. Beat sugar and *½ cup* butter in large mixer bowl until creamy. Beat in egg. Gradually beat in flour mixture. Stir in oats and nuts. Press *2 cups* oat mixture onto bottom of greased 13×9-inch baking pan with moistened fingers.

**MELT** morsels, sweetened condensed milk and *2 tablespoons* butter in heavy-duty saucepan over low heat, stirring constantly until smooth; pour over crust. Crumble *remaining* oat mixture over filling.

**BAKE** in preheated 350°F. oven for 25 to 30 minutes or until filling is set and topping begins to brown. Cool in pan on wire rack.
    *Makes about 2½ dozen squares*

## BOUNTIFUL BAR COOKIES

### 152 SWEET WALNUT MAPLE BARS

**CRUST**
1 package DUNCAN HINES® Moist Deluxe Yellow Cake Mix, divided
⅓ cup butter or margarine, melted
1 egg

**TOPPING**
1⅓ cups maple syrup (see Tip)
3 eggs
⅓ cup firmly packed light brown sugar
½ teaspoon maple flavoring or vanilla extract
1 cup chopped walnuts

**1.** Preheat oven to 350°F. Grease 13×9×2-inch pan.

**2. For crust,** reserve ⅔ cup cake mix; set aside. Combine remaining cake mix, melted butter and egg in large bowl. Stir until thoroughly blended. (Mixture will be crumbly.) Press into pan. Bake at 350°F for 15 to 20 minutes or until light golden brown.

**3. For topping,** combine reserved cake mix, maple syrup, eggs, brown sugar and maple flavoring in large bowl. Beat at low speed with electric mixer for 3 minutes. Pour over crust. Sprinkle with walnuts. Bake at 350°F for 30 to 35 minutes or until filling is set. Cool completely. Cut into bars. Store leftover cookie bars in refrigerator.

*Makes 24 bars*

**TIP:** You may substitute your favorite maple-flavored or imitation maple syrup for the pure maple syrup if desired.

### 153 PLUM OAT SQUARES

1 cup uncooked rolled oats
⅓ cup whole wheat flour
⅓ cup packed brown sugar
1 teaspoon ground cinnamon
¼ teaspoon baking soda
¼ teaspoon ground nutmeg
1 egg, slightly beaten
2 tablespoons unsalted butter, melted
2 tablespoons unsweetened apple juice concentrate, thawed
1 teaspoon vanilla
2 fresh California plums, finely chopped

Preheat oven to 350°F. Grease 11×7-inch baking pan; set aside. Combine oats, flour, sugar, cinnamon, baking soda and nutmeg in large bowl. Combine egg, butter, juice and vanilla in small bowl until well blended. Stir into oat mixture until well blended. Fold in plums. Spread evenly into prepared pan. Bake 25 minutes or until wooden pick inserted in center comes out clean. Cool in pan on wire rack 10 minutes. Cut into squares. Serve warm or cool completely.

*Makes 12 squares*

*Favorite recipe from* **California Tree Fruit Agreement**

*Sweet Walnut Maple Bars*

## BOUNTIFUL BAR COOKIES

### 154 CHOCOLATE MACADAMIA BARS

12 squares (1 ounce each) bittersweet
    chocolate or 1 package (12 ounces)
    semisweet chocolate chips
1 package (8 ounces) cream cheese
2/3 cup whipping cream or undiluted
    evaporated milk
1 cup chopped macadamia nuts or
    almonds
1 teaspoon vanilla, divided
1 cup butter or margarine, softened
1 1/2 cups sugar
1 egg
3 cups all-purpose flour
1 teaspoon baking powder
1/4 teaspoon salt

Preheat oven to 375°F. Lightly grease 13×9-
inch pan.

Combine chocolate, cream cheese and
cream in large heavy saucepan. Stir over low
heat until chocolate is melted and mixture is
smooth. Remove from heat; stir in nuts and
1/2 teaspoon vanilla.

Beat butter and sugar in large bowl. Beat in
egg and remaining 1/2 teaspoon vanilla. Add
flour, baking powder and salt, blending well.
Press half of dough onto bottom of prepared
pan. Spread chocolate mixture evenly over
top. Sprinkle remaining dough over
chocolate mixture.

Bake 35 to 40 minutes or until golden brown.
Cool in pan on wire rack. Cut into bars.
*Makes about 3 dozen bars*

### 155 ALMOND CHINESE CHEWS

1 cup granulated sugar
3 eggs
1 can SOLO® or 1 jar BAKER® Almond
    Filling
3/4 cup all-purpose flour
1 teaspoon baking powder
1/4 teaspoon salt
    Confectioners' sugar

Preheat oven to 300°F. Grease 13×9-inch
baking pan; set aside.

Beat granulated sugar and eggs in medium-
size bowl with electric mixer until
thoroughly blended. Add almond filling; beat
until blended. Stir flour, baking powder and
salt until mixed; fold into almond mixture.
Spread batter evenly in prepared pan.

Bake 40 to 45 minutes or until wooden
toothpick inserted in center comes out
clean. Cool completely in pan on wire rack.
Cut into 2×1 1/2-inch bars; dust with
confectioners' sugar.        *Makes 36 bars*

### 156 OASIS DATE BARS

1/2 cup (1 stick) butter or margarine,
    softened
3/4 cup firmly packed light brown sugar
2 large eggs
2 teaspoons vanilla extract
1 1/2 cups all-purpose flour
1/2 cup shredded coconut
1 teaspoon baking powder
1 3/4 cups "M&M's"® Chocolate Mini Baking
    Bits, divided
1 cup chopped pitted dates
1/2 cup chopped almonds
    Lemon Glaze (page 141)

## BOUNTIFUL BAR COOKIES

Preheat oven to 350°F. Lightly grease 13×9×2-inch baking pan; set aside. In large bowl cream butter and sugar until light and fluffy; beat in eggs and vanilla. In separate bowl combine flour, coconut and baking powder; blend into creamed mixture. Stir in *1¼ cups "M&M's"® Chocolate Mini Baking Bits,* dates and nuts. Dough will be stiff. Spread into prepared pan; sprinkle with remaining *½ cup "M&M's"® Chocolate Mini Baking Bits.* Bake 35 to 40 minutes or until toothpick inserted in center comes out clean. Cool completely; drizzle with Lemon Glaze. Cut into bars. Store in tightly covered container.          *Makes 24 bars*

**LEMON GLAZE:** Combine 1 cup powdered sugar, 2 tablespoons lemon juice and 1 tablespoon grated lemon zest until smooth. Place in resealable plastic sandwich bag; seal bag. Cut a tiny piece off one corner of the bag (not more than ⅛ inch). Drizzle glaze over bars.

**VARIATION:** For thicker bars, pour mixture into lightly greased 8×8×2-inch baking pan; bake 40 to 45 minutes. Reduce Lemon Glaze ingredients by half. Makes 16 bars.

*Oasis Date Bars*

## 157 CALIFORNIA APRICOT POWER BARS

2 cups (12 ounces) California dried apricot halves, coarsely chopped
1¼ cups (8 ounces) pitted dates, coarsely chopped
2½ cups (10 ounces) pecans, coarsely chopped
1¼ cups whole wheat flour
1 teaspoon baking powder
3 eggs
1 cup packed brown sugar
¼ cup apple juice or water
1½ teaspoons vanilla

Preheat oven to 350°F. Line 15½×10½×1-inch jelly roll pan with foil. In large bowl, stir together apricots, dates and pecans; divide in half. Combine flour and baking powder; add to half of fruit mixture. Toss to coat. In medium bowl, combine eggs, sugar, apple juice and vanilla; stir into flour mixture until thoroughly moistened. Spread batter evenly into prepared pan. Press remaining fruit mixture lightly on top.

Bake 20 minutes or until golden and bars spring back when pressed lightly. Cool in pan 5 minutes. Turn out onto wire rack; cool 45 minutes. Peel off foil and cut into bars. Store in airtight container.

*Makes about 32 bars*

*Favorite recipe from California Apricot Advisory Board*

## 158 CHOCOLATE MACAROON BARS

1¼ cups graham cracker crumbs
⅓ cup sugar
¼ cup HERSHEY'S Cocoa
⅓ cup butter or margarine, melted
1 can (14 ounces) sweetened condensed milk (not evaporated milk)
2⅔ cups MOUNDS® Sweetened Coconut Flakes
2 cups fresh white bread crumbs (4 slices)
2 eggs
2 teaspoons vanilla extract
1 cup HERSHEY'S MINI CHIPS Semi-Sweet Chocolate

1. Heat oven to 350°F.

2. In large bowl, stir together graham cracker crumbs, sugar, cocoa and butter; press firmly onto bottom of ungreased 13×9×2-inch baking pan.

3. Bake 10 minutes. Meanwhile, in medium bowl, combine sweetened condensed milk, coconut, bread crumbs, eggs, vanilla and small chocolate chips; stir until blended. Spoon evenly over prepared crust.

4. Bake 30 minutes or until lightly browned. Cool completely in pan on wire rack. Cut into bars. Store covered in refrigerator.

*Makes 24 to 36 bars*

*California Apricot Power Bars*

## BOUNTIFUL BAR COOKIES

### 159 SPECIAL TREAT NO–BAKE SQUARES

½ cup plus ⅓ cup plus 1 teaspoon butter
    or margarine, divided
¼ cup granulated sugar
¼ cup unsweetened cocoa
1 large egg
¼ teaspoon salt
1½ cups graham cracker crumbs (about
    18 graham crackers)
¾ cup flaked coconut
½ cup chopped pecans
1 package (3 ounces) cream cheese,
    softened
1 teaspoon vanilla
1 cup powdered sugar
2 ounces dark sweet or bittersweet
    chocolate candy bar, broken into
    ½-inch pieces

LINE 9-inch square pan with foil, shiny side
up, allowing 2-inch overhang on sides. Or,
lightly grease pan; set aside.

For crust, **COMBINE** ½ cup butter,
granulated sugar, cocoa, egg and salt in
medium saucepan. Cook over medium heat,
stirring constantly, until mixture thickens,
about 2 minutes. Remove from heat. Stir in
graham cracker crumbs, coconut and
pecans. Press evenly into prepared pan.

For filling, **BEAT** ⅓ cup butter, cream
cheese and vanilla in small bowl with
electric mixer at medium speed until
smooth. Gradually beat in powdered sugar.
Spread over crust; refrigerate 30 minutes.

For glaze, **COMBINE** candy bar and
remaining 1 teaspoon butter in small
resealable plastic food storage bag; seal bag.
Microwave on HIGH 50 seconds. Turn bag
over; microwave on HIGH 40 to 50 seconds
or until melted. Knead bag until mixture is
smooth.

**CUT** off very tiny corner of bag; drizzle
chocolate over filling. Refrigerate until firm,
about 20 minutes. Remove foil from pan. Cut
into 1½-inch squares. Store tightly covered
in refrigerator.          *Makes 25 squares*

### 160 PEANUT BUTTER 'N FUDGE FILLED BARS

1 cup (2 sticks) margarine or butter,
    softened
2 cups firmly packed brown sugar
¼ cup peanut butter
2 eggs
2 cups QUAKER® Oats (quick or old
    fashioned, uncooked)
2 cups all-purpose flour
1 teaspoon baking soda
¼ teaspoon salt (optional)
1 (14-ounce) can sweetened condensed
    milk (not evaporated milk)
1 (12-ounce) package (2 cups) semisweet
    chocolate pieces
2 tablespoons peanut butter
½ cup chopped peanuts

Heat oven to 375°F. Beat together margarine,
sugar and ¼ cup peanut butter until creamy.
Add eggs; beat well. Add combined oats,
flour, baking soda and salt; mix well.
Reserve 1 cup oat mixture for topping; set
aside. Spread remaining oat mixture onto
bottom of ungreased 13×9-inch baking pan.
In medium saucepan, combine condensed
milk, chocolate pieces and remaining
2 tablespoons peanut butter. Cook over low
heat until chocolate is melted, stirring
constantly. Remove from heat; stir in
peanuts. Spread mixture evenly over crust.
Drop reserved oat mixture by teaspoonfuls
over chocolate mixture. Bake 30 to
35 minutes or until light golden brown. Cool
completely; cut into bars. Store tightly
covered.          *Makes 32 bars*

## 161 RASPBERRY COCONUT LAYER BARS

1⅔ cups graham cracker crumbs
  ½ cup (1 stick) butter or margarine, melted
2⅔ cups (7-ounce package) flaked coconut
1¼ cups (14-ounce can) CARNATION® Sweetened Condensed Milk
  1 cup raspberry jam or preserves
  ⅓ cup finely chopped walnuts, toasted
  ½ cup NESTLÉ® TOLL HOUSE® Semi-Sweet Chocolate Morsels, melted
  ¼ cup (1½ ounces) NESTLÉ® Premier White Baking Bar, melted

**COMBINE** graham cracker crumbs and butter in medium bowl. Spread evenly over bottom of 13×9-inch baking pan; press in firmly. Sprinkle with coconut; pour sweetened condensed milk evenly over coconut.

**BAKE** in preheated 350°F. oven for 20 to 25 minutes or until lightly browned; cool for 15 minutes.

**SPREAD** jam over coconut layer; chill for 3 to 4 hours or until firm. Sprinkle with nuts. Drizzle with melted morsels and baking bar; chill. Cut into 3×1½-inch bars.

*Makes 24 bar cookies*

*Raspberry Coconut Layer Bars*

## BOUNTIFUL BAR COOKIES

### 162 FUDGE FILLED WALNUT–OATMEAL BARS

  1 cup (2 sticks) butter or margarine, softened
  2 cups packed light brown sugar
  2 eggs
  1 teaspoon vanilla extract
  ½ teaspoon powdered instant coffee (optional)
  3 cups quick-cooking oats
  2½ cups all-purpose flour
  1 teaspoon baking soda
  ½ teaspoon salt
  1½ cups chopped walnuts, divided
      Chocolate Filling (recipe follows)

Heat oven to 350°F. In large mixer bowl, beat butter and brown sugar until creamy. Add eggs, vanilla and instant coffee, if desired; beat well. Stir together oats, flour, baking soda, salt and 1 cup walnuts; gradually add to butter mixture, beating until well blended. (Batter will be stiff; stir in last part by hand.) Remove 2 cups dough. Press remaining dough onto bottom of 15½×10½×1-inch jelly-roll pan. Prepare Chocolate Filling; spread over mixture in pan. Sprinkle reserved dough over filling. Sprinkle with remaining ½ cup walnuts. Bake 25 minutes or until top is golden. (Chocolate will be soft.) Cool completely in pan on wire rack. Cut into bars.    *Makes about 48 bars*

#### CHOCOLATE FILLING
  1 tablespoon butter or margarine
  3½ bars (1 ounce each) HERSHEY'S Unsweetened Baking Chocolate, broken into pieces
  ½ cup sugar
  1 can (14 ounces) sweetened condensed milk (not evaporated milk)
  1½ teaspoons vanilla extract

In medium saucepan over low heat, melt butter. Add chocolate; cook until smooth and completely melted, stirring occasionally. Stir in sugar and sweetened condensed milk. Cook, stirring constantly, until mixture thickens and sugar is dissolved. Remove from heat. Stir in vanilla.

### 163 WALNUT APPLE DUMPLING BARS

  6 tablespoons (¾ stick) butter or margarine
  1 cup packed light brown sugar
  1 cup all-purpose flour
  1 teaspoon baking powder
  1½ teaspoons cinnamon
  2 eggs
  1½ cups coarsely chopped walnuts
  1 Granny Smith or Pippin apple, coarsely grated* (about 1 cup lightly packed)
      Powdered sugar

*It's not necessary to peel or core the apple. Simply use a hand grater, turning the apple as you go, until only the core remains.*

Melt butter in 3-quart saucepan. Add sugar. Stir until sugar is dissolved and mixture begins to bubble; cool. Combine flour, baking powder and cinnamon in medium bowl; blend thoroughly. Beat eggs, 1 at a time, into butter mixture; add flour mixture. Mix in walnuts and apple. Turn into buttered and floured 9-inch square baking pan; smooth top. Bake in preheated 350°F oven 25 to 35 minutes until pick inserted in center comes out clean and edges begin to pull away from sides of pan. Cool completely on wire rack. Cut into 24 1×3-inch bars.    *Makes 24 bars*

*Favorite recipe from* **Walnut Marketing Board**

*Fudge Filled Walnut-Oatmeal Bars*

## BOUNTIFUL BAR COOKIES

### 164 RASPBERRY & WHITE CHIP NUT BARS

1⅔ cups (10-ounce package) HERSHEY'S
    Premier White Chips, divided
¾ cup (1½ sticks) butter or margarine
2¼ cups all-purpose flour
¾ cup sugar
3 eggs
¾ teaspoon baking powder
1⅔ cups (10-ounce package) HERSHEY'S
    Raspberry Chips, divided
½ cup chopped pecans
    DOUBLE DRIZZLE (recipe follows)

**1.** Heat oven to 350°F. Grease 13×9×2-inch baking pan.

**2.** Reserve 2 tablespoons white chips for drizzle. In medium microwave-safe bowl, place remaining white chips and butter. Microwave at HIGH (100%) 1½ minutes; stir. If necessary, microwave at HIGH an additional 15 seconds at a time, stirring after each heating, just until chips are melted when stirred. In large bowl, combine flour, sugar, eggs and baking powder. Add white chip mixture; beat well. Reserve 2 tablespoons raspberry chips for drizzle. Chop remaining raspberry chips in food processor (use pulsing motion); stir into batter with pecans. Spread batter into prepared pan.

**3.** Bake 25 minutes or until edges pull away from sides of pan and top surface is golden. Cool completely in pan on wire rack. Prepare DOUBLE DRIZZLE; using one flavor at a time, drizzle over top of bars. Cut into bars.                    *Makes about 24 bars*

**DOUBLE DRIZZLE:** In small microwave-safe bowl, place 2 tablespoons HERSHEY'S Premier White Chips and ½ teaspoon shortening (do not use butter, margarine or oil). Microwave at HIGH (100%) 1 minute; stir. If necessary, microwave at HIGH an additional 15 seconds at a time, stirring after each heating, just until chips are melted when stirred. Repeat procedure with raspberry chips.

**PEANUT BUTTER AND CHOCOLATE BARS:** Omit HERSHEY'S Premier White Chips; replace with REESE'S Peanut Butter Chips. Omit HERSHEY'S Raspberry Chips; replace with HERSHEY'S Semi-Sweet Chocolate Chips. Omit chopped pecans; replace with ½ cup chopped peanuts.

**BUTTERSCOTCH AND CHOCOLATE BARS:** Omit HERSHEY'S Premier White Chips; replace with HERSHEY'S Butterscotch Chips. Omit HERSHEY'S Raspberry Chips; replace with HERSHEY'S Semi-Sweet Chocolate Chips. Omit chopped pecans; replace with ½ cup chopped walnuts.

*Apricot Meringue Squares*

## 165 APRICOT MERINGUE SQUARES

1 cup butter, softened
⅓ cup granulated sugar
1 teaspoon vanilla
2 teaspoons grated orange peel
2 cups all-purpose flour
1 jar (12 ounces) apricot jam
2 tablespoons orange juice
2 egg whites
1 cup powdered sugar
Slivered almonds (optional)

Preheat oven to 350°F. Beat butter, granulated sugar, vanilla and orange peel in large bowl with electric mixer at medium speed until light and fluffy. Gradually add flour, beating at low speed until smooth.

Press dough into ungreased 13×9-inch baking pan. Bake 15 minutes. Cool completely on wire rack. *Do not turn oven off.*

Combine jam and orange juice in small bowl; beat until smooth. Spread over cooled crust.

Beat egg whites in clean large bowl with electric mixer at high speed until foamy. Gradually beat in powdered sugar until stiff peaks form. Spread meringue over jam mixture with rubber spatula.

Bake 15 to 20 minutes or until light golden brown. Cool completely on wire rack. Cut into 2-inch squares. Garnish with almonds, if desired.          *Makes about 24 squares*

## BOUNTIFUL BAR COOKIES

### 166 OATMEAL PRALINE CHEESE BARS

**COOKIE BASE**

1 cup all-purpose flour
1 cup quick or old-fashioned oats, uncooked
1 cup very finely chopped pecans
2/3 cup firmly packed light brown sugar
1/4 cup toasted wheat germ
1/2 teaspoon salt
1/2 teaspoon cinnamon
1/8 teaspoon mace (optional)
1 BUTTER FLAVOR* CRISCO® Stick or
1 cup BUTTER FLAVOR CRISCO all-vegetable shortening

**FILLING**

1 package (8 ounces) cream cheese, softened
1/3 cup firmly packed light brown sugar
2 eggs
2 tablespoons flour
1/2 teaspoon vanilla
1/4 teaspoon salt

**TOPPING**

1 cup finely chopped toffee, almond brickle chips or butterscotch chips
1/2 cup very finely chopped pecans

*Butter Flavor Crisco is artificially flavored.*

**1.** Preheat oven to 350°F.

**2. For cookie base,** combine flour, oats, nuts, brown sugar, wheat germ, salt, cinnamon and mace. Cut in shortening using pastry blender (or 2 knives) until well blended. Press into 13×9×2-inch pan.

**3.** Bake at 350°F for 15 to 17 minutes, or until light golden brown and beginning to pull away from sides of pan.

**4. For filling,** combine cream cheese, brown sugar, eggs, flour, vanilla and salt in medium bowl. Beat at medium speed of electric mixer until smooth. Pour over baked base.

**5. For topping,** sprinkle toffee and nuts over filling.

**6.** Bake at 350°F for 15 to 17 minutes, or until filling is set. Cool. Cut into bars about 2×1¾ inches. Refrigerate.

*Makes about 2½ dozen bars*

### 167 SMUCKER'S® CRIMSON RIBBON BARS

6 tablespoons butter or margarine, softened
1/2 cup firmly packed brown sugar
1 teaspoon vanilla
1/2 cup all-purpose flour
1/4 teaspoon baking soda
1½ cups rolled oats
1 cup chopped walnuts
1/2 cup chopped figs
1/3 cup SMUCKER'S® Red Raspberry Preserves

Preheat oven to 375°F. Combine butter, brown sugar and vanilla; beat until well blended. Add flour and baking soda; mix well. Stir in oats and walnuts. Reserve ¾ cup oat mixture for topping. Press remaining oat mixture into 8-inch square baking pan coated with nonstick cooking spray. Combine figs and preserves; spread over oat mixture leaving ½-inch border. Sprinkle with reserved oat mixture; press lightly.

Bake 25 to 30 minutes or until golden brown. Cool in pan; cut into bars.

*Makes 20 bars*

*Smucker's® Crimson Ribbon Bars*

## BOUNTIFUL BAR COOKIES

### 168 CHOCOLATE CINNAMON NUT BARS

**COOKIE CRUST**
2 cups all-purpose flour
¾ cup (1½ sticks) butter or margarine, softened
⅓ cup granulated sugar
¾ teaspoon baking powder
¾ teaspoon ground cinnamon
1½ cups chopped nuts

**CHOCOLATE LAYER**
1 cup (6 ounces) NESTLÉ® TOLL HOUSE® Semi-Sweet Chocolate Morsels
¼ cup (½ stick) butter or margarine, cut into pieces
1¼ cups packed brown sugar
3 eggs
1 teaspoon vanilla extract
Powdered sugar

*FOR COOKIE CRUST:*
**BEAT** flour, butter, granulated sugar, baking powder and cinnamon in large mixer bowl until crumbly. Stir in nuts. Press onto bottom of ungreased 13×9-inch baking pan. **BAKE** in preheated 350°F. oven for 15 to 18 minutes or until firm.

*FOR CHOCOLATE LAYER:*
**MELT** morsels and butter in medium, heavy-duty saucepan over *lowest possible* heat; stir until smooth. Remove from heat; stir in brown sugar, eggs and vanilla. Pour over hot crust. **BAKE** at 350°F. for 20 to 25 minutes or until center is set. Cool in pan on wire rack. Sprinkle with powdered sugar.
*Makes about 2½ dozen bars*

### 169 CHOCOLATE AMARETTO BARS

**CRUST**
3 cups all-purpose flour
1 cup (2 sticks) butter or margarine, cut into pieces, softened
½ cup packed brown sugar

**FILLING**
4 eggs
¾ cup light corn syrup
¾ cup granulated sugar
¼ cup amaretto liqueur *or* ½ teaspoon almond extract
2 tablespoons butter or margarine, melted
1 tablespoon cornstarch
2 cups (about 7 ounces) sliced almonds
2 cups (12-ounce package) NESTLÉ® TOLL HOUSE® Semi-Sweet Chocolate Morsels, divided

*FOR CRUST:*
**BEAT** flour, butter and sugar in large mixer bowl until crumbly. Press into greased 13×9-inch baking pan. **BAKE** in preheated 350°F. oven for 12 to 15 minutes or until golden brown.

*FOR FILLING:*
**BEAT** eggs, corn syrup, sugar, liqueur, butter and cornstarch in medium bowl with wire whisk. Stir in almonds and 1⅔ cups morsels. Pour over hot crust; spread evenly. Bake at 350°F. for 25 to 30 minutes or until center is set. Cool to room temperature.

**PLACE** remaining morsels in heavy-duty plastic bag. Microwave on HIGH (100%) power for 45 seconds; knead. Microwave at 10 second intervals, kneading until smooth. Cut tiny corner from bag; squeeze to drizzle over bars. Chill for a few minutes to firm chocolate before cutting into bars.
*Makes about 2½ dozen bars*

## 170 WHITE CHIP MERINGUE DESSERT BARS

**CRUST**
- 2 cups all-purpose flour
- ½ cup powdered sugar
- 1 cup (2 sticks) butter or margarine, softened

**TOPPING**
- 2 cups (12-ounce package) NESTLÉ® TOLL HOUSE® Premier White Morsels
- 1¼ cups coarsely chopped nuts, *divided*
- 3 egg whites
- 1 cup packed brown sugar

**FOR CRUST:**
**COMBINE** flour, powdered sugar and butter with pastry blender or two knives in medium bowl until crumbly. Press evenly onto bottom of ungreased 13×9-inch baking pan. **BAKE** in preheated 375°F. oven for 10 to 12 minutes or until set. Remove from oven.

**FOR TOPPING:**
**SPRINKLE** morsels and *1 cup* nuts over hot crust. **BEAT** egg whites in small mixer bowl until frothy. Gradually add brown sugar. Beat until stiff peaks form when beaters are lifted. Carefully spread meringue over morsels and nuts. Sprinkle with *remaining* nuts. **BAKE** at 375°F. for 15 to 20 minutes or until golden brown. Serve warm or cool on wire rack.          *Makes about 2 dozen bars*

*White Chip Meringue Dessert Bars*

## BOUNTIFUL BAR COOKIES

## 171 CHIPPY CHEESEYS

**BASE**
1¼ cups firmly packed brown sugar
¾ BUTTER FLAVOR* CRISCO® Stick or
  ¾ cup BUTTER FLAVOR CRISCO
  all-vegetable shortening
2 tablespoons milk
1 tablespoon vanilla
1 egg
1¾ cups all-purpose flour
1 teaspoon salt
¾ teaspoon baking soda
1 cup semisweet mini chocolate chips
1 cup coarsely chopped walnuts

**FILLING**
2 (8-ounce) packages cream cheese,
  softened
2 eggs
¾ cup granulated sugar
1 teaspoon vanilla

*Butter Flavor Crisco is artificially flavored.*

1. **Heat** oven to 375°F. **Grease** 13×9-inch pan with shortening. **Place** cooling rack on countertop for cooling cookies.

2. *For base*, **combine** brown sugar, shortening, milk and vanilla in large bowl. **Beat** at medium speed of electric mixer until well blended. **Beat** in egg.

3. **Combine** flour, salt and baking soda. **Mix** into shortening mixture just until blended. **Stir** in chocolate chips and walnuts. **Spread** half of dough in prepared pan. **Bake** at 375°F for 8 minutes. *Do not overbake.*

4. *For filling*, **combine** cream cheese, eggs, granulated sugar and vanilla in medium bowl. **Beat** at medium speed of electric mixer until smooth. **Pour** over hot base.

5. **Roll** remaining half of dough into 13×9-inch rectangle between sheets of waxed

paper. **Remove** top sheet. **Flip** dough over onto filling. **Remove** waxed paper.

6. **Bake** at 375°F for 40 minutes or until top is set and light golden brown. *Do not overbake.* **Cool** on cooling rack. **Cut** into 2×1¾-inch bars. **Refrigerate.**
*Makes about 30 bars*

## 172 CHOCOLATE CHIPS AND RASPBERRY BARS

1½ cups all-purpose flour
½ cup sugar
½ teaspoon baking powder
½ teaspoon salt
½ cup (1 stick) butter or margarine, softened
1 egg, beaten
¼ cup milk
¼ teaspoon vanilla extract
¾ cup raspberry preserves
1 cup HERSHEY'S Semi-Sweet Chocolate Chips

1. Heat oven to 400°F. Grease 13×9×2-inch baking pan.

2. In large bowl, stir together first four ingredients. Cut in butter with pastry blender until mixture resembles coarse crumbs. Add egg, milk and vanilla; beat on medium speed of electric mixer until well blended.

3. Reserve ½ cup mixture for topping. Spread remaining mixture onto bottom of prepared pan (this will be a very thin layer). Spread preserves evenly over dough; sprinkle chocolate chips over top. Drop reserved dough by ½ teaspoons over chips.

4. Bake 25 minutes or until golden. Cool completely in pan on wire rack. Cut into bars. *Makes about 32 bars*

*Chippy Cheeseys*

## BOUNTIFUL BAR COOKIES

### 173 FABULOUS FRUIT BARS

1½ cups all-purpose flour, divided
1½ cups sugar, divided
½ cup MOTT'S® Apple Sauce, divided
½ teaspoon baking powder
2 tablespoons margarine
½ cup peeled, chopped apple
½ cup chopped dried apricots
½ cup chopped cranberries
1 whole egg
1 egg white
1 teaspoon lemon juice
½ teaspoon vanilla extract
1 teaspoon ground cinnamon

**1.** Preheat oven to 350°F. Spray 13×9-inch baking pan with nonstick cooking spray.

**2.** In medium bowl, combine 1¼ cups flour, ½ cup sugar, ⅓ cup apple sauce and baking powder. Cut in margarine with pastry blender or fork until mixture resembles coarse crumbs.

**3.** In large bowl, combine apple, apricots, cranberries, remaining apple sauce, whole egg, egg white, lemon juice and vanilla.

**4.** In small bowl, combine remaining 1 cup sugar, ¼ cup flour and cinnamon. Add to fruit mixture, stirring just until mixed.

**5.** Press half of crumb mixture evenly into bottom of prepared pan. Top with fruit mixture. Sprinkle with remaining crumb mixture.

**6.** Bake 40 minutes or until lightly browned. Broil, 4 inches from heat, 1 to 2 minutes or until golden brown. Cool on wire rack 15 minutes; cut into 16 bars.

*Makes 16 servings*

### 174 MICROWAVE CHEWY GRANOLA SQUARES

½ cup (1 stick) margarine or butter
½ cup firmly packed brown sugar
1 egg
½ teaspoon vanilla
1 cup quick oats, uncooked
½ cup all-purpose flour
½ teaspoon baking soda
½ teaspoon ground cinnamon
¼ teaspoon salt
1 cup BAKER'S® Semi-Sweet Real Chocolate Chips, divided
½ cup raisins

**To Microwave:** Beat margarine, sugar, egg and vanilla until light and fluffy in large bowl.

Stir in oats, flour, baking soda, cinnamon and salt. Stir in ½ cup chips and raisins. Spread into greased 8-inch square microwavable dish.

Microwave on HIGH (100% power) 2 minutes; rotate dish. Microwave 2 minutes longer or until wooden toothpick inserted into center comes out clean. Sprinkle with remaining ½ cup chips; microwave 1 minute longer. Cool in pan on counter top 15 minutes; cut into squares.

*Makes about 16 squares*

**Prep Time:** 15 minutes
**Microwave Time:** 5 minutes

*Fabulous Fruit Bars*

# Bevy of Brownies

## 175 GERMAN SWEET CHOCOLATE BROWNIES

1 package (4 ounces) BAKER'S® GERMAN'S® Sweet Chocolate
¼ cup (½ stick) margarine or butter
¾ cup sugar
2 eggs
1 teaspoon vanilla
½ cup all-purpose flour
½ cup chopped nuts

**HEAT** oven to 350°F.

**MICROWAVE** chocolate and margarine in large microwavable bowl on HIGH 2 minutes or until margarine is melted. **Stir until chocolate is completely melted.**

**STIR** sugar into chocolate mixture. Mix in eggs and vanilla until blended. Stir in flour and nuts. Spread in greased 8-inch square pan.

**BAKE** for 25 minutes or until toothpick inserted into center comes out with fudgy crumbs. **Do not overbake.** Cool in pan; cut into squares.          *Makes about 16 brownies*

**Prep Time:** 10 minutes
**Baking Time:** 25 minutes

## 176 OUTRAGEOUS BROWNIES

½ cup MIRACLE WHIP® Salad Dressing
2 eggs, beaten
¼ cup cold water
1 (21.5-ounce) package fudge brownie mix
3 (7-ounce) milk chocolate bars, divided
   Walnut halves (optional)

Preheat oven to 350°F.

Mix together salad dressing, eggs and water until well blended. Stir in brownie mix, mixing just until moistened.

Coarsely chop two chocolate bars; stir into brownie mixture. Pour into greased 13×9-inch baking pan.

Bake 30 to 35 minutes or until edges begin to pull away from sides of pan. Immediately top with 1 chopped chocolate bar. Let stand about 5 minutes or until melted; spread evenly over brownies. Garnish with walnut halves, if desired. Cool. Cut into squares.
          *Makes about 24 brownies*

**Prep Time:** 10 minutes
**Bake Time:** 35 minutes

*Outrageous Brownies*

## 177 IRISH BROWNIES

1 cup all-purpose flour
½ teaspoon baking powder
¼ teaspoon salt
4 squares (1 ounce each) semisweet
   baking chocolate, coarsely chopped
½ cup butter or margarine
½ cup sugar
2 large eggs
¼ cup Irish cream liqueur
   Irish Cream Frosting (recipe follows)

1. Preheat oven to 350°F. Grease 8-inch square baking pan; set aside. Place flour, baking powder and salt in small bowl; stir to combine.

2. Melt chocolate and butter in medium, heavy saucepan over low heat, stirring constantly. Stir in sugar. Beat in eggs, 1 at a time, with wire whisk. Whisk in Irish cream. Whisk flour mixture into chocolate mixture until just blended. Spread batter evenly into prepared baking pan. Bake 22 to 25 minutes or until center is set. Remove pan to wire rack; cool completely before frosting.

3. Prepare Irish Cream Frosting. Spread frosting over cooled brownies. Chill at least 1 hour or until frosting is set. Cut into 2-inch squares. Store tightly covered in refrigerator. These brownies do not freeze well.

*Makes 16 brownies*

**IRISH CREAM FROSTING**
   Powdered sugar
   2 ounces cream cheese (¼ cup), softened
   2 tablespoons butter or margarine,
      softened
   2 tablespoons Irish cream liqueur

1. Sift powdered sugar with sifter or fine-mesh strainer onto waxed paper. Gently spoon into measuring cups to measure 1½ cups.

2. Beat cream cheese and butter in small bowl with electric mixer at medium speed until smooth. Beat in Irish cream. Gradually beat in powdered sugar until smooth.

*Makes about ⅔ cup*

## 178 DOUBLE FUDGE SAUCEPAN BROWNIES

⅔ cup all-purpose flour
¼ teaspoon baking soda
¼ teaspoon salt
½ cup sugar
2 tablespoons butter or margarine
2 tablespoons water
2 cups (12-ounce package) HERSHEY'S
   Semi-Sweet Chocolate Chips, divided
2 eggs, slightly beaten
1 teaspoon vanilla extract
½ cup chopped nuts (optional)

1. Heat oven to 325°F. Grease 9-inch square baking pan.

2. Stir together flour, baking soda and salt. In medium saucepan, combine sugar, butter and water. Cook over low heat, stirring constantly, until mixture comes to boil. Remove from heat; immediately add 1 cup chocolate chips, stirring until melted. Stir in eggs and vanilla until blended. Gradually add flour mixture, blending well. Stir in remaining 1 cup chips and nuts, if desired. Pour batter into prepared pan.

3. Bake 25 to 30 minutes or until brownies begin to pull away from sides of pan. Cool completely in pan on wire rack. Cut into squares.

*Makes about 1½ dozen brownies*

*Irish Brownies*

BEVY OF BROWNIES

## 179 DOUBLE "TOPPED" BROWNIES

**BROWNIES**
1 package DUNCAN HINES® Double
   Fudge Brownie Mix
2 eggs
⅓ cup water
¼ cup CRISCO® Oil or CRISCO®
   PURITAN® Canola Oil
½ cup flaked coconut
½ cup chopped nuts

**FROSTING**
3 cups confectioners sugar
⅓ cup butter or margarine, softened
1½ teaspoons vanilla extract
2 to 3 tablespoons milk

**TOPPING**
3 squares (3 ounces) unsweetened
   chocolate
1 tablespoon butter or margarine

1. Preheat oven to 350°F. Grease bottom of 13×9×2-inch pan.

2. **For brownies,** combine brownie mix, fudge packet from Mix, eggs, water and oil in large bowl. Stir with spoon until well blended, about 50 strokes. Stir in coconut and nuts. Spread in pan. Bake at 350°F for 27 to 30 minutes or until set. Cool completely.

3. **For frosting,** combine confectioners sugar, ⅓ cup butter and vanilla extract. Stir in milk, 1 tablespoon at a time, until frosting is spreading consistency. Spread over brownies. Refrigerate until frosting is firm, about 30 minutes.

4. **For topping,** melt chocolate and 1 tablespoon butter in small bowl over hot water; stir until smooth. Drizzle over frosting. Refrigerate until chocolate is firm, about 15 minutes. Cut into bars.

*Makes 48 brownies*

**TIP:** Chocolate topping can be prepared in microwave oven. Place chocolate and butter in microwave-safe bowl and microwave at MEDIUM (50% power) for 2 to 2½ minutes; stir until smooth.

## 180 BLACK RUSSIAN BROWNIES

4 squares (1 ounce each) unsweetened
   chocolate
1 cup butter
¾ teaspoon ground black pepper
4 eggs, lightly beaten
1½ cups granulated sugar
1½ teaspoons vanilla
⅓ cup KAHLÚA®
2 tablespoons vodka
1⅓ cups all-purpose flour
½ teaspoon salt
¼ teaspoon baking powder
1 cup chopped walnuts or toasted sliced
   almonds
   Powdered sugar (optional)

Preheat oven to 350°F. Line bottom of 13×9-inch baking pan with waxed paper. Melt chocolate and butter with pepper in small saucepan over low heat, stirring until smooth. Remove from heat; cool.

Combine eggs, granulated sugar and vanilla in large bowl; beat well. Stir in cooled chocolate mixture, Kahlúa and vodka. Combine flour, salt and baking powder; add to chocolate mixture and stir until blended. Add walnuts. Spread evenly in prepared pan.

Bake just until wooden toothpick inserted into center comes out clean, about 25 minutes. *Do not overbake.* Cool in pan on wire rack. Cut into bars. Sprinkle with powdered sugar.
*Makes about 2½ dozen brownies*

**Double "Topped" Brownies**

## BEVY OF BROWNIES

### 181 MARBLE BROWNIES

½ cup plus 2 tablespoons all-purpose flour, divided
½ cup unsweetened cocoa powder
1 teaspoon baking powder
½ teaspoon salt
1¾ cups sugar, divided
2 tablespoons margarine, softened
½ cup MOTT'S® Natural Apple Sauce
3 egg whites, divided
1½ teaspoons vanilla extract, divided
4 ounces low-fat cream cheese (Neufchâtel), softened

1. Preheat oven to 350°F. Spray 8-inch square baking pan with nonstick cooking spray.

2. In small bowl, sift together ½ cup flour, cocoa, baking powder and salt.

3. In large bowl, beat 1½ cups sugar and margarine with electric mixer at medium speed until blended. Whisk in apple sauce, 2 egg whites and 1 teaspoon vanilla.

4. Add flour mixture to apple sauce mixture; stir until well blended. Pour batter into prepared pan.

5. In small bowl, beat cream cheese and remaining ¼ cup sugar with electric mixer at medium speed until blended. Stir in remaining egg white, 2 tablespoons flour and ½ teaspoon vanilla. Pour over brownie batter; run knife through batters to marble.

6. Bake 35 to 40 minutes or until firm. Cool on wire rack 15 minutes; cut into 12 bars.

*Makes 12 servings*

### 182 PEANUT BUTTER MARBLED BROWNIES

4 ounces cream cheese, softened
½ cup peanut butter
2 tablespoons sugar
1 egg
1 package (20 to 22 ounces) brownie mix plus ingredients to prepare mix
¾ cup lightly salted cocktail peanuts

**PREHEAT** oven to 350°F. Lightly grease 13×9-inch baking pan; set aside.

**BEAT** cream cheese, peanut butter, sugar and egg in medium bowl with electric mixer at medium speed until blended; set aside.

**PREPARE** brownie mix according to package directions.

**SPREAD** brownie mixture evenly in prepared pan. Spoon peanut butter mixture in dollops over brownie mixture. Swirl peanut butter mixture into brownie mixture with tip of knife. Sprinkle peanuts on top; lightly press peanuts down.

**BAKE** 30 to 35 minutes or until wooden pick inserted into center comes out almost clean. (Do not overbake.) Cool brownies completely in pan on wire rack. Cut into 2-inch squares.

**STORE** tightly covered at room temperature or freeze up to 3 months.

*Makes 2 dozen brownies*

*Peanut Butter Marbled Brownies*

## BEVY OF BROWNIES

### 183 FESTIVE FRUITED WHITE CHIP BLONDIES

½ cup (1 stick) butter or margarine
1⅔ cups (10-ounce package) HERSHEY'S Premier White Chips, divided
2 eggs
¼ cup granulated sugar
1¼ cups all-purpose flour
⅓ cup orange juice
¾ cup cranberries, chopped
¼ cup chopped dried apricots
½ cup coarsely chopped nuts
¼ cup packed light brown sugar

1. Heat oven to 325°F. Grease and flour 9-inch square baking pan.

2. In medium saucepan, melt butter; stir in 1 cup white chips. In large bowl, beat eggs until foamy. Add granulated sugar; beat until thick and pale yellow in color. Add flour, orange juice and white chip mixture; beat just until combined. Spread one-half of batter, about 1¼ cups, into prepared pan.

3. Bake 15 minutes until edges are lightly browned; remove from oven.

4. Stir cranberries, apricots and remaining ⅔ cup white chips into remaining one-half of batter; spread over top of hot baked mixture. Stir together nuts and brown sugar; sprinkle over top.

5. Bake 25 to 30 minutes or until edges are lightly browned. Cool completely in pan on wire rack. Cut into bars.

*Makes about 16 bars*

### 184 CHOCOLATE CHIP BROWNIES

¾ cup granulated sugar
½ cup butter or margarine
2 tablespoons water
2 cups semisweet chocolate chips or mini chocolate chips, divided
1½ teaspoons vanilla
1¼ cups all-purpose flour
½ teaspoon baking soda
½ teaspoon salt
2 eggs
Powdered sugar for garnish

**PREHEAT** oven to 350°F. Grease 9-inch square baking pan.

**COMBINE** sugar, butter and water in medium microwavable mixing bowl. Microwave on HIGH 2½ to 3 minutes or until butter is melted. Stir in 1 cup chocolate chips; stir gently until chips are melted and mixture is well blended. Stir in vanilla; let stand 5 minutes to cool.

**COMBINE** flour, baking soda and salt in small bowl. Beat eggs into chocolate mixture, 1 at a time. Add flour mixture; mix well. Stir in remaining 1 cup chocolate chips. Spread batter evenly into prepared pan.

**BAKE** 25 minutes for fudgy brownies or 30 to 35 minutes for cakelike brownies. Remove pan to wire rack to cool completely. Cut into 2¼-inch squares. Place powdered sugar in fine-mesh strainer and sprinkle over brownies, if desired. Store tightly covered at room temperature or freeze up to 3 months.

*Makes 16 brownies*

*Festive Fruited White Chip Blondies*

## 185 TRIPLE CHOCOLATE BROWNIES

3 squares (1 ounce each) unsweetened chocolate, coarsely chopped
2 squares (1 ounce each) semisweet chocolate, coarsely chopped
$\frac{1}{2}$ cup margarine or butter
1 cup all-purpose flour
$\frac{1}{2}$ teaspoon salt
$\frac{1}{4}$ teaspoon baking powder
$1\frac{1}{2}$ cups sugar
3 large eggs
1 teaspoon vanilla
$\frac{1}{4}$ cup sour cream
$\frac{1}{2}$ cup milk chocolate chips
  Powdered sugar (optional)

**PREHEAT** oven to 350°F. Lightly grease 13×9-inch baking pan.

**PLACE** unsweetened chocolate, semisweet chocolate and margarine in medium microwavable bowl. Microwave at HIGH 2 minutes or until butter is melted; stir until chocolate is completely melted. Cool to room temperature.

**PLACE** flour, salt and baking powder in small bowl; stir to combine.

**BEAT** sugar, eggs and vanilla in large bowl with electric mixer at medium speed until slightly thickened. Beat in chocolate mixture until well combined. Add flour mixture; beat at low speed until blended. Add sour cream; beat at low speed until combined. Stir in milk chocolate chips. Spread mixture evenly into prepared pan.

**BAKE** 20 to 25 minutes or until wooden pick inserted into center comes out almost clean. (Do not overbake.) Cool brownies completely in pan on wire rack. Cut into 2-inch squares. Place powdered sugar in fine-mesh strainer; sprinkle over brownies, if desired.

**STORE** tightly covered at room temperature or freeze up to 3 months.

*Makes 2 dozen brownies*

## 186 MADISON AVENUE MOCHA BROWNIES

1 (20- to 23-ounce) package brownie mix
1 (8-ounce) package PHILADELPHIA BRAND® Cream Cheese, softened
$\frac{1}{3}$ cup sugar
1 egg
$1\frac{1}{2}$ teaspoons MAXWELL HOUSE® Instant Coffee
1 teaspoon vanilla

• Preheat oven to 350°F.

• Prepare brownie mix according to package directions. Pour into greased 13×9-inch baking pan.

• Beat cream cheese, sugar and egg in small mixing bowl at medium speed with electric mixer until well blended.

• Dissolve coffee in vanilla; add to cream cheese mixture, mixing until well blended.

• Spoon cream cheese mixture over brownie batter; cut through batter with knife several times for marble effect.

• Bake 35 to 40 minutes or until set. Cool in pan on wire rack. Cut into bars.

*Makes about 4 dozen brownies*

**Prep Time:** 20 minutes
**Cook Time:** 40 minutes

*Triple Chocolate Brownies*

## 187 THREE GREAT TASTES BLOND BROWNIES

2 cups packed light brown sugar
1 cup (2 sticks) butter or margarine, melted
2 eggs
2 teaspoons vanilla extract
2 cups all-purpose flour
1 teaspoon salt
²/₃ cup (of each) HERSHEY'S Semi-Sweet Chocolate Chips, REESE'S® Peanut Butter Chips and HERSHEY'S Premier White Chips
   CHOCOLATE CHIP DRIZZLE (recipe follows)

1. Heat oven to 350°F. Grease 15½×10½×1-inch jelly-roll pan.

2. In large bowl, stir together brown sugar and butter; beat in eggs and vanilla until smooth. Add flour and salt, beating just until blended; stir in chocolate, peanut butter and white chips. Spread batter into prepared pan.

3. Bake 25 to 30 minutes or until wooden pick inserted in center comes out clean. Cool completely in pan on wire rack. Cut into bars. With tines of fork, drizzle CHOCOLATE CHIP DRIZZLE randomly over bars. *Makes about 72 bars*

**CHOCOLATE CHIP DRIZZLE:** In small microwave-safe bowl, place ¼ cup HERSHEY'S Semi-Sweet Chocolate Chips and ¼ teaspoon shortening (do not use butter, margarine or oil). Microwave at HIGH (100%) 30 seconds to 1 minute; stir until chips are melted and mixture is smooth.

## 188 FUDGEY HONEY BROWNIES

1 package (19.8 ounces) fudge brownie mix
⅓ cup vegetable oil
¼ cup water
2 tablespoons honey
1 egg
   Honey Whipped Cream (recipe follows)
   Bottled hot fudge topping

Combine brownie mix, oil, water, honey and egg in large bowl. Spread into greased and floured 5-cup heart-shaped baking pan*. Bake according to package directions for 8-inch square pan. Cool completely. Invert onto serving plate. Spread with Honey Whipped Cream or pipe cream through pastry tube. Drizzle with hot fudge topping.
*Makes 8 servings*

*An 8-inch square pan can be substituted.*

**HONEY WHIPPED CREAM:** Beat 1 cup whipping cream until mixture thickens; gradually add 3 tablespoons honey and beat until soft peaks form. Fold in 1 teaspoon vanilla. Makes about 2 cups.

*Favorite recipe from **National Honey Board***

*Three Great Tastes Blond Brownies*

## 189 DOUBLE DECKER BLACK & WHITE BROWNIES

2 cups all-purpose flour
1 teaspoon baking powder
¼ teaspoon salt
1 cup (2 sticks) butter or margarine, softened
2 cups packed light brown sugar
2 teaspoons vanilla extract
3 eggs
⅔ cup HERSHEY'S Semi-Sweet Chocolate Chips
⅓ cup HERSHEY'S Cocoa or HERSHEY'S European Style Cocoa
2 tablespoons vegetable oil
⅔ cup HERSHEY'S Premier White Chips
WHITE CHIP DRIZZLE (recipe follows)

**1.** Heat oven to 350°F. Grease and flour 13×9×2-inch baking pan.

**2.** Stir together flour, baking powder and salt; set aside. In large bowl, beat butter, brown sugar and vanilla until creamy; add eggs, beating well. Stir in flour mixture until well blended; divide batter in half.

**3.** Stir chocolate chips into one part; spread into prepared pan. Into remaining batter, stir cocoa, oil and white chips; spread gently and evenly over vanilla layer.

**4.** Bake 35 to 40 minutes or until brownies begin to pull away from sides of pan. Cool completely in pan on wire rack; cut into bars. Prepare WHITE CHIP DRIZZLE; drizzle over top of bars with tines of fork. Let stand until firm. *Makes about 36 brownies*

**WHITE CHIP DRIZZLE:** In small microwave-safe bowl, place ⅓ cup HERSHEY'S Premier White Chip and ½ teaspoon shortening. Microwave at HIGH (100%) 30 seconds; stir. If necessary, microwave at HIGH an additional 15 seconds at a time, stirring after each heating, just until chips are melted when stirred. Use immediately.

## 190 CHOCOLATE MINT BROWNIE BARS

⅔ cup butter or margarine
1⅔ cups (10-ounce package) HERSHEY'S Mint Chocolate Chips, divided
1½ cups sugar
1 cup all-purpose flour
⅓ cup HERSHEY'S Cocoa
1 teaspoon vanilla extract
½ teaspoon baking powder
½ teaspoon salt
3 eggs
1 cup coarsely chopped walnuts

**1.** Heat oven to 350°F. Grease 13×9×2-inch baking pan.

**2.** In large microwave-safe bowl, place butter and 1 cup mint chocolate chips. Microwave at HIGH (100%) 1 to 1½ minutes or until chips are melted when stirred. Add sugar, flour, cocoa, vanilla, baking powder, salt and eggs; stir with spoon until smooth. Stir in remaining ⅔ cup chips. Spread batter into prepared pan; sprinkle walnuts over top.

**3.** Bake 30 minutes or until center is set. Cool completely in pan on wire rack. Cut into bars. *Makes about 36 brownies*

## BEVY OF BROWNIES

## 191 ALMOND MACAROON BROWNIES

**BROWNIE LAYER**

  6 squares BAKER'S® Semi-Sweet Chocolate
  ½ cup (1 stick) margarine or butter
  ⅔ cup sugar
  2 eggs
  1 teaspoon vanilla
  1 cup all-purpose flour
  ⅓ cup chopped toasted almonds

**CREAM CHEESE TOPPING**

  4 ounces PHILADELPHIA BRAND® Cream
      Cheese, softened
  ⅓ cup sugar
  1 egg
  1 tablespoon all-purpose flour
  ⅓ cup chopped toasted almonds
  1 cup BAKER'S® ANGEL FLAKE® Coconut
      Whole almonds (optional)
  1 square BAKER'S® Semi-Sweet Chocolate,
      melted (optional)

Preheat oven to 350°F.

Microwave 6 squares chocolate and margarine in large microwavable bowl on HIGH (100% power) 2 minutes or until margarine is melted. Stir until chocolate is completely melted.

Stir ⅔ cup sugar into melted chocolate mixture. Mix in 2 eggs and vanilla until well blended. Stir in 1 cup flour and ⅓ cup chopped almonds. Spread in greased 8-inch square pan.

Mix cream cheese, ⅓ cup sugar, 1 egg and 1 tablespoon flour in small bowl until smooth. Stir in ⅓ cup chopped almonds and coconut. Spread over brownie batter. Garnish with whole almonds, if desired.

Bake for 35 minutes or until wooden toothpick inserted into center comes out with fudgy crumbs. Do not overbake. Cool in pan on wire rack. Drizzle with 1 square melted chocolate, if desired. Cool until chocolate is set. Cut into squares.

*Makes about 16 brownies*

## 192 PEAR BLONDIES

  1 cup packed brown sugar
  ¼ cup butter or margarine, melted
  1 egg
  ½ teaspoon vanilla
  ¾ cup all-purpose flour
  ½ teaspoon baking powder
  ½ teaspoon salt
  1 cup chopped firm-ripe fresh U.S.A.
      Anjou, Bosc, Bartlett, Nelis or Seckel
      pears
  ⅓ cup semisweet chocolate chips

Preheat oven to 350°F. Grease 8-inch square baking pan. Set aside.

Combine brown sugar, butter, egg and vanilla in medium bowl; blend well. Combine flour, baking powder and salt in small bowl; stir into brown sugar mixture. Stir in pears and chips. Spread in prepared baking pan. Bake 30 to 35 minutes or until golden brown. Cool completely in pan on wire rack. Cut into 2-inch squares.

*Makes 16 squares*

*Favorite recipe from **Oregon Washington California Pear Bureau***

## BEVY OF BROWNIES

## 193 CARAMEL FUDGE BROWNIES

1 jar (12 ounces) hot caramel ice cream topping
1¼ cups all-purpose flour, divided
¼ teaspoon baking powder
    Dash salt
4 squares (1 ounce each) unsweetened chocolate, coarsely chopped
¾ cup margarine or butter
2 cups sugar
3 eggs
2 teaspoons vanilla
¾ cup semisweet chocolate chips
¾ cup chopped pecans

**PREHEAT** oven to 350°F. Lightly grease 13×9-inch baking pan.

**COMBINE** caramel topping and ¼ cup flour in small bowl; set aside.

**COMBINE** remaining 1 cup flour, baking powder and salt in small bowl; mix well.

**PLACE** unsweetened chocolate squares and margarine in medium microwavable bowl. Microwave at HIGH 2 minutes or until margarine is melted; stir until chocolate is completely melted.

**STIR** sugar into melted chocolate with mixing spoon. Add eggs and vanilla; stir until combined. Add flour mixture, stirring until well blended. Spread chocolate mixture evenly into prepared pan.

**BAKE** 25 minutes. Immediately after removing brownies from oven, spread caramel mixture over brownies. Sprinkle top evenly with chocolate chips and pecans.

**RETURN** pan to oven; bake 20 to 25 minutes or until topping is golden brown and bubbling. (Do not overbake.) Cool brownies completely in pan on wire rack. Cut into 2×1½-inch bars.

**STORE** tightly covered at room temperature or freeze up to 3 months.

*Makes 3 dozen brownies*

## 194 HERSHEY'S CHOCOLATE MINT BROWNIES

¾ cup HERSHEY'S Cocoa
½ teaspoon baking soda
⅔ cup butter or margarine, melted and divided
½ cup boiling water
2 cups sugar
2 eggs
1⅓ cups all-purpose flour
1 teaspoon vanilla extract
¼ teaspoon salt
1⅔ cups (10-ounce package) HERSHEY'S Mint Chocolate Chips

**1.** Heat oven to 350°F. Grease 13×9×2-inch baking pan.

**2.** In large bowl, stir together cocoa and baking soda; stir in ⅓ cup butter. Add water; stir until mixture thickens. Stir in sugar, eggs and remaining ⅓ cup butter; stir until smooth. Add flour, vanilla and salt; stir until well blended. Stir in mint chocolate chips. Spread batter into prepared pan.

**3.** Bake 35 to 40 minutes or until brownies begin to pull away from sides of pan. Cool completely in pan on wire rack. Cut into bars. *Makes about 36 brownies*

**GLAZE:** In small bowl, combine ⅔ cup powdered sugar and 2 to 3 teaspoons milk; stir in few drops green food color, if desired.

*Caramel Fudge Brownies*

## 195 RICH 'N' CREAMY BROWNIE BARS

**BROWNIES**
1 package DUNCAN HINES® Double Fudge Brownie Mix
2 eggs
1/3 cup water
1/4 cup CRISCO® Oil or CRISCO® PURITAN® Canola Oil
1/2 cup chopped pecans

**TOPPING**
1 package (8 ounces) cream cheese, softened
2 eggs
1 pound (3 1/2 cups) confectioners' sugar
1 teaspoon vanilla extract

1. Preheat oven to 350°F. Grease bottom of 13×9×2-inch pan.

2. **For brownies,** combine brownie mix, contents of fudge packet from Mix, 2 eggs, water and oil in large bowl. Stir with spoon until well blended, about 50 strokes. Stir in pecans. Spread evenly into prepared pan.

3. **For topping,** beat cream cheese in large bowl at medium speed with electric mixer until smooth. Beat in 2 eggs, confectioners' sugar and vanilla extract until smooth. Spread evenly over brownie mixture. Bake at 350°F for 45 to 50 minutes or until edges and top are golden brown and shiny. Cool completely. Refrigerate until well chilled. Cut into bars.          *Makes 48 bars*

## 196 CREAMY CAPPUCCINO BROWNIES

1 package (21- to 24-ounce) brownie mix
1 tablespoon coffee crystals *or* 1 teaspoon espresso powder
2 tablespoons warm water
1 cup (8-ounces) Wisconsin Mascarpone cheese
3 tablespoons sugar
1 egg
Powdered sugar

Grease bottom of 13×9-inch baking pan. Prepare brownie mix according to package directions. Pour half of batter into prepared pan. Dissolve coffee crystals in water; add Mascarpone, sugar and egg. Blend until smooth. Drop by spoonfuls over brownie batter; top with remaining brownie batter. With knife, swirl cheese mixture through brownies creating a marbled effect. Bake at 375°F 30 to 35 minutes or until toothpick inserted in center comes out clean. Sprinkle with powdered sugar.

*Makes 2 dozen brownies*

*Favorite recipe from* **Wisconsin Milk Marketing Board**

*Rich 'n' Creamy Brownie Bars*

## BEVY OF BROWNIES

## 197 ALMOND CHEESECAKE BROWNIES

4 squares (1 ounce each) semisweet
    chocolate
5 tablespoons butter or margarine,
    divided
1 package (3 ounces) cream cheese,
    softened
1 cup granulated sugar, divided
3 eggs, divided
½ cup plus 1 tablespoon all-purpose flour
1½ teaspoons vanilla, divided
½ teaspoon baking powder
¼ teaspoon salt
½ teaspoon almond extract
½ cup chopped or slivered almonds
    Almond Icing (recipe follows)

Preheat oven to 350°F. Butter 8-inch square
pan. Melt chocolate and 3 tablespoons
butter in small heavy saucepan over low
heat; set aside. Mix cream cheese with
remaining 2 tablespoons butter in small
bowl. Slowly add ¼ cup granulated sugar,
blending well. Add 1 egg, 1 tablespoon flour
and ½ teaspoon of the vanilla; set aside. Beat
remaining 2 eggs and ¾ cup granulated sugar
in large bowl until light. Add baking powder,
salt and ½ cup flour. Blend in chocolate
mixture, remaining 1 teaspoon vanilla and
almond extract. Stir in almonds. Spread half
the chocolate mixture into prepared pan.
Cover with cream cheese mixture; spoon
remaining chocolate mixture over top. Swirl
with knife or spatula to create a marbled
effect. Bake 30 to 35 minutes or until set in
center. Do not overbake. Meanwhile,
prepare Almond Icing. Cool brownies
5 minutes; spread icing evenly over the top.
Cool completely in pan on wire rack. Cut
into 2-inch squares.       *Makes 16 brownies*

### ALMOND ICING
½ cup semisweet chocolate chips
2 tablespoons butter or margarine
3 tablespoons milk
¼ teaspoon almond extract
1 cup powdered sugar

Combine chocolate chips, butter, milk and
almond extract in small heavy saucepan. Stir
over low heat until chocolate is melted. Add
powdered sugar; beat until glossy and easy
to spread.

## 198 MOIST AND MINTY BROWNIES

1¼ cups all-purpose flour
½ teaspoon baking soda
¼ teaspoon salt
¾ cup granulated sugar
½ cup (1 stick) butter or margarine
2 tablespoons water
1½ cups (10-ounce package) NESTLÉ® TOLL
    HOUSE® Mint-Chocolate Morsels,
    divided
1 teaspoon vanilla extract
2 eggs

**COMBINE** flour, baking soda and salt in
small bowl; set aside. Combine sugar, butter
and water in medium saucepan. Bring *just to
a boil* over medium heat, stirring constantly;
remove from heat. Add *1 cup* morsels and
vanilla; stir until smooth. Add eggs one at a
time, stirring well after each addition. Stir in
flour mixture and *remaining* morsels. Spread
into greased 9-inch-square baking pan.

**BAKE** in preheated 350°F oven for 20 to
30 minutes or until center is set. Cool in pan
on wire rack (center will sink).
                    *Makes about 16 brownies*

*Moist and Minty Brownies*

## 199 PEANUT BUTTER CHEESECAKE BROWNIE BARS

**PEANUT BUTTER CHEESECAKE FILLING (recipe follows)**
1 cup HERSHEY'S Semi-Sweet Chocolate Chips, divided
½ cup (1 stick) butter or margarine, softened
1 cup sugar
1 egg
1 teaspoon vanilla extract
1¼ cups all-purpose flour
¼ cup HERSHEY'S Cocoa
½ teaspoon baking soda
¼ teaspoon salt
½ teaspoon shortening (do not use butter, margarine or oil)

1. Heat oven to 350°F.

2. Prepare PEANUT BUTTER CHEESECAKE FILLING.

3. Reserve 1 tablespoon chocolate chips for drizzle. In large bowl, beat butter, sugar, egg and vanilla until well blended. Stir together flour, cocoa, baking soda and salt; gradually add to butter mixture, beating until blended. Stir in remaining chips. Spread batter into 13×9×2-inch baking pan. Spread cheesecake filling over brownie batter.

4. Bake 25 to 30 minutes or until wooden pick inserted in center comes out clean. Cool completely in pan on wire rack.

5. Place reserved chips and shortening in small microwave-safe bowl. Microwave at HIGH (100%) 30 seconds or until chips are melted and smooth when stirred. Drizzle over surface. Cover; refrigerate until ready to serve. Cut into bars. Allow to soften slightly. Refrigerate leftover bars.

*Makes about 36 bars*

**PEANUT BUTTER CHEESECAKE FILLING**
1 package (8 ounces) cream cheese, softened
½ cup REESE'S Creamy or REESE'S Crunchy Peanut Butter
½ cup sugar
1 tablespoon all-purpose flour
1 egg
1 teaspoon vanilla extract

In small bowl, beat cream cheese and peanut butter. Add sugar, flour, egg and vanilla; beat well.

## 200 WHITE CHOCOLATE BROWNIES

1 package DUNCAN HINES® Milk Chocolate Chunk Brownie Mix
2 eggs
⅓ cup water
⅓ cup CRISCO® Oil or CRISCO® PURITAN® Canola Oil
¾ cup coarsely chopped white chocolate
¼ cup sliced natural almonds

1. Preheat oven to 350°F. Grease bottom of 13×9×2-inch pan.

2. Combine brownie mix, eggs, water and oil in large bowl. Stir with spoon until well blended, about 50 strokes. Stir in white chocolate. Spread in pan. Sprinkle top with almonds. Bake at 350°F for 25 to 28 minutes or until set. Cool completely. Cut into bars.
*Makes 48 small or 24 large brownies*

**TIP:** For decadent brownies, combine 2 ounces coarsely chopped white chocolate and 2 teaspoons Crisco® Shortening in small heavy saucepan. Melt over low heat, stirring constantly. Drizzle over brownies.

*White Chocolate Brownies*

## BEVY OF BROWNIES

### 201 CHOCOLATE ESPRESSO BROWNIES

4 squares (1 ounce each) unsweetened chocolate
1 cup sugar
¼ cup Prune Purée (recipe follows) or prepared prune butter
3 egg whites
1 to 2 tablespoons instant espresso coffee powder
1 teaspoon baking powder
1 teaspoon salt
1 teaspoon vanilla
½ cup all-purpose flour
    Powdered sugar (optional)

Preheat oven to 350°F. Coat 8-inch square baking pan with vegetable cooking spray. In small heavy saucepan, melt chocolate over very low heat, stirring until melted and smooth. Remove from heat; cool. In mixer bowl, beat chocolate and remaining ingredients except flour and powdered sugar at medium speed until well blended; mix in flour. Spread batter evenly in prepared pan. Bake in center of oven about 30 minutes until pick inserted into center comes out clean. Cool completely in pan on wire rack. Dust with powdered sugar. Cut into 1⅓-inch squares. *Makes 36 brownies*

**PRUNE PURÉE:** Combine 1⅓ cups (8 ounces) pitted prunes and 6 tablespoons hot water in container of food processor or blender. Pulse on and off until prunes are finely chopped and smooth. Store leftovers in a covered container in the refrigerator for up to two months. Makes 1 cup.

*Favorite recipe from* **California Prune Board**

### 202 SUPER EASY CHOCOLATE FUDGE BROWNIES

1⅔ cups granulated sugar
½ cup (1 stick) butter or margarine
2 tablespoons water
2 bars (4 ounces) NESTLÉ® TOLL HOUSE® Unsweetened Baking Chocolate, broken into pieces
2 eggs
1½ teaspoons vanilla extract
1⅓ cups all-purpose flour
¼ teaspoon baking soda
¼ teaspoon salt
½ cup chopped nuts (optional)

**MICROWAVE** sugar, butter and water in large, microwave-safe bowl on HIGH (100%) power for 4 to 5 minutes or until mixture bubbles, stirring once. (Or, heat sugar, butter and water in medium saucepan just to boiling, stirring constantly. Remove from heat). Add baking bars; stir until melted.

**STIR** in eggs one at a time until blended. Stir in vanilla. Add flour, baking soda and salt; stir well. Stir in nuts. Pour into greased 13×9-inch baking pan.

**BAKE** in preheated 350°F. oven for 15 to 20 minutes or until wooden pick inserted in center comes out slightly sticky. Cool in pan on wire rack. *Makes 2 dozen brownies*

*Chocolate Espresso Brownies*

## BEVY OF BROWNIES

### 203 ROCKY ROAD BROWNIES

1 cup HERSHEY'S Semi-Sweet Chocolate Chips
1¼ cups miniature marshmallows
1 cup chopped nuts
½ cup (1 stick) butter or margarine
1 cup sugar
1 teaspoon vanilla extract
2 eggs
½ cup all-purpose flour
⅓ cup HERSHEY'S Cocoa
½ teaspoon baking powder
½ teaspoon salt

**1.** Heat oven to 350°F. Grease 9-inch square baking pan.

**2.** Stir together chocolate chips, marshmallows and nuts; set aside. In large microwave safe bowl, place butter. Microwave at HIGH (100% power) 1 to 1½ minutes or until melted. Add sugar, vanilla and eggs, beating with spoon until well blended. Add flour, cocoa, baking powder and salt; blend well. Spread batter into prepared pan.

**3.** Bake 22 minutes. Sprinkle chocolate chip mixture over top. Continue baking 5 minutes or until marshmallows have softened and puffed slightly. Cool completely. With wet knife, cut into squares.

*Makes about 20 brownies*

### 204 RICOTTA CHEESE BROWNIES

**BROWNIE LAYER**
½ cup butter or margarine
⅓ cup unsweetened cocoa
1 cup sugar
2 eggs, slightly beaten
1 teaspoon vanilla
½ cup all-purpose flour
½ teaspoon baking powder
¼ teaspoon salt

**CHEESE LAYER**
¾ cup (6 ounces) SARGENTO® Part-Skim Ricotta Cheese
¼ cup sugar
1 egg, slightly beaten
2 tablespoons butter or margarine, softened
1 tablespoon all-purpose flour
½ teaspoon vanilla

For brownie layer, preheat oven to 350°F. Melt butter in small saucepan; remove from heat. Stir in cocoa; cool. In large bowl of electric mixer, beat sugar, eggs and vanilla on medium speed until light and fluffy. In small bowl, stir together flour, baking powder and salt. Add to egg mixture; beat until blended. Add cocoa mixture; beat until thoroughly combined. Reserve 1 cup batter; spread remaining batter into greased 8-inch square baking pan.

For cheese layer, in small bowl of electric mixer, beat ricotta cheese, sugar, egg, butter, flour and vanilla on medium speed until well blended. Spread over brownie layer in pan. Drop teaspoonfuls of reserved brownie batter over cheese mixture; spread batter with spatula to cover cheese mixture. Bake 40 minutes. Cool. *Makes 16 brownies*

*Rocky Road Brownies*

## 205 CRUNCHY BROWNIE BARS

### CRUNCHY LAYER
1½ cups quick-cooking oats (not instant or old fashioned)
¾ cup firmly packed light brown sugar
¾ cup all-purpose flour
¼ teaspoon baking soda
¼ teaspoon salt
¾ cup butter or margarine, melted

### BROWNIE LAYER
1 package DUNCAN HINES® Fudge Brownie Mix
2 eggs
⅓ cup water
¼ cup CRISCO® Oil or CRISCO® PURITAN® Canola Oil

### FROSTING
1½ squares (1½ ounces) unsweetened chocolate, chopped
3 tablespoons butter or margarine
2¼ cups confectioners sugar (sift if lumpy)
1½ teaspoons vanilla extract
3 tablespoons hot water

1. Preheat oven to 350°F.

2. **For crunchy layer,** combine oats, brown sugar, flour, baking soda and salt in large bowl. Add melted butter; stir until blended. Press mixture into bottom of ungreased 13×9×2-inch pan. Bake at 350°F for 10 minutes. (Mixture will not be completely baked.)

3. **For brownie layer,** combine brownie mix, contents of fudge packet from Mix, eggs, water and oil in large bowl. Stir until thoroughly blended. Pour batter slowly over hot crunchy layer; spread evenly. Bake at 350°F for 40 to 45 minutes or until set. *DO NOT OVERBAKE.* Cool completely.

4. **For frosting,** place chocolate and butter in medium saucepan. Heat on low heat until melted. Add confectioners sugar, vanilla extract and **hot** water. Stir until smooth. Immediately pour hot frosting on brownies; spread evenly. Let stand until frosting is set. Cut into bars.

*Makes 24 large or 32 small bars*

**TIP:** Always use the pan size called for in Duncan Hines® recipes. Using a different size can give the brownies an altogether different texture.

## 206 NUGGETS O' GOLD BROWNIES

3 ounces unsweetened baking chocolate
¼ cup WESSON® Oil
2 eggs
1 cup sugar
¼ teaspoon salt
1 teaspoon vanilla extract
½ cup all-purpose flour
1 (3.8-ounce) BUTTERFINGER® Candy Bar, coarsely chopped

In microwave-safe measuring cup, heat chocolate 2 minutes on HIGH in microwave oven. Stir and continue heating in 30 second intervals until chocolate is completely melted. Stir in oil and set aside to cool. In mixing bowl, beat eggs until foamy. Whisk in sugar then add salt and vanilla. Stir in chocolate mixture then mix in flour until all ingredients are moistened. Gently, fold in candy. Pour batter into a 9-inch greased baking pan and bake at 350°F for 25 to 30 minutes or until edges begin to leave sides of pan. Cool before cutting.

*Makes 20 brownies*

*Crunchy Brownie Bars*

# Kid
# Pleasers

## 207 CHOCOLATE CHIP LOLLIPOPS

1 package DUNCAN HINES® Chocolate
    Chip Cookie Mix
1 egg
⅓ cup CRISCO® Oil or CRISCO®
    PURITAN® Canola Oil
2 tablespoons water
    Flat ice cream sticks
    Assorted decors

1. Preheat oven to 375°F.

2. Combine cookie mix, egg, oil and water in large bowl. Stir until thoroughly blended. Shape dough into 32 (1-inch) balls. Place balls 3 inches apart on ungreased baking sheets. Push ice cream stick into center of each ball. Flatten dough ball with hand to form round lollipop. Decorate by pressing decors onto dough. Bake at 375°F for 8 to 9 minutes or until light golden brown. Cool 1 minute on baking sheets. Remove to cooling racks. Cool completely. Store in airtight container.

*Makes 2½ to 3 dozen cookies*

TIP: For best results, use shiny baking sheets for baking cookies. Dark baking sheets cause cookie bottoms to become too brown.

## 208 CAP'N'S COOKIES

1 cup firmly packed brown sugar
½ cup (1 stick) margarine or butter,
    softened
2 eggs
1 teaspoon vanilla
1½ cups all-purpose flour
1 teaspoon baking powder
½ teaspoon salt (optional)
2 cups CAP'N CRUNCH® Cereal, any
    flavor
1 cup raisins or semi-sweet chocolate
    pieces

Preheat oven to 375°F. Lightly grease cookie sheet. Beat sugar and margarine until fluffy. Blend in eggs and vanilla. Add combined flour, baking powder and salt; mix well. Stir in cereal and raisins. Drop by rounded teaspoonfuls onto prepared cookie sheet.

Bake 10 to 12 minutes or until light golden brown. Cool 2 minutes on cookie sheet; remove to wire rack. Cool completely. Store tightly covered.

*Makes about 3 dozen cookies*

*Chocolate Chip Lollipops*

## 209 BROWNIE PIZZA

**BROWNIE LAYER:**
   4 squares BAKER'S® Unsweetened
      Chocolate
   ¾ cup (1½ sticks) margarine or butter
   2 cups sugar
   4 eggs
   1 teaspoon vanilla
   1 cup all-purpose flour

**TOPPING:**
   1 package (8 ounces) PHILADELPHIA
      BRAND® Cream Cheese, softened
   ¼ cup sugar
   1 egg
   ½ teaspoon vanilla
      Assorted sliced fruit
   2 squares BAKER'S® Semi-Sweet
      Chocolate, melted

**HEAT** oven to 350°F. Line 12×½-inch pizza pan with foil (to lift brownie from pan after baking); grease foil.

**MICROWAVE** unsweetened chocolate and margarine in large microwavable bowl on HIGH 2 minutes or until margarine is melted. **Stir until chocolate is completely melted.**

**STIR** 2 cups sugar into melted chocolate mixture. Mix in 4 eggs and 1 teaspoon vanilla until well blended. Stir in flour. Spread in prepared pan. Bake for 30 minutes.

**MIX** cream cheese, ¼ cup sugar, 1 egg and ½ teaspoon vanilla in same bowl until well blended. Pour over baked brownie crust.

**BAKE** 10 minutes longer or until toothpick inserted into center comes out with fudgy crumbs. **Do not overbake.** Cool in pan. Lift brownie pizza out of pan; peel off foil. Place brownie pizza on serving plate. Arrange fruit over cream cheese layer. Drizzle with melted semi-sweet chocolate.

*Makes 12 servings*

**Prep Time:** 30 minutes
**Baking Time:** 40 minutes

## 210 OREO® BROWNIE TREATS

   15 OREO® Chocolate Sandwich Cookies,
      coarsely chopped
   1 (21½-ounce) package deluxe fudge
      brownie mix, batter prepared
      according to package directions
   2 pints ice cream, any flavor

Stir cookie pieces into prepared brownie batter. Grease 13×9-inch baking pan; pour batter into pan. Bake according to brownie mix package directions for time and temperature. Cool. To serve, cut into 12 squares and top each with a scoop of ice cream.

*Makes 12 servings*

*Brownie Pizza*

## 211 CHOCOLATE SURPRISE COOKIES

2¾ cups all-purpose flour
¾ cup unsweetened cocoa powder
½ teaspoon baking powder
½ teaspoon baking soda
1 cup margarine or butter, softened
1½ cups packed light brown sugar
½ cup plus 1 tablespoon granulated sugar,
    divided
2 eggs
1 teaspoon vanilla
1 cup chopped pecans, divided
1 package (9 ounces) caramels coated in
    milk chocolate
3 squares (1 ounce each) white chocolate,
    coarsely chopped

**PREHEAT** oven to 375°F. Place flour, cocoa, baking powder and baking soda in medium bowl; stir to combine. Set aside.

**BEAT** margarine, brown sugar and ½ cup granulated sugar with electric mixer at medium speed until light and fluffy; beat in eggs and vanilla. Gradually add flour mixture and ½ cup pecans. Beat at low speed, scraping down side of bowl occasionally. Refrigerate dough, covered, 15 minutes or until firm enough to roll into balls.

**PLACE** remaining ½ cup nuts and remaining 1 tablespoon sugar in shallow dish. Roll tablespoonful of dough around 1 caramel candy, covering completely; press one side into nut mixture. Place, nut-side up, on ungreased cookie sheet. Repeat with additional dough and candies, placing 3 inches apart.

**BAKE** 10 to 12 minutes or until set and slightly cracked. Let stand on cookie sheet 2 minutes. Transfer cookies to wire rack; cool completely.

**PLACE** white chocolate pieces in small resealable plastic freezer bag; seal bag. Microwave at MEDIUM (50% power) 2 minutes. Turn bag over; microwave at MEDIUM 2 to 3 minutes or until melted. Knead bag until chocolate is smooth. Cut off tiny corner of bag; drizzle white chocolate onto cookies. Let stand until white chocolate is set, about 30 minutes.

*Makes about 3½ dozen cookies*

## 212 KARA'S KRUNCHIE KOOKIES

1 cup semi-sweet chocolate chips
7 tablespoons margarine or butter
4 cups RICE CHEX® brand Cereal, crushed
    to 2½ cups
4 SNICKERS® candy bars (2.07 ounces
    each), cut into ½-inch pieces
½ cup raisins
    Powdered sugar

Paper line twenty-four 2½-inch muffin cups. Combine chocolate chips and margarine in saucepan. Cook over low heat until melted, stirring frequently. Stir in cereal, candy bars and raisins. Divide evenly among prepared muffins cups; press firmly onto bottom of muffin cups with back of buttered spoon or buttered hands. Chill 1 hour. Sprinkle with powdered sugar. Store in airtight container in refrigerator.          *Makes 24 kookies*

*Chocolate Surprise Cookies*

## KID PLEASERS

### 213 TONY'S TIGER BITES™

1 package (10 ounces) regular-size
    marshmallows (about 40)
¼ cup margarine
⅓ cup peanut butter
7½ cups KELLOGG'S FROSTED FLAKES®
    Cereal

**1.** In 4-quart microwave-safe bowl, melt marshmallows and margarine at HIGH (100%) 3 minutes or until melted, stirring after 1½ minutes.

**2.** Stir in peanut butter until mixture is smooth. Add KELLOGG'S FROSTED FLAKES cereal, stirring until well coated.

**3.** Using a buttered spatula or waxed paper, press mixture into a 13×9×2-inch pan coated with cooking spray. Cut into 1½×2-inch bars when cool.

*Makes 32 bars*

**NOTE:** Use fresh marshmallows for best results. Do not use diet or reduced fat margarine. This recipe was tested in 700-watt microwave oven. Cooking time may vary.

**RANGETOP DIRECTIONS:** Melt margarine over low heat in large saucepan. Add marshmallows, stirring until completely melted. Remove from heat. Follow steps 2 and 3 above.

### 214 PEANUT BUTTER BEARS

1 cup SKIPPY® Creamy Peanut Butter
1 cup (2 sticks) MAZOLA® Margarine or
    butter, softened
1 cup packed brown sugar
⅔ cup KARO® Light or Dark Corn Syrup
2 eggs
4 cups all-purpose flour, divided
1 tablespoon baking powder
1 teaspoon cinnamon (optional)
¼ teaspoon salt

**1.** In large bowl with mixer at medium speed, beat peanut butter, margarine, brown sugar, corn syrup and eggs until smooth. Reduce speed; beat in 2 cups of the flour, the baking powder, cinnamon and salt. With spoon stir in remaining 2 cups flour. Wrap dough in plastic wrap; refrigerate 2 hours.

**2.** Preheat oven to 325°F. Divide dough in half; set aside half.

**3.** On floured surface roll out half the dough to ⅛-inch thickness. Cut with floured bear cookie cutter. Repeat with remaining dough.

**4.** Bake bears on ungreased cookie sheets 10 minutes or until lightly browned. Remove from cookie sheets; cool completely on wire rack. Decorate as desired.

*Makes about 3 dozen bears*

**Prep Time:** 35 minutes plus chilling
**Bake Time:** 10 minutes plus cooling

**NOTE:** Use scraps of dough to make bear faces. Make one small ball of dough for muzzle. Form 3 smaller balls of dough and press gently to create eyes and nose; bake as directed. If desired, use frosting to create paws, ears and bow ties.

*Peanut Butter Bears*

## 215 PB & J COOKIE SANDWICHES

½ cup butter or margarine, softened
½ cup creamy peanut butter
¼ cup solid vegetable shortening
 1 cup firmly packed light brown sugar
 1 large egg
 1 teaspoon vanilla extract
1⅔ cups all-purpose flour
 1 teaspoon baking soda
½ teaspoon baking powder
 1 cup "M&M's"® Milk Chocolate Mini
     Baking Bits
½ cup finely chopped peanuts
½ cup grape or strawberry jam

Preheat oven to 350°F. In large bowl cream
butter, peanut butter, shortening and sugar
until light and fluffy; beat in egg and vanilla.
In medium bowl combine flour, baking soda
and baking powder; blend into creamed
mixture. Stir in "M&M's"® Milk Chocolate
Mini Baking Bits and nuts. Drop by rounded
teaspoonfuls onto ungreased cookie sheets.
Bake 8 to 10 minutes or until light golden.
Let cool 2 minutes on cookie sheets; remove
to wire racks to cool completely. Just before
serving, spread ½ teaspoon jam on bottom
of one cookie; top with second cookie. Store
in tightly covered container.

*Makes about 2 dozen sandwich cookies*

## 216 MOVIETIME CRUNCH BARS

6 cups CAP'N CRUNCH® Cereal, Regular
     Flavor, divided
1 cup salted peanuts
1 cup raisins
1 cup semi-sweet chocolate pieces
     One 14-ounce can sweetened
     condensed milk

Preheat oven to 350°F. Grease 13×9-inch
baking pan. Crush 4 cups of the cereal;
spread evenly in bottom of prepared pan.
Top with peanuts, raisins, chocolate pieces
and remaining 2 cups uncrushed cereal.
Drizzle sweetened condensed milk evenly
over mixture. Bake 25 to 30 minutes or until
golden brown. Cool completely; cut into
2×1½-inch bars. Store tightly covered.

*Makes 24 bars*

## 217 TEDDY WANTS S'MORES

9 NABISCO® Grahams, cut in half
8 ounces milk chocolate
2 cups Honey, Cinnamon or Chocolate
     TEDDY GRAHAMS® Graham Snacks,
     divided
1½ cups miniature marshmallows

Grease and waxed paper-line 8×8×2-inch
baking pan. Cover bottom of pan with
graham cracker halves; set aside.

In small saucepan over very low heat, melt
chocolate. Remove from heat. Stir in
1½ cups TEDDY GRAHAMS® and
marshmallows. Spread mixture evenly over
graham cracker halves. Press remaining
TEDDY GRAHAMS® on top of chocolate
mixture. Let stand until firm. Cut into bars.

*Makes about 1½ dozen bars*

## 218 PEANUT BUTTER HANDPRINTS

1 package DUNCAN HINES® Peanut
   Butter Cookie Mix
1 egg
¼ cup CRISCO® Oil or CRISCO®
   PURITAN® Canola Oil
1 tablespoon water
   Assorted candies such as gumdrops, jelly
   beans, cinnamon candies and decors

1. Preheat oven to 375°F.

2. Trace child's hand on piece of paper and
cut out.

3. Combine cookie mix, peanut butter
packet from Mix, egg, oil and water in large
bowl. Stir until thoroughly blended. Roll
dough on lightly floured surface to ¼-inch
thickness. Place hand pattern on dough. Cut
around pattern with knife. Carefully transfer
to ungreased baking sheets. Press assorted
candies on "hands." Bake at 375°F for 6 to
7 minutes or until set. Cool 1 minute on
baking sheets. Remove to cooling racks.
Cool completely. Store between layers of
waxed paper in airtight container.

*Makes about 1½ dozen cookies*

**TIP:** Allow your children to have fun
decorating handprints with candies to form
fingernails, rings and bracelets.

*Peanut Butter Handprints*

## 219 GIANT RAISIN–CHIP FRISBEES

1 cup butter or margarine, softened
1 cup packed brown sugar
½ cup granulated sugar
2 eggs
1 teaspoon vanilla
1½ cups all-purpose flour
¼ cup unsweetened cocoa
1 teaspoon baking soda
1 cup (6 ounces) semisweet chocolate chips
¾ cup raisins
¾ cup chopped walnuts

Preheat oven to 350°F. Line cookie sheets with parchment paper or lightly grease and dust with flour.

Cream butter with sugars in large bowl. Add eggs and vanilla; beat until light. Combine flour, cocoa and baking soda in small bowl. Add to creamed mixture with chocolate chips, raisins and walnuts; stir until well blended.

Scoop out about ½ cupful of dough for each cookie. Place on prepared cookie sheets, spacing about 5 inches apart. Using knife dipped in water, smooth balls of dough out to 3½ inches in diameter. Bake 10 to 12 minutes or until golden. Remove to wire racks to cool.        *Makes about 16 cookies*

## 220 CHEERY CHOCOLATE ANIMAL COOKIES

1⅔ cups REESE'S® Peanut Butter Chips
1 cup HERSHEY'S Semi-Sweet Chocolate Chips
2 tablespoons shortening (do not use butter, margarine or oil)
1 package (20 ounces) chocolate sandwich cookies
1 package (11 ounces) animal crackers

Line trays or cookie sheets with waxed paper. In 2-quart glass measuring cup with handle, combine chips and shortening. Microwave on HIGH (100% power) 1½ to 2 minutes or until chips are melted and mixture is smooth when stirred. With fork, dip each cookie into melted chip mixture; gently tap fork on side of cup to remove excess chocolate. Place chocolate-coated cookies on prepared trays; top each cookie with an animal cracker. Chill until chocolate is set, about 30 minutes. Store in airtight container in a cool, dry place.
        *Makes about 4 dozen cookies*

*Cheery Chocolate Animal Cookies*

## KID PLEASERS

## 221 GINGERBREAD TEDDIES

1 cup butter or margarine
²/₃ cup JACK FROST® Light Brown Sugar, packed
¹/₃ cup JACK FROST® Granulated Sugar
¹/₂ cup molasses
1 egg, beaten
2 teaspoons vanilla
4 cups all-purpose flour
¾ teaspoon baking soda
1¹/₂ teaspoon ground cinnamon
1 teaspoon ground ginger
¹/₂ teaspoon ground cloves
Chocolate chips

In medium saucepan, combine butter, sugars and molasses. Heat and stir over medium heat until butter is melted and sugars are dissolved. Pour into large mixing bowl; cool 10 minutes. Add egg and vanilla; mix well. Stir together flour, baking soda, cinnamon, ginger and cloves. Add to butter mixture; beat until well mixed. Divide dough in half. Wrap in plastic wrap; chill at least 2 hours.

For each bear, shape dough into one 3-inch ball, one 2-inch ball, six ¾-inch balls and five ¹/₂-inch balls.

On ungreased cookie sheet, flatten 3-inch ball to ¹/₂-inch thickness for body. Attach 2-inch ball for the head; flatten. Attach ¾-inch balls for arms, legs and ears. Place ¹/₂-inch balls at end of the arms and legs to make paws. Add the last ball to the face to make the nose. Use chocolate chips for eyes and navel. Melt 1 to 2 tablespoons chocolate chips. Using a decorators tip, pipe on mouth.

Bake in a 350° oven for 10 minutes or until lightly browned. Remove and cool on wire rack. Decorate with red satin ribbon.
*Makes 4 Gingerbread Teddies*

## 222 CINNAMON STARS

2 tablespoons sugar
¾ teaspoon ground cinnamon
¾ cup butter or margarine, softened
2 egg yolks
1 teaspoon vanilla extract
1 package DUNCAN HINES® Moist Deluxe French Vanilla Cake Mix

**1.** Preheat oven to 375°F. Combine sugar and cinnamon in small bowl. Set aside.

**2.** Combine butter, egg yolks and vanilla extract in large bowl. Blend in cake mix gradually. Roll to ¹/₈-inch thickness on lightly floured surface. Cut with 2¹/₂-inch star cookie cutter. Place 2 inches apart on ungreased baking sheet.

**3.** Sprinkle cookies with cinnamon-sugar mixture. Bake at 375°F for 6 to 8 minutes or until edges are light golden brown. Cool 1 minute on baking sheet. Remove to cooling rack. Cool completely. Store in airtight container. *Makes 3 to 3¹/₂ dozen cookies*

**TIP:** You can use your favorite cookie cutter in place of the star cookie cutter.

*Cinnamon Stars*

## 223 PEANUTTY CRISSCROSSES

3 cups QUAKER® Oats (quick or old
   fashioned, uncooked)
1½ cups all-purpose flour
½ teaspoon baking soda
1½ cups firmly packed brown sugar
1 cup peanut butter
¾ cup (1½ sticks) margarine or butter,
   softened
⅓ cup water
1 egg
1 teaspoon vanilla

Combine oats, flour and baking soda; set
aside. In large bowl, beat brown sugar,
peanut butter and margarine until creamy.
Blend in water, egg and vanilla. Add dry
ingredients; mix well. Chill dough about
1 hour.

Preheat oven to 350°F. Shape dough into
1-inch balls. Place on ungreased cookie
sheet; flatten with tines of fork dipped in
granulated sugar to form crisscross pattern.

Bake 9 to 10 minutes or until edges are
golden brown. Cool 2 minutes on cookie
sheet. Remove to wire rack to cool
completely. Store tightly covered.

*Makes about 7 dozen cookies*

## 224 GIANT PEANUT BUTTER CUP COOKIES

½ cup (1 stick) butter or margarine,
   softened
¾ cup sugar
⅓ cup REESE'S® Creamy or Crunchy Peanut
   Butter
1 egg
½ teaspoon vanilla extract
1¼ cups all-purpose flour
½ teaspoon baking soda
¼ teaspoon salt
16 REESE'S® Peanut Butter Cup Miniatures,
   cut into fourths

Heat oven to 350°F. In small mixer bowl,
beat butter, sugar and peanut butter until
creamy. Add egg and vanilla; beat well. Stir
together flour, baking soda and salt. Add to
butter mixture; blend well. Drop dough by
level ¼ cup measurements onto ungreased
cookie sheets, three cookies per sheet.
(Cookies will spread while baking.) Push
about seven pieces of peanut butter cup into
each cookie, flattening cookie slightly. Bake
15 to 17 minutes or until light golden brown
around the edges. Centers will be pale and
slightly soft. Cool 1 minute on cookie sheet.
Remove to wire rack; cool completely.

*Makes 9 cookies*

*Giant Peanut Butter Cup Cookies*

## 225 SWEET AS ANGELS' KISSES

4 egg whites, at room temperature
1/4 teaspoon cream of tartar
1/8 teaspoon salt
1 cup granulated sugar
1/4 teaspoon peppermint or mint extract or desired fruit-flavored flavoring
Few drops red or green food color
Cookie decorations or colored sugar

1. Preheat oven to 250°F. Cover baking sheets with parchment paper or aluminum foil; set aside.

2. Beat egg whites in large bowl with electric mixer until foamy. Add cream of tartar and salt; beat until soft peaks form. Gradually add sugar, beating until stiff peaks form. Beat in extract and food color.

3. Drop rounded tablespoonfuls of egg white mixture onto prepared baking sheets; sprinkle with cookie decorations.

4. Bake until cookies are firm to the touch and just beginning to brown around the edges, 35 to 45 minutes. Remove to wire rack to cool completely.

*Makes 20 servings*

**COCOA KISSES:** Omit extract, food color and decorations. Beat egg white mixture as directed until stiff peaks form; fold in 1/3 cup unsweetened cocoa powder. Drop rounded tablespoons of egg white mixture onto prepared baking sheets as directed; sprinkle lightly with chocolate sprinkles or finely chopped nuts. Continue as directed.

## 226 GRAPE-FILLED COOKIES

2 cups coarsely chopped seedless California grapes
1/4 cup packed brown sugar
1/2 teaspoon ground cinnamon
1 teaspoon lemon juice
Sugar Cookie Dough

Combine grapes, sugar and cinnamon in saucepan. Bring to boil; cook and stir over medium heat 35 minutes or until thickened. Stir in lemon juice; cool. Roll Sugar Cookie Dough to 1/8-inch thickness. Cut into 24 (2½-inch) circles. Place 12 circles on greased cookie sheet. Place a heaping teaspoonful of grape mixture on each circle leaving 1/8-inch border around edges. Place remaining circles on filling; press together with fork. Cut 3 to 5 slits through top circles of dough. Bake at 400°F 6 to 8 minutes or until lightly browned. Cool on wire rack.

*Makes about 1 dozen*

**SUGAR COOKIE DOUGH:** Beat 1/3 cup butter or margarine and 2 tablespoons sugar until smooth. Beat in 1 egg and 1/2 teaspoon vanilla. Combine 1 cup all-purpose flour, 3/4 teaspoon baking powder and dash salt; stir into butter mixture. Wrap and refrigerate at least 1 hour.

*Favorite recipe from California Table Grape Commission*

*Grape-Filled Cookies*

## 227 DINOSAUR COOKIES

1 cup FLEISCHMANN'S® Margarine,
  softened
1 cup sugar
1 egg
1 teaspoon vanilla extract
3 cups all-purpose flour
2 teaspoons DAVIS® Baking Powder
  Decorator icing (assorted colors), for
  decorating

With electric mixer, blend margarine and sugar until creamy. Beat in egg and vanilla. Combine flour and baking powder; blend into margarine mixture. Beat at medium speed until mixture forms a ball. Let dough rest 15 minutes; do not refrigerate.

On floured surface, roll dough to ⅛-inch thickness. With floured 5-inch cookie cutters, cut dough into desired shapes, rerolling scraps as necessary. Place on lightly greased baking sheet. Bake at 400°F for 4 to 6 minutes. Do not brown. Cool completely on wire rack. Decorate cookies as desired with icing.

*Makes about 20 cookies*

## 228 CHOCOLATE CHIP DESSERT PIZZA

1 package DUNCAN HINES® Chocolate
  Chip Cookie Mix
1 egg
⅓ cup CRISCO® Oil or CRISCO®
  PURITAN® Canola Oil
3 teaspoons water
2 cups miniature marshmallows
½ cup semi-sweet chocolate chips
½ cup chopped pecans

**1.** Preheat oven to 375°F. Grease 12-inch pizza pan.

**2.** Combine cookie mix, egg, oil and water in large bowl. Stir until thoroughly blended. Spread dough evenly on pan. Bake at 375°F for 12 minutes or until lightly browned. Remove from oven. Sprinkle marshmallows, chocolate chips and pecans on baked cookie. Return to oven. Bake 5 to 7 minutes longer or until marshmallows are lightly browned. Cool. Cut into wedges for serving.

*Makes 12 to 16 servings*

**TIP:** To cut cookie wedges easily, use pizza cutter.

*Monster Pops*

## 229 MONSTER POPS

1²/₃ cups all-purpose flour
1 teaspoon baking soda
½ teaspoon salt
1 cup (2 sticks) butter or margarine, softened
¾ cup granulated sugar
¾ cup packed brown sugar
2 teaspoons vanilla extract
2 eggs
2 cups (12-ounce package) NESTLÉ® TOLL HOUSE® Semi-Sweet Chocolate Morsels
2 cups quick or old-fashioned oats
1 cup raisins
About 24 wooden craft sticks
1 container (16 ounces) prepared vanilla frosting, colored as desired, or colored icing in tubes

**COMBINE** flour, baking soda and salt in small bowl. Beat butter, granulated sugar, brown sugar and vanilla in large mixer bowl until creamy. Beat in eggs. Gradually beat in flour mixture. Stir in morsels, oats and raisins. Drop dough by level ¼-cup measure 3 inches apart onto ungreased baking sheets. Shape into round mounds. Insert wooden stick into side of each mound.

**BAKE** in preheated 325°F. oven for 14 to 18 minutes or until golden brown. Cool on baking sheet for 2 minutes; remove to wire racks to cool completely.

**DRAW** Halloween characters on pops using frosting and icing.

*Makes about 2 dozen cookies*

## 230 MARSHMALLOW SANDWICH COOKIES

  2 cups all-purpose flour
  ½ cup unsweetened cocoa
  2 teaspoons baking soda
  ¼ teaspoon salt
  ⅔ cup butter or margarine, softened
  1¼ cups sugar
  ¼ cup light corn syrup
  1 large egg
  1 teaspoon vanilla
    Additional sugar
  24 large marshmallows

Preheat oven to 350°F.

Place flour, cocoa, baking soda and salt in medium bowl; stir to combine.

Beat butter and 1¼ cups sugar in large bowl with electric mixer at medium speed until light and fluffy, scraping down side of bowl once. Beat in corn syrup, egg and vanilla, scraping down side of bowl once. Gradually add flour mixture. Beat at low speed, scraping down side of bowl occasionally. Cover and refrigerate dough 15 minutes or until firm enough to roll into balls.

Place additional sugar in shallow dish. Roll tablespoonfuls of dough into 1-inch balls; roll in sugar to coat. Place 3 inches apart on ungreased cookie sheets.

Bake 10 to 11 minutes or until set. Remove cookies with spatula to wire rack; cool completely.

To assemble sandwiches,* place one marshmallow on flat side of one cookie on paper plate. Microwave at HIGH (100% power) 12 seconds or until marshmallow is hot. Immediately place another cookie, flat side down over marshmallow; press together slightly. Store tightly covered at room temperature.

*Makes about 2 dozen sandwich cookies*

*Cookies also taste great just as they are!*

NOTE: These cookies do not freeze well.

## 231 MINI PIZZA COOKIES

  1 20-ounce tube of refrigerated sugar
    cookie dough
  2 cups (16 ounces) prepared pink frosting
    "M&M's"® Chocolate Mini Baking Bits
    Variety of additional toppings such as
    shredded coconut, granola, raisins,
    nuts, small pretzels, snack mixes,
    sunflower seeds, popped corn and
    mini marshmallows

Preheat oven to 350°F. Lightly grease cookie sheets; set aside. Divide dough into 8 equal portions. On lightly floured surface, roll each portion of dough into ¼-inch-thick circle; place about 2 inches apart onto prepared cookie sheets. Bake 10 to 13 minutes or until golden brown on edges. Cool completely on wire racks. Spread top of each pizza with frosting; sprinkle with "M&M's"® Chocolate Mini Baking Bits and 2 or 3 suggested toppings. *Makes 8 cookies*

*Marshmallow Sandwich Cookies*

**KID PLEASERS**

## 232 PEANUT BUTTER CHIPS AND JELLY BARS

1½ cups all-purpose flour
½ cup sugar
¾ teaspoon baking powder
½ cup (1 stick) cold butter or margarine
1 egg, beaten
¾ cup grape jelly
1⅔ cups (10-ounce package) REESE'S® Peanut Butter Chips, divided

**1.** Heat oven to 375°F. Grease 9-inch square baking pan.

**2.** Stir together flour, sugar and baking powder. Cut in butter with pastry blender until mixture resembles coarse crumbs. Add egg; blend well. Reserve one-half of mixture; press remaining mixture onto bottom of prepared pan. Spread jelly evenly over crust. Sprinkle 1 cup peanut butter chips over jelly. Stir together remaining crumb mixture with remaining ⅔ cup chips; sprinkle over top.

**3.** Bake 25 to 30 minutes or until lightly browned. Cool completely in pan on wire rack. Cut into bars.    *Makes about 16 bars*

**HIGH ALTITUDE DIRECTIONS:** Increase flour to 1½ cups plus 1 tablespoon. Add 1 tablespoon water with egg. Do not change baking time or temperature.

## 233 P. B. GRAHAM SNACKERS

½ BUTTER FLAVOR* CRISCO® Stick or ½ cup BUTTER FLAVOR CRISCO all-vegetable shortening
2 cups powdered sugar
¾ cup creamy peanut butter
1 cup graham cracker crumbs
½ cup semisweet chocolate chips
½ cup graham cracker crumbs or crushed peanuts or chocolate sprinkles (optional)

*\*Butter Flavor Crisco is artificially flavored.*

**1.** Combine shortening, powdered sugar and peanut butter in large bowl. Beat at low speed of electric mixer until well blended. Stir in 1 cup crumbs and chocolate chips. Cover and refrigerate 1 hour.

**2.** Form dough into 1-inch balls. Roll in ½ cup crumbs. Cover and refrigerate until ready to serve.
    *Makes about 3 dozen cookies*

*Peanut Butter Chips and Jelly Bars*

## 234 HAPPY COOKIE POPS

1½ cups granulated sugar
1 cup butter-flavored solid vegetable
    shortening
2 large eggs
1 teaspoon vanilla extract
2¾ cups all-purpose flour
1 teaspoon baking powder
½ teaspoon baking soda
1¾ cups "M&M's"® Chocolate Mini Baking
    Bits, divided
    Additional granulated sugar
2½ dozen flat wooden ice cream sticks
    Prepared frostings
    Tubes of decorator's icing

In large bowl cream 1½ cups sugar and
shortening until light and fluffy; beat in eggs
and vanilla. In medium bowl combine flour,
baking powder and baking soda; blend into
creamed mixture. Stir in *1¼ cups
"M&M's"® Chocolate Mini Baking Bits.*
Wrap and refrigerate dough 1 hour.

Preheat oven to 375°F. Roll 1½ tablespoons
dough into ball and roll in granulated sugar.
Insert ice cream stick into each ball. Place
about 2 inches apart onto ungreased cookie
sheets; gently flatten, using bottom of small
plate. On half the cookies, make a smiling
face by placing some of the remaining
*"M&M's"® Chocolate Mini Baking Bits*
on the surface; leave other cookies for
decorating after baking. Bake all cookies
10 to 12 minutes or until golden. Cool
2 minutes on cookie sheets; cool completely
on wire racks. Decorate cookies as desired
using frostings, decorator's icing and
remaining *"M&M's"® Chocolate Mini
Baking Bits.* Store in single layer in tightly
covered container.

*Makes 2½ dozen cookies*

**VARIATION:** For chocolate cookies,
combine ⅓ cup unsweetened cocoa powder
with flour, baking powder and baking soda;
continue as directed.

## 235 CHOCOLATE PEANUT BUTTER COOKIES

1 package DUNCAN HINES® Moist
    Deluxe Devil's Food Cake Mix
¾ cup JIF® Extra Crunchy Peanut Butter
2 eggs
2 tablespoons milk
1 cup candy-coated peanut butter pieces

**1.** Preheat oven to 350°F. Grease baking
sheets.

**2.** Combine cake mix, peanut butter, eggs
and milk in large bowl. Mix at low speed
with electric mixer until blended. Stir in
peanut butter pieces. Drop dough by slightly
rounded tablespoonfuls onto prepared
baking sheets. Bake at 350°F for 7 to
9 minutes or until lightly browned. Cool
2 minutes on baking sheets. Remove to
cooling racks. Cool completely. Store in
airtight container.

*Makes about 3½ dozen cookies*

**TIP:** You can use 1 cup peanut butter chips in
place of peanut butter pieces.

*Chocolate Peanut Butter Cookies*

## KID PLEASERS

### 236 COLOR–BRIGHT ICE CREAM SANDWICHES

¾ cup (1½ sticks) butter or margarine, softened
¾ cup creamy peanut butter
1¼ cups firmly packed light brown sugar
1 large egg
1 teaspoon vanilla extract
1½ cups all-purpose flour
1 teaspoon baking soda
¼ teaspoon salt
1¾ cups "M&M's"® Chocolate Mini Baking Bits, divided
2 quarts vanilla or chocolate ice cream, slightly softened

Preheat oven to 350°F. In large bowl cream butter, peanut butter and sugar until light and fluffy; beat in egg and vanilla. In medium bowl combine flour, baking soda and salt; blend into creamed mixture. Stir in *1⅓ cups "M&M's"® Chocolate Mini Baking Bits.* Shape dough into 1¼-inch balls. Place about 2 inches apart on ungreased cookie sheets. Gently flatten to about ½-inch thickness with fingertips. Place 7 or 8 of the remaining *"M&M's"® Chocolate Mini Baking Bits* on each cookie; press in lightly. Bake 10 to 12 minutes or until edges are light brown. *Do not overbake.* Cool about 1 minute on cookie sheets; cool completely on wire racks. Assemble cookies in pairs with about ⅓ cup ice cream; press cookies together lightly. Wrap each sandwich in plastic wrap; freeze until firm.

*Makes about 24 ice cream sandwiches*

### 237 TRACY'S PIZZA–PAN COOKIES

1 cup butter or margarine, softened
¾ cup granulated sugar
¾ cup packed brown sugar
1 package (8 ounces) cream cheese, softened
1 teaspoon vanilla
2 eggs
2¼ cups all-purpose flour
1 teaspoon baking soda
¼ teaspoon salt
1 package (12 ounces) semisweet chocolate chips
1 cup chopped walnuts or pecans

Preheat oven to 375°F. Lightly grease 2 (12-inch) pizza pans.

Beat butter, sugars, cream cheese and vanilla in large bowl. Add eggs; beat until well blended. Combine flour, baking soda and salt in small bowl. Add to butter mixture; blend well. Stir in chocolate chips and nuts. Divide dough in half; press each half evenly into a prepared pan.

Bake 20 to 25 minutes or until lightly browned around edges. Cool completely in pans on wire racks. To serve, cut into slim wedges or break into pieces.

*Makes 2 (12-inch) cookies*

*Tracy's Pizza-Pan Cookies*

# Special Occasions

## 238 CHOCOLATE–DIPPED BRANDY SNAPS

½ cup (1 stick) butter
½ cup granulated sugar
⅓ cup dark corn syrup
½ teaspoon ground cinnamon
¼ teaspoon ground ginger
1 cup all-purpose flour
2 teaspoons brandy
1 cup (6 ounces) NESTLÉ® TOLL HOUSE®
     Semi-Sweet Chocolate Morsels
1 tablespoon shortening
⅓ cup finely chopped nuts

**MELT** butter, sugar, corn syrup, cinnamon and ginger in medium, heavy-duty saucepan over low heat, stirring until smooth. Remove from heat; stir in flour and brandy. Drop mixture by rounded teaspoon onto ungreased baking sheets about 3 inches apart, baking no more than six cookies at a time.

**BAKE** in preheated 300°F for 10 to 14 minutes or until deep caramel color. Cool for 10 seconds. Remove from baking sheets and immediately roll around wooden spoon handle; cool completely on wire racks.

**MICROWAVE** morsels and shortening in medium, microwave-safe bowl on HIGH (100%) power for 45 seconds; stir. Microwave an additional 10- to 20-second intervals, stirring until smooth. Dip cookies halfway in melted chocolate; shake off excess. Sprinkle with nuts; set on waxed paper-lined baking sheets. Chill for 10 minutes or until chocolate is set. Store in airtight container in refrigerator.

*Makes about 3 dozen cookies*

*Chocolate-Dipped Brandy Snaps*

## 239 CHOCOLATE FUDGE COOKIE CAKES

**CHOCOLATE FILLING**
1 square (1 ounce) unsweetened chocolate
3 tablespoons water
1 tablespoon light corn syrup
2 tablespoons sugar
1 tablespoon unsweetened cocoa powder
½ teaspoon cornstarch
½ teaspoon vanilla

**CHOCOLATE DOUGH**
1 cup sugar
¼ cup Prune Purée (recipe, page 182) or prepared prune butter or 1 jar (2½ ounces) first-stage baby food prunes
2 egg whites
2 tablespoons water*
1 teaspoon instant espresso coffee powder
1 teaspoon vanilla
1¾ cups all-purpose flour
½ cup unsweetened cocoa powder
1 teaspoon baking soda
½ teaspoon salt

*Omit water if using baby food prunes.*

To make filling, in small heavy saucepan, melt chocolate with water over very low heat, stirring until smooth. Remove from heat; whisk in corn syrup, sugar, cocoa and cornstarch. Bring to a boil over medium heat, whisking occasionally. Cook 1 minute, whisking constantly, until slightly thickened. Remove from heat; stir in vanilla. Let cool, stirring occasionally.

Preheat oven to 350°F. Coat baking sheets with vegetable cooking spray. To make dough, in mixer bowl, beat sugar, prune purée, egg whites, water, espresso powder and vanilla at high speed 1 minute until fluffy and light in color. Combine flour, cocoa,

baking soda and salt; stir into prune purée mixture until well blended. Shape dough into thirty balls.** Place on prepared baking sheets, spacing 3 inches apart. Bake in center of oven 11 to 12 minutes. Remove from oven; immediately make 1-inch-wide indentation in each cookie with handle of wooden spoon. Spoon scant ½ teaspoon of filling into each cookie. Cool completely on baking sheets. *Makes 30 cookies*

***If dough is sticky, moisten your hands lightly with cold water.*

*Favorite recipe from **California Prune Board***

## 240 ALMOND RASPBERRY MACAROONS

2 cups BLUE DIAMOND® Blanched Almond Paste
1 cup granulated sugar
6 large egg whites
   Powdered sugar
   Seedless raspberry jam, stirred until smooth

Beat almond paste and granulated sugar until mixture resembles coarse cornmeal. Beat in egg whites, a little at a time, until thoroughly combined. Place heaping teaspoonfuls onto cookie sheet lined with waxed paper or parchment paper. Coat finger with powdered sugar and make an indentation in the middle of each cookie. (Coat finger with powdered sugar each time.) Bake at 350°F for 15 to 20 minutes or until lightly browned. Remove from oven and fill each indentation with about ¼ teaspoon raspberry jam. Cool. If using waxed paper, carefully peel paper off cookies when cooled.
*Makes about 30 cookies*

*Chocolate Fudge Cookie Cakes*

## SPECIAL OCCASIONS

### 241 KENTUCKY BOURBON PECAN TARTS

Cream Cheese Pastry (recipe follows)
2 eggs
½ cup granulated sugar
½ cup KARO® Light or Dark Corn Syrup
2 tablespoons bourbon
1 tablespoon MAZOLA® Margarine or butter, melted
½ teaspoon vanilla
1 cup chopped pecans
Confectioners' sugar (optional)

1. Preheat oven to 350°F. Prepare Cream Cheese Pastry. Divide dough in half; set aside half.

2. On floured surface, roll out pastry to ⅛-inch thickness. *If necessary, add small amount of flour to keep pastry from sticking.* Cut into 12 (2¼-inch) rounds. Press evenly into bottoms and up sides of 1¾-inch muffin pan cups. Repeat with remaining pastry. Refrigerate.

3. In medium bowl, beat eggs slightly. Stir in granulated sugar, corn syrup, bourbon, margarine and vanilla until well blended. Spoon 1 heaping teaspoon pecans into each pastry-lined cup; top with 1 tablespoon corn syrup mixture.

4. Bake 20 to 25 minutes or until lightly browned and toothpick inserted into center comes out clean. Cool in pans 5 minutes. Remove; cool completely on wire rack. If desired, sprinkle cookies with confectioners' sugar.        *Makes about 2 dozen cookies*

**Prep Time:** 45 minutes
**Bake Time:** 25 minutes plus cooling

CREAM CHEESE PASTRY
1 cup all-purpose flour
¾ teaspoon baking powder
Pinch salt
½ cup (1 stick) MAZOLA® Margarine or butter, softened
1 package (3 ounces) cream cheese, softened
2 teaspoons sugar

In small bowl, combine flour, baking powder and salt. In large bowl, mix margarine, cream cheese and sugar until well combined. Stir in flour mixture until well blended. Press firmly into ball with hands.

### 242 HONEY SHORTBREAD

1 cup butter
⅓ cup honey
1 teaspoon vanilla
2½ cups all-purpose flour
¾ cup chopped pecans

Preheat oven to 300°F. Beat butter, honey and vanilla in large bowl with electric mixer at medium speed until mixture is light and fluffy. Add flour, 1 cup at a time, beating well after each addition. If dough becomes too stiff to stir, knead in remaining flour by hand. Knead in nuts. Pat dough into shortbread mold or ungreased 9-inch cast iron skillet. Score surface with knife so it can be divided into 24 wedges. With fork, prick deeply into the scores. Bake 35 to 40 minutes. Cool in pan on wire rack 10 minutes. Remove from pan. Cut into wedges while warm.

*Makes 2 dozen wedges*

*Favorite recipe from **National Honey Board***

## 243 CHOCOLATE ALMOND BUTTONS

1⅓ cups flour
⅓ cup cocoa powder
¼ teaspoon salt
1 cup BLUE DIAMOND® Blanched Almond Paste
½ cup plus 1½ tablespoons softened butter, divided
¼ cup corn syrup
1 teaspoon vanilla extract
3 ounces semisweet chocolate, melted
⅔ cup BLUE DIAMOND® Blanched Whole Almonds, toasted

Sift flour, cocoa powder and salt; reserve. Cream almond paste and ½ cup butter until smooth. Beat in corn syrup and vanilla. Beat in flour mixture, scraping sides of bowl occasionally, until well-blended. Shape into ¾-inch balls. Place on lightly greased cookie sheet; indent center of cookies with finger. Bake at 350°F for 8 to 10 minutes or until done. (Cookies will be soft but will become firm when cooled.) In a double boiler, stir chocolate and remaining 1½ tablespoons butter over simmering water until smooth. With spoon, drizzle small amount of chocolate into center of each cookie. Press an almond into chocolate on each cookie.

*Makes 6 dozen*

**Honey Shortbread**

## 244 CHOCOLATE LACE CORNUCOPIAS

½ cup firmly packed brown sugar
½ cup corn syrup
¼ cup (½ stick) margarine or butter
4 squares BAKER'S® Semi-Sweet Chocolate
1 cup all-purpose flour
1 cup finely chopped nuts
   Whipped cream or COOL WHIP®
   Whipped Topping, thawed

**HEAT** oven to 350°F.

**MICROWAVE** sugar, corn syrup and margarine in large microwavable bowl on HIGH 2 minutes or until boiling. Stir in chocolate until completely melted. Gradually stir in flour and nuts until well blended.

**DROP** by level tablespoonfuls, 4 inches apart, onto foil-covered cookie sheets.

**BAKE** for 10 minutes. Lift foil and cookies onto wire rack. Cool on wire rack 3 to 4 minutes or until cookies can be easily peeled off foil. Remove foil; finish cooling cookies on wire rack that has been covered with paper towels.

**PLACE** several cookies, lacy side down, on foil-lined cookie sheet. Heat at 350° for 2 to 3 minutes or until slightly softened. Remove from foil, one at a time, and roll lacy side out to form cones. Cool completely. Just before serving, fill with whipped cream.

*Makes about 30 cornucopias*

**Prep Time:** 20 minutes
**Bake Time:** 12 to 13 minutes

**SAUCEPAN PREPARATION:** Mix sugar, corn syrup and margarine in 2-quart saucepan. Bring to boil over medium heat, stirring constantly. Remove from heat; stir in chocolate until melted. Continue as above.

## 245 CHOCOLATE PISTACHIO FINGERS

¾ cup butter or margarine, softened
⅓ cup sugar
3 ounces (about ⅓ cup) almond paste
1 egg yolk
1⅔ cups all-purpose flour
1 cup (6 ounces) semisweet chocolate chips
½ cup finely chopped natural pistachios

Preheat oven to 350°F. Line cookie sheets with parchment paper or lightly grease and dust with flour.

Beat butter and sugar in large bowl until blended. Add almond paste and egg yolk; beat until light. Blend in flour to make a smooth dough. (If dough is too soft to handle, cover and refrigerate until firm.) Turn out onto lightly floured surface. Divide into 8 equal pieces; divide each piece in half. Roll each half into a 12-inch rope; cut each rope into 2-inch lengths. Place 2 inches apart on prepared cookie sheets.

Bake 10 to 12 minutes or until edges just begin to brown. Remove to wire racks to cool. Melt chocolate chips in small bowl over hot water. Stir until smooth. Dip both ends of cookies about ½ inch into melted chocolate; dip chocolate ends into pistachios. Place on waxed paper; let stand until chocolate is set.

*Makes 8 dozen cookies*

*Chocolate Lace Cornucopias*

## SPECIAL OCCASIONS

## 246 CHOCOLATE CHIP CORDIALS

**COOKIES**
1 package DUNCAN HINES® Chocolate
   Chip Cookie Mix
1 egg
⅓ cup CRISCO® Oil or CRISCO®
   PURITAN® Canola Oil
3 tablespoons water
1⅓ cups chopped pecans
⅓ cup chopped red candied cherries
⅓ cup flaked coconut
   Pecan halves, for garnish
   Red or green candied cherry halves, for
   garnish

**CHOCOLATE GLAZE**
1½ squares (1½ ounces) semi-sweet
   chocolate
3 tablespoons butter or margarine

**1.** Preheat oven to 375°F. Place 1¾-inch paper liners in 42 mini-muffin cups.

**2. For cookies,** combine cookie mix, egg, oil and water in large bowl. Stir until thoroughly blended. Stir in chopped pecans, chopped cherries and coconut. Fill cups with cookie dough. Top with pecan or cherry halves. Bake at 375°F for 13 to 15 minutes or until light golden brown. Cool completely.

**3. For chocolate glaze,** melt chocolate and butter in small bowl over hot water. Stir until smooth. Drizzle over cordials. Refrigerate until chocolate is firm. Store in airtight containers.          *Makes 42 cordials*

**TIP:** You can also prepare glaze in microwave oven. Place chocolate and butter in microwave-safe bowl. Microwave at MEDIUM (50% power) for 45 to 60 seconds; stir until smooth.

## 247 CALIFORNIA APRICOT PISTACHIO BISCOTTI

1¼ cups all-purpose flour
½ cup whole-wheat flour
1 cup sugar
½ teaspoon baking powder
¼ teaspoon salt
5 tablespoons cold unsalted butter, cut
   into pieces
¾ teaspoon vanilla extract
2 eggs, slightly beaten
⅔ cup coarsely chopped California dried
   apricots
1 cup shelled natural California pistachios
1 teaspoon sugar

Preheat oven to 350°F. Lightly grease large baking sheet.

In food processor or blender, process flours, 1 cup sugar, baking powder and salt until blended. Add butter and vanilla; process until mixture resembles coarse crumbs. Add eggs; process until blended. Add apricots and pistachios; process just until dough is evenly moistened.

Remove dough from food processor; form into 2 balls. On prepared baking sheet, shape each half of dough into a 12-inch log. With hands, flatten each log to a width of 2 inches. Sprinkle each log with ½ teaspoon sugar. Bake 25 minutes or until golden brown. Remove logs to cooling rack; cool 10 minutes. *Do not turn oven off.* With serrated knife, carefully cut logs diagonally into ½-inch slices. Place on baking sheet with cut sides up; return to oven and bake 7 minutes or until very lightly browned. Transfer to wire rack; cool completely.
              *Makes 4 dozen cookies*

*Favorite recipe from* **California Apricot Advisory Board**

*Chocolate Chip Cordials*

## 248 CHOCOLATE PECAN TASSIES

**CRUST**
- ½ cup (1 stick) margarine or butter
- 1 package (3 ounces) PHILADELPHIA BRAND® Cream Cheese, softened
- 1 cup all-purpose flour

**FILLING**
- 1 square BAKER'S® Unsweetened Chocolate
- 1 tablespoon margarine or butter
- ¾ cup firmly packed brown sugar
- 1 egg
- 1 teaspoon vanilla
- 1 cup chopped pecans
- Powdered sugar (optional)

**BEAT** ½ cup margarine and cream cheese until well blended. Beat in flour until just blended. Wrap dough in plastic wrap; refrigerate 1 hour.

**HEAT** oven to 350°F. Microwave chocolate and 1 tablespoon margarine in large microwavable bowl on HIGH 1 minute or until margarine is melted. **Stir until chocolate is completely melted.**

**BEAT** in sugar, egg and vanilla until thickened. Stir in pecans.

**SHAPE** chilled dough into 36 (1-inch) balls. Flatten each ball and press onto bottom and up sides of ungreased miniature muffin cups. Spoon about 1 teaspoon filling into each cup.

**BAKE** for 20 minutes. Cool in pans on wire racks 15 minutes. Remove from pans. Sprinkle with powdered sugar, if desired.

*Makes 36 tassies*

**Prep Time:** 45 minutes
**Chill Time:** 1 hour
**Baking Time:** 20 minutes

## 249 CHOCOLATE COVERED CHERRY COOKIES

- 1 cup sugar
- ½ cup butter, softened
- 1 egg
- 1½ teaspoons vanilla
- 1½ cups all-purpose flour
- ¼ cup unsweetened cocoa powder
- ¼ teaspoon baking powder
- ¼ teaspoon baking soda
- ¼ teaspoon salt
- 42 maraschino cherries, well-drained
- 1 (6-ounce) package semi-sweet chocolate pieces
- ½ cup sweetened condensed milk
- 4 to 5 teaspoons maraschino cherry juice

Beat sugar and butter in large bowl until light and fluffy. Blend in egg and vanilla. Combine flour, cocoa, baking powder, baking soda and salt in small bowl. Add to sugar mixture; mix well. Shape dough into 1-inch balls; place on ungreased cookie sheet. Indent centers; fill each with one cherry. Combine chocolate pieces and sweetened condensed milk in small saucepan; stir over low heat until smooth. Blend in enough cherry juice to make nice spreading consistency. Drop 1 teaspoon chocolate mixture over each cherry, spreading to cover cherry. Bake in preheated 350°F oven 12 minutes or until set.

*Makes 3½ dozen*

*Favorite recipe from **Wisconsin Milk Marketing Board.***

## 250 CHOCOLATE–DIPPED ALMOND HORNS

1 can SOLO® Almond Paste
3 egg whites
½ cup superfine sugar
½ teaspoon almond extract
¼ cup plus 2 tablespoons all-purpose flour
½ cup sliced almonds
5 squares (1 ounce each) semisweet chocolate, melted and cooled

Preheat oven to 350°F. Grease 2 cookie sheets; set aside. Break almond paste into small pieces and place in medium bowl or container of food processor. Add egg whites, sugar and almond extract. Beat with electric mixer or process until mixture is very smooth. Add flour and beat or process until blended.

Spoon almond mixture into pastry bag fitted with ½-inch (#8) plain tip. Pipe mixture into 5- or 6-inch crescent shapes on prepared cookie sheets about 1½ inches apart. Sprinkle with sliced almonds.

Bake 13 to 15 minutes or until edges are golden. Cool on cookie sheets on wire racks 2 minutes. Remove from cookie sheets and cool completely on wire racks. Dip ends of cookies in melted chocolate and place on sheet of foil. Let stand until chocolate is set.
*Makes about 16 cookies*

**Chocolate-Dipped Almond Horns**

## 251 BLACK FOREST OATMEAL FANCIES

1 BUTTER FLAVOR* CRISCO® Stick or
   1 cup BUTTER FLAVOR CRISCO
   all-vegetable shortening
1 cup packed brown sugar
1 cup granulated sugar
2 eggs
2 teaspoons vanilla
1⅔ cups all-purpose flour
1 teaspoon baking soda
1 teaspoon salt
½ teaspoon baking powder
3 cups quick oats (not instant or old
   fashioned), uncooked
1 baking bar (6 ounces) white chocolate,
   coarsely chopped
6 squares (1 ounce each) semisweet
   chocolate, coarsely chopped
½ cup coarsely chopped red candied
   cherries
½ cup sliced almonds

*Butter Flavor Crisco is artificially flavored.*

**1. Heat** oven to 375°F. **Place** sheets of foil on countertop for cooling cookies.

**2. Combine** shortening, brown sugar, granulated sugar, eggs and vanilla in large bowl. **Beat** at medium speed of electric mixer until well blended.

**3. Combine** flour, baking soda, salt and baking powder. **Mix** into shortening mixture at low speed until well blended. **Stir** in, one at a time, oats, white chocolate, semisweet chocolate, cherries and nuts with spoon.

**4. Drop** rounded tablespoonfuls of dough 2 inches apart onto ungreased baking sheets.

**5. Bake** one baking sheet at a time at 375°F for 9 to 11 minutes or until set. *Do not overbake.* **Cool** 2 minutes on baking sheets. **Remove** cookies to foil to cool completely.

*Makes about 3 dozen cookies*

## 252 BUTTER PECAN CRISPS

1 cup unsalted butter, softened
¾ cup granulated sugar
¾ cup firmly packed brown sugar
½ teaspoon salt
2 eggs
1 teaspoon vanilla
1½ cups finely ground pecans
2½ cups sifted all-purpose flour
1 teaspoon baking soda
30 pecan halves
4 squares (1 ounce each) semisweet
   chocolate
1 tablespoon shortening

Preheat oven to 375°F. Beat butter, sugars and salt in large bowl until light and fluffy. Add eggs, 1 at a time, beating well after each addition. Beat in vanilla and ground pecans. Combine flour and baking soda in small bowl. Gradually stir flour mixture into butter mixture. Spoon dough into large pastry bag fitted with ⅜-inch round tip; fill bag halfway. Shake down dough to remove air bubbles. Hold bag perpendicular to and about ½ inch above parchment paper-lined cookie sheets. Pipe dough into 1¼-inch balls, spacing 3 inches apart. Cut each pecan half lengthwise into 2 slivers. Press 1 sliver in center of each dough ball.

Bake 9 to 12 minutes or until lightly browned. Cool 5 minutes on cookie sheets. Remove to wire racks; cool completely. Melt chocolate and shortening in small, heavy saucepan over low heat; stir to blend. Drizzle chocolate mixture over cookies. Let stand until chocolate is set.

*Makes about 5 dozen cookies*

*Black Forest Oatmeal Fancies*

## 253 CHOCOLATE BANANA BISCOTTI

4 cups all-purpose flour
2 teaspoons baking powder
½ teaspoon salt
¼ cup margarine, softened
1½ cups sugar
2 eggs
2 medium, ripe DOLE® Bananas, mashed
(about ¾ cup)
1 teaspoon vanilla extract
1 cup DOLE® Whole Almonds, toasted
Vegetable cooking spray
2 cups white or milk chocolate chips,
melted

• **Combine** flour, baking powder and salt in large bowl; set aside.

• **Beat** together margarine and sugar in large bowl until light and fluffy. Beat in eggs, bananas and vanilla until blended. Stir in flour mixture and almonds until combined.

• **Divide** dough in half. On lightly floured surface, form each half into 12×3-inch logs. Place 3 inches apart on baking sheet sprayed with vegetable cooking spray.

• **Bake** at 325°F 25 to 30 minutes or until firm to touch and lightly brown. Cool logs on wire rack 15 minutes.

• **Cut** logs diagonally into ½-inch thick slices. Place slices flat, in single layer, on two baking sheets.

• **Bake** 10 minutes more. Turn slices over; bake 10 to 15 minutes more or until lightly browned on top and bottom of biscotti. Remove to wire rack; cool completely. Biscotti will become harder as they cool.

• **Spread** melted chocolate on one side of each biscotti. Place on baking sheets, chocolate side up, and chill 10 minutes or until chocolate is set. Store in air-tight container in cool area.　　*Makes 4 dozen*

**Prep:** 20 minutes
**Bake:** 50 minutes

## 254 CHOCOLATE ALMOND SHORTBREAD

¾ cup (1½ sticks) butter or margarine,
softened
1¼ cups powdered sugar
6 squares BAKER'S® Semi-Sweet
Chocolate, melted and cooled
1 teaspoon vanilla
1 cup all-purpose flour
¼ teaspoon salt
1 cup toasted ground blanched almonds
½ cup toasted chopped almonds

**HEAT** oven to 250°F.

**BEAT** butter and sugar until light and fluffy. Stir in chocolate and vanilla. Mix in flour, salt and ground almonds.

**PRESS** dough into 12×9-inch rectangle on ungreased cookie sheet. Sprinkle with chopped almonds; press lightly into dough.

**BAKE** for 45 to 50 minutes or until set. Cool on cookie sheet; cut into bars.
　　　　　　　　　*Makes about 36 bars*

**Prep Time:** 30 minutes
**Baking Time:** 45 to 50 minutes

*Top to bottom: Chocolate Almond*
*Shortbread and Chocolate Chip Rugalach*
*(page 42)*

SPECIAL OCCASIONS

## 255 MARBLED BISCOTTI

½ cup (1 stick) butter or margarine, softened
1 cup granulated sugar
2 large eggs
1 teaspoon vanilla extract
2½ cups all-purpose flour
1 teaspoon baking powder
1 teaspoon baking soda
1¾ cups "M&M's"® Chocolate Mini Baking Bits, divided
1 cup slivered almonds, toasted*
¼ cup unsweetened cocoa powder
2 tablespoons instant coffee granules

*To toast almonds, spread in single layer on baking sheet. Bake at 350°F for 7 to 10 minutes until light golden, stirring occasionally. Remove almonds from pan and cool completely before using.*

Preheat oven to 350°F. Lightly grease cookie sheets; set aside. In large bowl cream butter and sugar until light and fluffy; beat in eggs and vanilla. In medium bowl combine flour, baking powder and baking soda; blend into creamed mixture. *Dough will be stiff.* Stir in **1¼ cups "M&M's"® Chocolate Mini Baking Bits** and nuts. Divide dough in half. Add cocoa powder and coffee granules to half of the dough, mixing to blend. On well-floured surface, gently knead doughs together just enough to marble. Divide dough in half and gently roll each half into 12×2-inch log; place on prepared cookie sheets at least 4 inches apart. Press remaining ½ **cup "M&M's"® Chocolate Mini Baking Bits** onto outside of both logs. Bake 25 minutes. *Dough will spread.* Cool logs 15 to 20 minutes. Slice each log into 12 slices; arrange on cookie sheet cut-side down. Bake an additional 10 minutes. (For softer biscotti, omit second baking.) Cool completely. Store in tightly covered container. *Makes 24 pieces*

## 256 CHOCOLATE–GILDED DANISH SUGAR CONES

½ cup butter or margarine, softened
½ cup sugar
½ cup all-purpose flour
2 egg whites
1 teaspoon vanilla
3 ounces bittersweet chocolate or ½ cup semisweet chocolate chips

Preheat oven to 400°F. Generously grease 4 cookie sheets. Beat butter and sugar in large bowl until light and fluffy. Blend in flour. In clean, dry bowl, beat egg whites until frothy. Blend into butter mixture with vanilla. Using a teaspoon, place 4 mounds of dough 4 inches apart on each prepared cookie sheet. Spread mounds with small spatula dipped in water to 3-inch diameter. Bake 1 sheet at a time 5 to 6 minutes or until edges are just barely golden. (Do not overbake or cookies become crisp too quickly and are difficult to shape.) Remove from oven and quickly loosen each cookie from cookie sheet with a thin spatula. Shape each into a cone; cones become firm as they cool. (If cookies become too firm to shape, return to oven for a few seconds to soften.) Melt chocolate in small bowl over hot water. Stir until smooth. When all cookies are baked and cooled, dip flared ends into melted chocolate; let stand until chocolate is set. If desired, serve cones by standing them in a bowl. (Adding about 1 inch of sugar to bottom of bowl may be necessary to hold them upright.) *Makes 16 cookies*

## SPECIAL OCCASIONS

### 257 ABSOLUTELY WONDERFUL PECAN BARS

1½ cups quick or old-fashioned oats
1½ cups all-purpose flour
  2 cups JACK FROST® Dark Brown Sugar, packed, divided
  ½ cup butter (we do not recommend margarine)
1½ cups or 1 (7-ounce) package pecan halves
  1 cup JACK FROST® Granulated Sugar
  1 cup butter
  ⅓ cup heavy cream
  2 teaspoons vanilla

In large bowl, combine oats, flour and 1 cup dark brown sugar. Cut ½ cup butter into mixture until coarse and crumbly. Press into 13×9-inch baking pan. Place pecans evenly over crumb mixture.

In heavy saucepan, combine remaining 1 cup brown sugar, sugar and 1 cup butter. Bring to rolling boil over medium heat, stirring constantly. Boil 3 minutes; remove from heat. Stir in cream and vanilla until well blended; pour over pecans. Bake in preheated 350° oven 35 to 40 minutes. Cool in pan; cut into bars. *Makes 48 bars*

*Chocolate-Gilded Danish Sugar Cones*

## 258 CAPPUCCINO COOKIES

1¼ cups firmly packed light brown sugar
 1 Butter Flavor* CRISCO® Stick or 1 cup Butter Flavor CRISCO® all-vegetable shortening
 2 eggs
¼ cup light corn syrup
 1 teaspoon vanilla
 1 teaspoon rum extract
 2 tablespoons instant espresso or coffee powder
 3 cups all-purpose flour
¾ teaspoon baking powder
½ teaspoon baking soda
½ teaspoon salt
½ teaspoon nutmeg
   Chocolate jimmies

*Butter Flavor Crisco is artificially flavored.*

**1.** Place brown sugar and shortening in large bowl. Beat at medium speed of electric mixer until well blended. Add eggs, corn syrup, vanilla, rum extract and coffee; beat until well blended and fluffy.

**2.** Combine flour, baking powder, baking soda, salt and nutmeg. Add gradually to shortening mixture, beating at low speed until blended. Divide dough in half. Roll each half into two logs approximately 2 inches in diameter. Wrap in waxed paper. Refrigerate several hours.

**3.** Heat oven to 350°F. Place sheets of foil on countertop for cooling cookies.

**4.** Cut cookies into ¼-inch-thick slices. Place 2 inches apart on ungreased baking sheet. Sprinkle center of each cookie with jimmies.

**5.** Bake one baking sheet at a time for 10 to 12 minutes or until golden brown. *Do not overbake.* Cool 2 minutes on baking sheet. Remove cookies to foil to cool completely
*Makes about 4½ dozen cookies*

## 259 "PHILLY" APRICOT COOKIES

1½ cups butter or margarine, softened
1½ cups granulated sugar
 1 (8-ounce) package PHILADELPHIA BRAND® Cream Cheese, softened
 2 eggs
1½ teaspoons grated lemon peel
 2 tablespoons lemon juice
4½ cups all-purpose flour
1½ teaspoons baking powder
   KRAFT® Apricot Preserves
   Powdered sugar

• Combine butter, granulated sugar and cream cheese in large bowl, mixing until well blended. Blend in eggs, peel and juice. Add combined flour and baking powder; mix well. Cover; refrigerate several hours.

• Preheat oven to 350°F.

• Shape level measuring tablespoonfuls of dough into balls. Place on ungreased cookie sheet; flatten slightly. Indent centers; fill with preserves.

• Bake 15 minutes or until lightly browned. Cool on wire rack; sprinkle with powdered sugar. *Makes about 7 dozen cookies*

***Top to bottom: Cappuccino Cookies and Oatmeal Praline Cheese Bars (page 150)***

## 260 CHOCO–COCO PECAN CRISPS

½ cup butter or margarine, softened
1 cup packed light brown sugar
1 egg
1 teaspoon vanilla
1½ cups all-purpose flour
1 cup chopped pecans
⅓ cup unsweetened cocoa powder
½ teaspoon baking soda
1 cup flaked coconut

Cream butter and sugar in large bowl until light and fluffy. Beat in egg and vanilla. Combine flour, pecans, cocoa and baking soda in small bowl until well blended. Add to creamed mixture, blending until stiff dough is formed. Sprinkle coconut on work surface. Divide dough into 4 parts. Shape each part into a roll about 1½ inches in diameter; roll in coconut until thickly coated. Wrap in plastic wrap; refrigerate until firm, at least 1 hour or up to 2 weeks. (For longer storage, wrap in foil and freeze up to 6 weeks.)

Preheat oven to 350°F. Cut rolls into ⅛-inch-thick slices. Place 2 inches apart on ungreased cookie sheets. Bake 10 to 13 minutes or until firm, but not overly browned. Remove to wire racks to cool.

*Makes about 6 dozen cookies*

## 261 WALNUT MERINGUES

3 egg whites
Pinch of salt
¾ cup sugar
⅓ cup finely chopped California walnuts

Preheat oven to 350°F. Place egg whites and salt in large mixing bowl. Beat with an electric mixer or by hand with a wire whisk until soft peaks form. Gradually add sugar, beating until stiff peaks form. Gently fold in walnuts. Spoon mounds about 1 inch in diameter 1 inch apart onto parchment-lined baking sheet. Bake 20 minutes or until lightly browned and dry to the touch. Let cool completely before removing from baking sheet. Store in airtight container.

*Makes 48 cookies*

## 262 CHOCOLATE ALMOND BISCOTTI

2 cups (12-ounce package) NESTLÉ® TOLL HOUSE® Semi-Sweet Chocolate Morsels, *divided*
2 cups all-purpose flour
¼ cup NESTLÉ® TOLL HOUSE® Baking Cocoa
1½ teaspoons baking powder
¼ teaspoon baking soda
¼ teaspoon salt
½ cup granulated sugar
½ cup packed brown sugar
¼ cup (½ stick) butter or margarine, softened
½ teaspoon vanilla extract
½ teaspoon almond extract
3 eggs
1 cup slivered almonds, toasted
Chocolate Coating (optional, page 237)

## SPECIAL OCCASIONS

**MICROWAVE** *1 cup* morsels in small, microwave-safe bowl on HIGH (100%) power for 1 minute; stir. Microwave at additional 10- to 20-second intervals, stirring until smooth; cool to room temperature. Combine flour, cocoa, baking powder, baking soda and salt in medium bowl.

**BEAT** granulated sugar, brown sugar, butter, vanilla and almond extracts until crumbly. Add eggs one at a time, beating well after each addition. Beat in melted chocolate. Gradually beat in flour mixture. Stir in nuts. Chill for 15 minutes or until firm.

**SHAPE** dough into two (3-inch-wide by 1-inch-high) loaves with floured hands on 1 large or 2 small greased baking sheets.

**BAKE** in preheated 325°F. oven for 40 to 50 minutes or until firm. Cool on baking sheets for 15 minutes. Cut into ¾-inch-thick slices; turn slices onto their sides. Bake for 10 minutes on *each* side until dry. Remove to wire racks to cool completely.

*Makes about 2½ dozen cookies*

**FOR CHOCOLATE COATING:**
**MICROWAVE** *remaining* morsels and 2 tablespoons shortening in medium, microwave-safe bowl on HIGH (100%) power for 1 minute; stir. Microwave at 10- to 20-second intervals, stirring until smooth. Dip biscotti halfway into chocolate coating, pushing mixture up with a spatula; shake off excess. Place on waxed paper-lined tray. Chill for 10 minutes or until chocolate is set. Store in airtight containers in cool place or in refrigerator.

*Chocolate Almond Biscotti*

## 263 EXQUISITE BROWNIE TORTE

**FILLING**
1 package (3 ounces) cream cheese, softened
⅓ cup confectioners sugar
¼ teaspoon almond extract
1 package whipped topping mix
½ cup milk

**RASPBERRY SAUCE**
1 tablespoon cornstarch
2 tablespoons cold water
1 package (10 ounces) frozen raspberries in light syrup, thawed
2 tablespoons seedless red raspberry jam
¼ teaspoon lemon juice
1 tablespoon Amaretto (optional)

**BROWNIE**
1 package DUNCAN HINES® Walnut Brownie Mix
½ pint fresh raspberries
½ cup fresh blueberries
Mint leaves, for garnish

1. For filling, combine cream cheese, confectioners sugar and almond extract in large bowl. Beat at medium speed with electric mixer until softened and blended. Add whipped topping mix and milk. Beat at high speed for 4 minutes or until mixture thickens and forms peaks. Cover. Refrigerate for 2 to 3 hours or until thoroughly chilled.

2. For raspberry sauce, dissolve cornstarch in water in medium saucepan. Add thawed raspberries, raspberry jam and lemon juice. Cook on medium heat until mixture comes to a boil. Remove from heat; add Amaretto, if desired. Push mixture through sieve into small bowl to remove seeds. Refrigerate for 2 to 3 hours or until thoroughly chilled.

3. Preheat oven to 350°F. Line 9-inch springform pan with aluminum foil. Grease bottom of foil.

4. For brownie, prepare brownies following package directions for basic recipe. Spread in prepared pan. Bake for 35 to 37 minutes or until set. Cool completely. Remove from pan. Peel off aluminum foil.

5. To assemble, place brownie torte on serving plate. Spread filling over top of brownie. Place ¼ cup raspberry sauce in small resealable plastic bag. Snip pinpoint hole in bottom corner of bag. Drizzle sauce in three concentric rings one inch apart. Draw toothpick in straight line from center to edge through topping and sauce to form web design. Arrange fresh berries in center. Garnish. Serve with remaining sauce.

*Makes 12 to 16 servings*

## 264 ALMOND LACE COOKIES

¼ cup butter
½ cup sugar
½ cup BLUE DIAMOND® Blanched Almond Paste
¼ cup all-purpose flour
¼ teaspoon salt
½ teaspoon almond extract
2 tablespoons milk
2 teaspoons grated orange peel

Cream butter and sugar. Beat in almond paste. Add remaining ingredients. Mix well. Drop rounded teaspoonfuls onto cookie sheet, 3 inches apart. Cookies will spread. Bake at 350°F for 8 to 10 minutes or until edges are lightly browned. Cool 3 to 4 minutes on cookie sheet; remove and cool on wire rack. *Makes 1½ dozen cookies*

*Exquisite Brownie Torte*

## 265 CHOCOLATE– RASPBERRY KOLACHY

2 squares (1 ounce each) semisweet
   chocolate, coarsely chopped
1½ cups all-purpose flour
  ¼ teaspoon baking soda
  ¼ teaspoon salt
  ½ cup butter or margarine, softened
  3 ounces cream cheese or light cream
   cheese, softened
  ⅓ cup granulated sugar
  1 teaspoon vanilla
   Seedless raspberry jam
   Powdered sugar

Place chocolate in 1-cup glass measure. Microwave at HIGH (100% power) 1 to 2 minutes or until chocolate is melted, stirring after 1 minute; set aside.

Combine flour, baking soda and salt in small bowl; stir well. Beat butter and cream cheese in large bowl with electric mixer at medium speed until well blended, scraping down side of bowl occasionally. Beat in granulated sugar until light and fluffy, scraping down side of bowl once. Beat in vanilla and chocolate. Gradually add flour mixture. Beat at low speed, scraping down side of bowl once. Divide dough in half; flatten each half into a disc. Wrap separately in plastic wrap. Refrigerate until firm, 1 to 2 hours.

Preheat oven to 375°F. Lightly grease cookie sheets; set aside.

Roll each dough disc on well-floured surface with stockinette-covered rolling pin to ¼- to ⅛-inch thickness. Cut out with 3-inch round cookie cutter. Place 2 inches apart on prepared cookie sheets. Place rounded ½ teaspoon jam in center of each circle. Bring three edges of dough circles up over jam; pinch edges together to seal, leaving center of triangle slightly open.

Bake 10 minutes or until set. Let cookies stand on cookie sheets 2 minutes. Remove cookies with spatula to wire racks; cool completely. Just before serving, sprinkle with powdered sugar. Store tightly covered in refrigerator; let stand for 30 minutes at room temperature before serving.
*Makes about 1½ dozen cookies*

NOTE: These cookies do not freeze well.

## 266 CHEWY HAZELNUT BARS

1 pound JACK FROST® Dark Brown Sugar
   (2⅓ cups, packed)
¾ cup (1½ sticks) butter
2 eggs
2 teaspoons vanilla
2 cups all-purpose flour
2 teaspoons baking powder
½ teaspoon salt
1 cup chopped hazelnuts*
1 cup semi-sweet chocolate chips

*Substitute pecans or walnuts if desired.*

In microwave-safe bowl, heat brown sugar and butter on HIGH about 2 minutes or until butter melts. Let cool to room temperature.

In medium bowl, beat brown sugar mixture, eggs and vanilla until well blended. In large bowl, combine flour, baking powder and salt; add to butter mixture. Stir in nuts and chocolate chips. Spread mixture evenly into buttered 11×8-inch baking pan. Bake in preheated 350° oven 35 to 40 minutes.

Cool completely and cut into 2-inch squares.
*Makes 20 bars*

*Chocolate-Raspberry Kolachy*

## 267 CHOCOLATE FLORENTINES

¼ cup CANDIED ORANGE PEEL (recipe follows)
½ cup (1 stick) butter (no substitutes)
⅔ cup sugar
2 tablespoons milk
2 tablespoons light corn syrup
⅓ cup all-purpose flour
1 cup sliced almonds
1 teaspoon vanilla extract
CHOCOLATE FILLING (recipe follows)

1. Prepare CANDIED ORANGE PEEL.

2. Heat oven to 350°F. Line cookie sheets with heavy duty foil; smooth out wrinkles.

3. In medium saucepan, place butter, sugar, milk and corn syrup. Cook over medium heat, stirring constantly, until mixture boils. Continue cooking, without stirring, until syrup reaches 230°F on candy thermometer or until syrup spins 2-inch thread when dropped from fork or spoon. Remove from heat. Stir in flour, candied orange peel, almonds and vanilla. (To keep mixture from hardening, immediately place pan over hot water.) Drop mixture by level teaspoons onto prepared cookie sheets, placing at least 4 inches apart. (Cookies will spread.)

4. Bake 8 to 11 minutes or until cookies are bubbly and light brown caramel color. Remove from oven; cool. (Carefully slide foil off cookie sheet to reuse cookie sheet; prepare with foil for next use.) Cool cookies completely on foil; gently peel off foil.

5. Prepare CHOCOLATE FILLING; spread thin layer on flat side of one cookie; gently press on another cookie, flat sides together. Wrap individually in plastic wrap. Repeat with remaining cookies and filling. Store tightly covered in refrigerator.

*Makes about 1½ dozen filled cookies*

**CANDIED ORANGE PEEL:** Cut outer peel (no white membrane) of 2 small naval oranges into ½ inch wide strips. Cut across strips to make ½×⅛-inch pieces. In small saucepan, place peel, ¼ cup sugar and ½ cup water. Cook over very low heat until bottom of pan is covered only with glazed peel; do not caramelize. Remove from heat; spoon onto wax paper. Cool.

**CHOCOLATE FILLING:** In small microwave-safe bowl, place 1 cup HERSHEY'S Semi-Sweet Chocolate Chips. Microwave at HIGH (100%) 1 minute; stir. If necessary, microwave at HIGH an additional 15 seconds at a time, stirring after each heating, just until chips are melted when stirred.

## 268 DATE–NUT MACAROONS

1 (8-ounce) package pitted dates, chopped
1½ cups flaked coconut
1 cup PLANTERS® Pecan Halves, chopped
¾ cup sweetened condensed milk (not evaporated milk)
½ teaspoon vanilla

Preheat oven to 350°F.

In medium bowl, combine dates, coconut and nuts; blend in sweetened condensed milk and vanilla. Drop by rounded tablespoonfuls onto greased and floured cookie sheets. Bake for 10 to 12 minutes or until light golden brown. Carefully remove from cookie sheets; cool completely on wire racks. Store in airtight container.

*Makes about 2 dozen cookies*

## 269 CHOCOLATE JEWEL COOKIES

1 cup butter, softened
1 cup sugar
1 egg
1 teaspoon vanilla
2¼ cups all-purpose flour
¼ cup unsweetened cocoa powder
1 teaspoon baking powder
1 (16-ounce) can OCEAN SPRAY® Jellied Cranberry Sauce

Preheat oven to 350°F.

Beat butter and sugar in medium bowl with electric mixer at medium speed until light and fluffy. Add egg and vanilla; mix well. Combine flour, cocoa and baking powder in separate medium bowl. Add to butter mixture; mix well.

Roll dough between hands to form 1-inch balls. Place on ungreased cookie sheets. Press thumb into center of each ball. Place cranberry sauce in small bowl; beat with whisk or fork until smooth. Place ½-rounded teaspoonful cranberry sauce in indent of each cookie.

Bake about 13 minutes or until slightly firm to the touch.           *Makes 3½ dozen*

*Date-Nut Macaroons*

## 270 CHOCOLATE–DIPPED CINNAMON THINS

1¼ cups all-purpose flour
1½ teaspoons ground cinnamon
1 cup unsalted butter, softened
1 cup powdered sugar
1 large egg
1 teaspoon vanilla
¼ teaspoon salt
4 ounces broken bittersweet chocolate

Place flour and cinnamon in small bowl; stir to combine.

Beat butter in large bowl with electric mixer at medium speed until light and fluffy, scraping down side of bowl once. Add sugar; beat well. Add egg, vanilla and salt; beat well, scraping down side of bowl once. Gradually add flour mixture. Beat at low speed, scraping down side of bowl occasionally, until well blended.

Place dough on sheet of waxed paper. Using waxed paper to hold dough, roll it back and forth to form a log about 12 inches long and 2½ inches wide. Securely wrap log in plastic wrap. Refrigerate at least 2 hours or until firm. (Log may be frozen up to 3 months; thaw in refrigerator before baking).

Preheat oven to 350°F. Cut dough with long, sharp knife into ¼-inch-thick slices. Place 2 inches apart on ungreased cookie sheets.

Bake 10 minutes or until set. Let cookies stand on cookie sheets 2 minutes. Remove cookies with spatula to wire racks; cool completely.

Melt chocolate in 1-cup glass measure set in bowl of very hot water, stirring twice. Dip each cookie into chocolate, coating 1 inch up sides. Let excess chocolate drip back into cup.

Transfer to wire racks or waxed paper; let stand at cool room temperature about 40 minutes until chocolate is set. Store between sheets of waxed paper at cool room temperature or in refrigerator.

*Makes about 2 dozen*

NOTE: These cookies do not freeze well.

## 271 PECAN DROPS

¾ cup sugar
½ cup margarine, softened
¼ cup EGG BEATERS® Real Egg Product
1 teaspoon vanilla extract
2 cups all-purpose flour
⅔ cup PLANTERS® Pecans, finely chopped
3 tablespoons jam, jelly or preserves, any flavor

In small bowl, with electric mixer at medium speed, beat sugar and margarine. Add egg product and vanilla; beat for 1 minute. Stir in flour until blended. Chill dough 1 hour.

Preheat oven to 350°F. Form dough into 36 (1¼-inch) balls; roll in pecans, pressing into dough. Place 2 inches apart on greased cookie sheets. Indent center of each ball with thumb or back of wooden spoon. Bake for 10 minutes; remove from oven. Spoon ¼ teaspoon jam into each cookie indentation. Bake for 2 to 5 more minutes or until lightly browned. Remove from cookie sheets; cool on wire racks.

*Makes 3 dozen cookies*

*Chocolate-Dipped Cinnamon Thins*

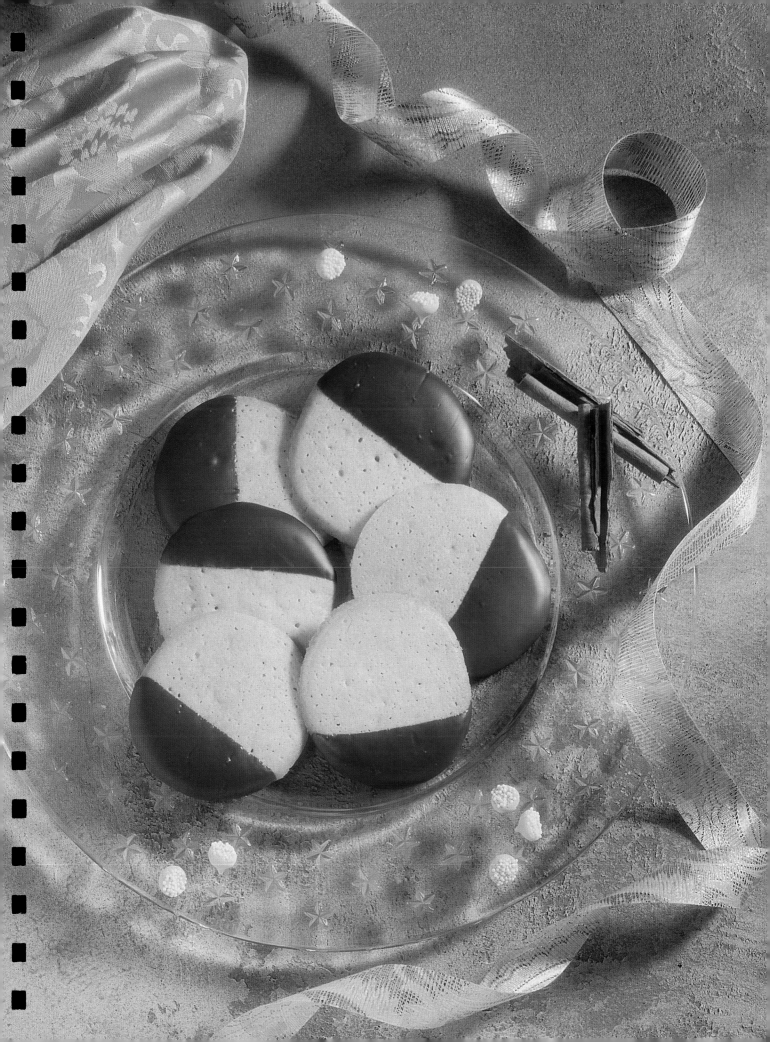

## SPECIAL OCCASIONS

### 272 WALNUT BISCOTTI

    2 cups unbleached all-purpose flour
    1 cup sugar
    ¼ teaspoon baking soda
    1 egg
    1 egg white
    ½ cup chopped California walnuts

Preheat oven to 350°F. Combine flour, sugar and baking soda in large bowl; blend well. Add egg, egg white and walnuts. Mix until mixture forms a smooth dough. (This recipe has no oil, so it must be blended until the oil from walnuts is released.) Shape into logs 8 inches long and 2 inches across. Place onto parchment-lined baking sheets. Bake 20 minutes or until golden brown. Slice diagonally into ¼-inch slices. Place slices on baking sheet; return to oven 5 minutes or until dry.          *Makes 4 dozen biscotti*

*Favorite recipe from* **Walnut Marketing Board**

### 273 BROWNIE BON BONS

    2 jars (10 ounces each) maraschino
        cherries with stems
        Cherry liqueur (optional)*
    4 squares BAKER'S® Unsweetened
        Chocolate
    ¾ cup (1½ sticks) margarine or butter
    2 cups granulated sugar
    4 eggs
    1 teaspoon vanilla
    1 cup all-purpose flour
        Chocolate Fudge Filling (recipe follows)
    ½ cup powdered sugar

*\*For liqueur-flavored cherries, drain liquid from cherries. Do not remove cherries from jars. Refill jars with liqueur to completely cover cherries; cover tightly. Let stand at least 24 hours for best flavor.*

**HEAT** oven to 350°F.

**MICROWAVE** chocolate and margarine in large microwavable bowl on HIGH 2 minutes or until margarine is melted. **Stir until chocolate is completely melted.**

**STIR** granulated sugar into chocolate mixture. Mix in eggs and vanilla until blended. Stir in flour. Fill greased 1¾×1-inch muffin cups ⅔ full with batter.

**BAKE** for 20 minutes or until toothpick inserted into center comes out with fudgy crumbs. **Do not overbake.** Cool slightly in muffin pans. Turn each brownie onto wax paper-lined tray while warm. Make ½-inch indentation into top of each brownie with end of wooden spoon. Cool completely.

**PREPARE** Chocolate Fudge Filling. Drain cherries, reserving liquid or liqueur. Let cherries stand on paper towels to dry. Combine powdered sugar with enough reserved liquid to form a thin glaze.

**SPOON** or pipe about 1 teaspoon Chocolate Fudge Filling into indentation of each brownie. Gently press cherry into filling. Drizzle with powdered sugar glaze.
          *Makes about 48 bon bons*

**Prep Time:** 1 hour
**Baking Time:** 20 minutes

#### CHOCOLATE FUDGE FILLING
    1 package (3 ounces) PHILADELPHIA
        BRAND® Cream Cheese, softened
    1 teaspoon vanilla
    ¼ cup corn syrup
    3 squares BAKER'S® Unsweetened
        Chocolate, melted and cooled
    1 cup powdered sugar

**BEAT** cream cheese and vanilla in small bowl until smooth. Slowly pour in corn syrup, beating until blended. Add chocolate; beat until smooth. Gradually add sugar, beating until blended.          *Makes about 1 cup*

*Brownie Bon Bons*

## 274 EUROPEAN KOLACKY

1 cup butter or margarine, softened
1 package (8 ounces) cream cheese, softened
1 tablespoon milk
1 tablespoon granulated sugar
1 egg yolk
1½ cups all-purpose flour
½ teaspoon baking powder
1 can SOLO® or 1 jar BAKER® Filling (any flavor)
Confectioners' sugar

Beat butter, cream cheese, milk and granulated sugar in medium bowl with electric mixer until thoroughly blended. Beat in egg yolk. Sift together flour and baking powder; stir into butter mixture to make stiff dough. Cover and refrigerate several hours or overnight.

Preheat oven to 400°F. Roll out dough on lightly floured surface to ¼-inch thickness. Cut dough with floured 2-inch round cookie cutter. Place on ungreased cookie sheets about 1 inch apart. Make depression in centers of dough rounds with thumb or back of spoon. Spoon 1 teaspoon filling into centers of depression.

Bake 10 to 12 minutes or until lightly browned. Remove from cookie sheets and cool completely on wire racks. Sprinkle with confectioners' sugar just before serving.

*Makes about 3 dozen cookies*

## 275 CASHEW–LEMON SHORTBREAD COOKIES

½ cup roasted cashews
1 cup butter or margarine, softened
½ cup sugar
2 teaspoons lemon extract
1 teaspoon vanilla
2 cups all-purpose flour

1. Preheat oven to 325°F. Place cashews in food processor; process until finely ground. Add butter, sugar, lemon extract and vanilla; process until well blended. Add flour; process using on/off pulsing action until dough is blended and begins to form ball.

2. Shape dough into 1½-inch balls; roll in additional sugar. Place about 2 inches apart onto ungreased baking sheets; flatten with bottom of glass.

3. Bake cookies 17 to 19 minutes or just until set and edges are lightly browned. Remove cookies from baking sheets to wire rack to cool.

*Makes 2 to 2½ dozen cookies*

**Prep and Bake Time:** 30 minutes

## 276 CHOCOLATE–DIPPED ORANGE LOGS

3¼ cups all-purpose flour
⅛ teaspoon salt
1 cup butter, softened
1 cup sugar
2 eggs
1½ teaspoons grated orange peel
1 teaspoon vanilla
1 package (12 ounces) semisweet chocolate chips
1½ cups pecan pieces, finely chopped

## SPECIAL OCCASIONS

**COMBINE** flour and salt in medium bowl. Beat butter in large bowl with electric mixer at medium speed until smooth. Gradually beat in sugar; increase speed to high and beat until light and fluffy. Beat in eggs, 1 at a time, blending well after each addition. Beat in orange peel and vanilla until blended. Gradually stir in flour mixture until blended. (Dough will be crumbly.)

**GATHER** dough together and press gently to form a ball. Flatten into disk; wrap in plastic wrap and refrigerate 2 hours or until firm. (Dough can be prepared one day in advance and refrigerated overnight.)

**PREHEAT** oven to 350°F. Shape dough into 1-inch balls. Roll balls on flat surface with fingertips to form 3-inch logs about ½ inch thick. Place logs 1 inch apart on *ungreased* cookie sheets.

**BAKE** 14 minutes or until bottoms of cookies are golden brown. (Cookies will feel soft and look white on top; they will become crisp when cool.) Transfer to wire racks to cool completely.

*For coating:* **MELT** chocolate chips in medium heavy saucepan over low heat. Place chopped pecans on sheet of waxed paper. Dip one end of each cookie in chocolate, shaking off excess. Roll chocolate-covered ends in pecans. Place on waxed paper-lined cookie sheets and let stand until chocolate is set, or refrigerate about 5 minutes to set chocolate. Store in airtight container.

*Makes about 36 cookies*

**Chocolate-Dipped Orange Logs**

## SPECIAL OCCASIONS

## 277 MINI BROWNIE CUPS

¼ cup (½ stick) 56-60% vegetable oil
    spread
 2 egg whites
 1 egg
¾ cup sugar
⅔ cup all-purpose flour
⅓ cup HERSHEY'S Cocoa
½ teaspoon baking powder
¼ teaspoon salt
    Mocha Glaze (recipe follows)

Heat oven to 350°F. Line small muffin cups (1¾ inches in diameter) with paper bake cups or spray with vegetable cooking spray. In small saucepan over low heat, melt corn spread; cool slightly. In small mixer bowl, beat egg whites and egg on medium speed of electric mixer until foamy; gradually add sugar, beating until slightly thickened and light in color. Stir together flour, cocoa, baking powder and salt; add gradually to egg mixture, beating until blended. Gradually add melted spread beating just until blended. Fill muffin cups ⅔ full with batter.

Bake 15 to 18 minutes or until wooden pick inserted in center comes out clean. Remove from pan to wire racks. Cool completely. Drizzle Mocha Glaze over tops of brownie cups. Let stand until set. Store, covered, at room temperature.

*Makes 2 dozen brownie cups*

### MOCHA GLAZE
¼ cup powdered sugar
¾ teaspoon HERSHEY'S Cocoa
¼ teaspoon powdered instant coffee
 2 teaspoons hot water
¼ teaspoon vanilla extract

In small bowl, stir together powdered sugar and cocoa. Dissolve coffee in water; add to sugar mixture, stirring until well blended. Stir in vanilla.

## 278 BISCOTTI FOR DUNKING

¾ cup sugar
¼ cup Prune Purée (recipe, page 182) or
    prepared prune butter
    Grated peel of 1 orange
½ cup egg substitute
½ teaspoon almond extract
2½ cups all-purpose flour
¼ cup toasted whole almonds, cut in half
1½ teaspoons baking powder
¼ teaspoon salt
 1 tablespoon anise seeds (optional)

Preheat oven to 325°F. Coat baking sheet with vegetable cooking spray and dust with flour. In mixer bowl, beat sugar, prune purée and orange peel at low speed until well blended. Add egg substitute and almond extract; beat until blended. In medium bowl, combine remaining ingredients; mix into sugar mixture until well blended. Divide mixture in half and form into two equal 14-inch logs. Place on prepared baking sheet, spacing at least 2 inches apart. Bake in center of oven about 30 minutes until golden brown. Remove from baking sheet to wire rack to cool 5 minutes. With serrated knife, cut diagonally into ½-inch slices. Lay slices flat on baking sheet and bake about 15 minutes longer, turning once, until dry. Remove from baking sheet to wire rack to cool completely. Store in airtight container. Biscotti can be dunked in coffee, tea, hot chocolate, milk or wine.

*Makes 56 cookies*

TIP: Biscotti, a twice-baked Italian cookie, is traditionally flavored with anise, almonds or hazelnuts.

*Favorite recipe from **California Prune Board***

***Mini Brownie Cups***

## SPECIAL OCCASIONS

## 279 KAHLÚA® KISSES

¾ teaspoon instant coffee powder
⅓ cup water
1 cup plus 2 tablespoons sugar, divided
¼ cup KAHLÚA®
3 egg whites
¼ teaspoon cream of tartar
   Dash salt

Set oven rack in center of oven. Preheat oven to 200°F.

In heavy 2-quart saucepan, dissolve coffee powder in water. Add 1 cup sugar; stir over low heat until sugar dissolves. Do not boil. Stir in Kahlúa®. Brush down sides of pan often with pastry brush dipped in cold water. Bring mixture to a boil over medium heat. *Do not stir.* Boil until candy thermometer registers 240° to 242°F, about 15 minutes, adjusting heat if necessary to prevent boiling over. (Mixture will be very thick.) Remove from heat (temperature will continue to rise).

Immediately beat egg whites with cream of tartar and salt until soft peaks form. Add remaining 2 tablespoons sugar; continue beating until stiff peaks form. Gradually beat hot Kahlúa® mixture into egg white mixture. Continue beating 4 to 5 minutes or until meringue is very thick, firm and cooled to lukewarm.

Line cookie sheet with aluminum foil, shiny side down. Using pastry bag fitted with large (#6) star tip, pipe meringue into kisses about 1½ inches wide at base and 1½ inches high onto cookie sheet.

Bake for 4 hours. Turn oven off. Without opening oven door, let kisses dry in oven 2 more hours or until crisp. Remove from oven; cool completely on cookie sheet. Store in airtight container up to 1 week.

*Makes about 2½ dozen cookies*

## 280 APRICOT–PECAN TASSIES

**PASTRY**
1 cup all-purpose flour
½ cup butter, cut into pieces
6 tablespoons light cream cheese

**FILLING**
¾ cup packed light brown sugar
1 egg, lightly beaten
1 tablespoon butter, softened
½ teaspoon vanilla
¼ teaspoon salt
⅔ cup California dried apricot halves, diced (about 4 ounces)
⅓ cup chopped pecans

For Pastry, combine flour, ½ cup butter and cream cheese in food processor; process until dough forms a ball and cleans sides of bowl. Wrap in plastic wrap; chill 15 minutes.

For Filling, preheat oven to 325°F. In large bowl, combine brown sugar, egg, 1 tablespoon butter, vanilla and salt; beat until smooth. Stir in apricots and pecans.

Shape dough into 1-inch balls; place each in paper-lined or greased miniature muffin cup or tart pan. Press dough on bottom and up side of each cup; fill each with 1 teaspoon filling.

Bake 25 minutes or until golden and filling is set. Cool in pans on wire racks. Cookies can be wrapped tightly in plastic and frozen up to six weeks. *Makes 24 cookies*

*Favorite recipe from **California Apricot Advisory Board***

*Apricot-Pecan Tassies*

## SPECIAL OCCASIONS

### 281 CRANBERRY ALMOND BISCOTTI

2¼ cups all-purpose flour
1 cup sugar
1 teaspoon baking powder
½ teaspoon baking soda
1 teaspoon ground cinnamon
½ teaspoon ground nutmeg
2 eggs
2 egg whites
1 tablespoon almond or vanilla extract
¾ cup sliced almonds
1 (6-ounce) package CRAISINS®
   Sweetened Dried Cranberries

Preheat oven to 325°F.

Combine flour, sugar, baking powder, baking soda, cinnamon and nutmeg in medium bowl. Whisk together eggs, egg whites and almond extract in separate medium bowl. Add to flour mixture. Beat with electric mixer on medium speed just until moist. Add almonds and dried cranberries; mix thoroughly.

On lightly floured surface, divide batter in half and pat each half into a log approximately 14-inches long and 1½-inches wide. Place on cookie sheet and bake 30 minutes.

Reduce oven temperature to 300°F. Cut biscotti into ½-inch slices. Stand upright on cookie sheet and bake for an additional 20 minutes. Let cool and store in loosely covered container. *Makes 2½ dozen*

### 282 ALMOND–ORANGE SHORTBREAD

1 cup (4 ounces) sliced almonds, divided
1 orange
2 cups all-purpose flour
1 cup cold butter, cut into pieces
½ cup sugar
½ cup cornstarch
1 teaspoon almond extract

**1.** Preheat oven to 350°F. To toast almonds, spread ¾ cup almonds in single layer in large baking pan. Bake 6 minutes or until golden brown, stirring frequently. Remove almonds from oven. Cool completely in pan. *Reduce oven temperature to 325°F.*

**2.** Place almonds in food processor. Process using on/off pulsing action until almonds are coarsely chopped.

**3.** Finely grate colored portion of orange peel. Measure 2 tablespoons orange peel.

**4.** Add flour, butter, sugar, cornstarch, orange peel and almond extract to food processor. Process using on/off pulsing action until mixture resembles coarse crumbs. Press dough firmly and evenly into 10½×8½-inch rectangle on large *ungreased* baking sheet with fingers. Score dough into 1¼-inch squares with utility knife. Press one slice of remaining almonds in center of each square.

**5.** Bake 30 to 40 minutes or until shortbread is firm when pressed and lightly browned. Immediately cut into squares along score lines with sharp knife. Remove cookies with spatula to wire racks; cool completely. Store loosely covered at room temperature up to 1 week. *Makes 5 dozen cookies*

## 283 RASPBERRY–FILLED CHOCOLATE RAVIOLI

2 squares (1 ounce each) bittersweet or
    semisweet chocolate
1 cup butter or margarine, softened
½ cup granulated sugar
1 egg
1 teaspoon vanilla
½ teaspoon chocolate extract
¼ teaspoon baking soda
    Dash salt
2½ cups all-purpose flour
1 to 1¼ cups seedless raspberry jam
    Powdered sugar

Melt chocolate in top of double boiler over
hot, not boiling, water. Remove from heat;
cool. Beat butter and granulated sugar in
large bowl until blended. Add egg, vanilla,
chocolate extract, baking soda, salt and
melted chocolate; beat until light. Blend in
flour to make a stiff dough. Divide dough in
half. Cover; refrigerate until firm.

Preheat oven to 350°F. Lightly grease cookie
sheets or line with parchment paper. Roll
out dough, half at a time, ⅛ inch thick
between 2 sheets of plastic wrap. Remove
top sheet of plastic. (If dough gets too soft
and sticks to plastic, refrigerate until firm.)
Cut dough into 1½-inch squares. Place half
of the squares 2 inches apart on prepared
cookie sheets. Place about ½ teaspoon jam
in center of each square; top with another
square. Using fork, press edges of squares
together to seal, then pierce center of each
square. Bake 10 minutes or just until edges
are browned. Remove to wire racks to cool.
Dust lightly with powdered sugar.

*Makes about 6 dozen cookies*

**Raspberry-Filled Chocolate Ravioli**

## SPECIAL OCCASIONS

## 284 AUSTRIAN TEA COOKIES

1½ cups sugar, divided
½ cup butter, softened
½ cup vegetable shortening
1 egg, beaten
½ teaspoon vanilla extract
2 cups all-purpose flour
2 cups ALMOND DELIGHT® brand Cereal, crushed to 1 cup
½ teaspoon baking powder
¼ teaspoon ground cinnamon
14 ounces almond paste
2 egg whites
5 tablespoons raspberry or apricot jam, warmed

In large bowl, beat 1 cup sugar, butter and shortening until well blended. Add egg and vanilla; mix well. Stir in flour, cereal, baking powder and cinnamon until well blended. Cover; refrigerate 1 to 2 hours or until firm.

Preheat oven to 350°F. Roll out dough on lightly floured surface to ¼-inch thickness; cut into 2-inch circles with floured cookie cutter. Place 2 inches apart on ungreased cookie sheet; set aside. In small bowl, beat almond paste, egg whites and remaining ½ cup sugar until smooth. With pastry tube fitted with medium-sized star tip, pipe almond paste mixture ½ inch thick on top of each cookie along outside edge. Place ¼ teaspoon jam in center of each cookie, spreading out to almond paste border.

Bake 8 to 10 minutes or until lightly browned. Let stand 1 minute on cookie sheet. Remove to wire rack; cool completely.

*Makes about 3½ dozen cookies*

## 285 CHOCOLATE–FLECKED PIROUETTES

½ cup butter or margarine, softened
½ cup sugar
2 egg whites
1 teaspoon vanilla
½ cup all-purpose flour
⅓ cup coarsely grated bittersweet or dark sweet chocolate bar (about 2 ounces)

**1.** Preheat oven to 400°F. Well-grease cookie sheets; set aside.

**2.** Beat butter and sugar in small bowl with electric mixer at medium speed until light and fluffy, scraping down side of bowl once. Beat in egg whites, 1 at a time, scraping down side of bowl after each addition. Beat in vanilla. Add flour. Beat at low speed, scraping down side of bowl once. Gently fold in grated chocolate with rubber spatula.

**3.** Drop teaspoonfuls of batter 4 inches apart onto prepared cookie sheets. Spread dough into 2-inch rounds with small spatula. Make only 3 or 4 rounds per sheet.

**4.** Bake, 1 sheet at a time, 4 to 5 minutes until edges are barely golden. *Do not overbake.*

**5.** Remove from oven and quickly loosen edge of 1 cookie from baking sheet with thin spatula. Quickly roll cookie around clean handle of wooden spoon overlapping edges to form a cigar shape. Repeat with remaining cookies. (If cookies become too firm to shape, return to oven for a few seconds to soften.) Slide cookie off handle to wire rack; cool completely.

**6.** Store tightly covered at room temperature or freeze up to 3 months.

*Makes about 3 dozen cookies*

*Chocolate-Flecked Pirouettes*

## SPECIAL OCCASIONS

### 286 CHOCOLATE CHERRY OATMEAL FANCIES

½ cup sliced almonds
1¼ cups firmly packed light brown sugar
¾ BUTTER FLAVOR* CRISCO® Stick or
    ¾ cup BUTTER FLAVOR CRISCO
    all-vegetable shortening
1 egg
⅓ cup milk
1 teaspoon vanilla
½ teaspoon almond extract
3 cups quick oats, uncooked
1 cup all-purpose flour
½ teaspoon baking soda
½ teaspoon salt
6 ounces white baking chocolate, coarsely
    chopped
6 ounces semisweet chocolate, coarsely
    chopped
½ cup coarsely chopped red candied
    cherries or well-drained, chopped
    maraschino cherries

*Butter Flavor Crisco is artificially flavored.*

**1.** Heat oven to 350°F. Spread almonds on baking sheet. Bake for 5 to 7 minutes or until almonds are golden brown. Cool completely; reserve.

**2.** *Increase oven temperature to 375°F.* Grease baking sheets. Place sheets of foil on countertop for cooling cookies.

**3.** Place brown sugar, shortening, egg, milk, vanilla and almond extract in large bowl. Beat at medium speed of electric mixer until well blended.

**4.** Combine oats, flour, baking soda and salt. Add to shortening mixture; beat at low speed just until blended. Stir in white chocolate, semisweet chocolate, cherries and reserved almonds.

**5.** Drop by rounded tablespoonfuls 2 inches apart onto prepared baking sheets.

**6.** Bake one baking sheet at a time at 375°F for 10 to 12 minutes or until cookies are lightly browned. *Do not overbake.* Cool 2 minutes on baking sheet. Remove cookies to foil to cool completely.

*Makes about 4 dozen cookies*

### 287 CINNAMON NUT CHOCOLATE SPIRALS

1½ cups all-purpose flour
¼ teaspoon salt
⅓ cup butter or margarine, softened
¾ cup sugar, divided
1 egg
1 cup semisweet mini chocolate chips
1 cup finely chopped walnuts
2 teaspoons ground cinnamon
3 tablespoons butter or margarine, melted

Combine flour and salt in small bowl; set aside. Beat butter and ½ cup sugar in large bowl with electric mixer at medium speed until light and fluffy. Beat in egg. Gradually mix in flour mixture with spoon.

Roll out dough between two sheets of waxed paper into 12×10-inch rectangle. Remove waxed paper from top of rectangle. Combine chocolate chips, walnuts, remaining ¼ cup sugar and cinnamon in medium bowl. Pour butter over mixture; mix well. Spread mixture evenly over dough, leaving ½-inch border on long (12-inch) edges. Starting at long side, tightly roll up dough jelly-roll style. Wrap roll in plastic wrap; refrigerate 30 minutes to 1 hour.

Preheat oven to 350°F. Lightly grease 2 cookie sheets. Unwrap dough; cut into ½-inch slices. Place slices 2 inches apart on prepared cookie sheets. Bake 14 minutes or until edges are light golden brown. Remove cookies to wire racks; cool completely.

*Makes about 2 dozen cookies*

## 288 RASPBERRY ALMOND SANDWICH COOKIES

1 package DUNCAN HINES® Golden
    Sugar Cookie Mix
1 egg
¼ cup CRISCO® Oil or CRISCO®
    PURITAN® Canola Oil
1 tablespoon water
¾ teaspoon almond extract
1⅓ cups sliced natural almonds, broken
    Seedless red raspberry jam

1. Preheat oven to 375°F.

2. Combine cookie mix, egg, oil, water and almond extract in large bowl. Stir until thoroughly blended. Drop half the dough by level measuring teaspoons 2 inches apart onto ungreased baking sheets. (It is a small amount of dough but will spread during baking to 1½ to 1¾ inches.)

3. Place almonds on waxed paper. Drop other half of dough by level measuring teaspoons onto nuts. Place almond side up 2 inches apart on baking sheets.

4. Bake both plain and almond cookies at 375°F for 6 minutes or until set but not browned. Cool 1 minute on baking sheets. Remove to cooling racks. Cool completely.

5. Spread bottoms of plain cookies with jam; top with almond cookies. Press together to make sandwiches. Store in airtight containers.

*Makes 6 dozen sandwich cookies*

TIP: For evenly baked cookies, place the baking sheet in the center of the oven, not touching the sides.

*Raspberry Almond Sandwich Cookies*

## 289 VALENTINE STAINED GLASS HEARTS

½ **cup butter or margarine, softened**
¾ **cup granulated sugar**
2 **eggs**
1 **teaspoon vanilla extract**
2⅓ **cups all-purpose flour**
1 **teaspoon baking powder**
   **Red hard candies, crushed**
      **(about ⅓ cup)**
   **Frosting (optional)**

Beat butter and sugar in large bowl until well blended. Beat in eggs and vanilla. Sift flour and baking powder together. Gradually stir in flour mixture until dough is very stiff. Cover and chill 3 hours to overnight.

Preheat oven to 375°F. Roll dough to ⅛-inch thickness on lightly floured surface. To prevent cookies from becoming tough and brittle, try not to incorporate a lot of flour. Cut out cookies using large heart-shaped cookie cutter or use sharp knife and cut around a heart pattern. Transfer cookies to foil-lined baking sheet. Using small heart-shaped cookie cutter, cut out and remove heart design from center of each cookie. Fill cut-out sections with crushed candy. Bake 7 to 9 minutes or until cookies are lightly browned and candy has melted. Do not overbake. When done, slide foil off baking sheet. Carefully loosen cookies from foil when cooled. Pipe decorative borders with frosting around edges, if desired.

*Makes about 2½ dozen*
*medium cookies*

*Favorite recipe from* **The Sugar Association, Inc.**

*Valentine Stained Glass Hearts*

## 290 GIANT CHOCOLATE AND BUTTERSCOTCH HEARTS

1 (12-ounce) package milk chocolate chips
1 (12-ounce) package butterscotch chips
2 cups creamy peanut butter
2 cups chopped pecans
2 cups coconut, toasted*
1 cup butter or margarine
1 (3⅛-ounce) package coconut cream pudding and pie filling (cook and serve)
½ cup evaporated milk
2 pounds JACK FROST® Confectioners Sugar
2 teaspoons vanilla

*To toast coconut, spread coconut in shallow pan and bake in 350° oven 7 to 12 minutes, stirring frequently.

In large microwave-safe bowl, melt chocolate chips and butterscotch chips on MEDIUM-HIGH 1½ to 2 minutes, stirring every 30 seconds. When chips are melted, stir in peanut butter and mix well. Add pecans and coconut. Spread half of mixture in large foil-lined heart-shaped pan. Refrigerate heart. Set aside remaining chocolate mixture.

In microwave-safe bowl, melt butter on HIGH 90 seconds. Add pudding mixture and evaporated milk; stir until combined. Microwave an additional 2 minutes until slightly thickened. (Do not boil.) Remove from microwave oven; stir in confectioners sugar and vanilla. Cool slightly. Carefully spread pudding mixture over chilled chocolate layer. Refrigerate 30 minutes; spread reserved chocolate mixture over chilled pudding layer. Refrigerate until firm.

Lift chilled chocolate out of pan and place on serving plate or gift box. Keep refrigerated. Cut into serving pieces.

*Makes 60 to 70 (1-inch) pieces*

## 291 HEAVENLY OATMEAL HEARTS

COOKIES
1 cup plus 2 tablespoons BUTTER FLAVOR* CRISCO® all-vegetable shortening
1 cup firmly packed brown sugar
½ cup granulated sugar
2 eggs
1 teaspoon vanilla
1½ cups plus ⅓ cup all-purpose flour
1½ teaspoons baking soda
¾ teaspoon salt
3 cups rolled oats, uncooked
1 cup milk chocolate chips
1 cup vanilla chips
1 cup plus 2 tablespoons cinnamon-roasted peanuts,** chopped

DRIZZLE
½ cup milk chocolate chips
½ cup vanilla chips
1 teaspoon BUTTER FLAVOR CRISCO all-vegetable shortening, divided

*Butter Flavor Crisco is artificially flavored

**Substitute honey-roasted peanuts combined with 1½ teaspoons ground cinnamon if cinnamon-roasted peanuts are unavailable.

1. Preheat oven to 375°F.

2. For Cookies, combine 1 cup plus 2 tablespoons shortening, brown sugar and granulated sugar in large bowl. Beat at medium speed of electric mixer until light and fluffy. Beat in eggs and vanilla until creamy.

## HOLIDAY HAPPENINGS

**3.** Combine flour, baking soda and salt. Add gradually to creamed mixture at low speed. Mix until well blended. Stir in oats, 1 cup chocolate chips, 1 cup vanilla chips and nuts with spoon.

**4.** Place 3-inch heart-shaped cookie cutter on ungreased cookie sheet. Place ⅓ cup dough inside cutter. Press to edges and level. Remove cutter. Repeat to form remaining cookies, spacing 2½ inches apart.

**5.** Bake at 375°F for 9 minutes or until light golden brown. Cool on cookie sheet until slightly warm before removing to wire rack. Cool completely.

**6.** For Drizzle, place ½ cup chocolate chips and ½ cup vanilla chips in separate heavy resealable sandwich bags. Add ½ teaspoon shortening to each bag. Seal. Microwave 1 bag at MEDIUM (50% power). Knead bag after 1 minute. Repeat until mixture is smooth (or melt by placing each in bowl of hot water). Repeat with remaining bag. Cut tiny piece off corner of each bag. Squeeze out and drizzle both mixtures over cookies. To serve, cut cookies in half, if desired.

*Makes about 2 dozen heart cookies*

**Heavenly Oatmeal Heart**

## 292 ALMOND HEARTS

1 package DUNCAN HINES® Golden
    Sugar Cookie Mix
¾ cup ground almonds
2 egg yolks
⅓ cup CRISCO® Oil or CRISCO®
    PURITAN® Canola Oil
1½ tablespoons water
14 ounces (6 cubes) vanilla flavored candy
    coating
    Pink candy coating, for garnish

1. Preheat oven to 375°F.

2. Combine cookie mix, ground almonds, egg yolks, oil and water in large bowl. Stir until thoroughly blended.

3. Divide dough in half. Roll half the dough between 2 sheets of waxed paper into 11-inch circle. Slide onto flat surface. Refrigerate about 15 minutes. Repeat with remaining dough. Loosen top sheet of waxed paper from dough. Turn over and remove second sheet of waxed paper. Cut dough with 2½-inch heart cookie cutter. Place cut-outs 2 inches apart on ungreased cookie sheets. (Roll leftover cookie dough to ⅛-inch thickness between sheets of waxed paper. Chill before cutting.) Repeat cutting with remaining dough circle. Bake at 375°F for 6 to 8 minutes or until light golden brown. Cool 1 minute on cookie sheets. Remove to cooling racks. Cool completely.

4. Place vanilla candy coating in 1-quart saucepan on low heat; stir until melted and smooth. Dip half of one heart cookie into candy coating. Allow excess to drip back into pan. Place cookie on waxed paper. Repeat with remaining cookies. Place pink candy coating in small saucepan on low heat. Stir until melted and smooth. Pour into pastry bag fitted with small writing tip. Decorate top of cookies as desired.
    *Makes about 5 dozen cookies*

## 293 COFFEE CHIP DROPS

1¼ cups firmly packed light brown sugar
¾ BUTTER FLAVOR* CRISCO® Stick or
    ¾ cup BUTTER FLAVOR CRISCO
    all-vegetable shortening
2 tablespoons cold coffee
1 teaspoon vanilla
1 egg
1¾ cups all-purpose flour
1 tablespoon finely ground French roast
    or espresso coffee beans
1 teaspoon salt
¾ teaspoon baking soda
½ cup semisweet chocolate chips
½ cup milk chocolate chips
½ cup coarsely chopped walnuts
30 to 40 chocolate kiss candies, unwrapped

*Butter Flavor Crisco is artificially flavored.*

1. Heat oven to 375°F. Place sheets of foil on countertop for cooling cookies.

2. Place brown sugar, shortening, coffee and vanilla in large bowl. Beat at medium speed of electric mixer until well blended. Add egg; beat well.

3. Combine flour, ground coffee, salt and baking soda. Add to shortening mixture; beat at low speed just until blended. Stir in chocolate chips and walnuts.

4. Drop dough by rounded measuring tablespoonfuls 2 inches apart onto ungreased baking sheets.

5. Bake one baking sheet at a time at 375°F for 8 to 10 minutes or until cookies are lightly browned and just set. *Do not overbake.* Place 1 candy in center of each cookie. Cool 2 minutes on baking sheet. Remove cookies to foil to cool completely.
    *Makes about 3 dozen cookies*

*Almond Hearts*

## 294 SUGAR COOKIES

1 cup sugar
1 cup butter or margarine
2 eggs
½ teaspoon lemon extract
½ teaspoon vanilla
3 cups all-purpose flour, divided
1 teaspoon baking powder
¼ teaspoon salt
Egg Yolk Paint (recipe follows)
Royal Icing (page 267)
Decorator Frosting (page 267)

**EQUIPMENT AND DECORATIONS:**
Liquid or paste food coloring
Small paint brushes
Sponges

**1.** Beat sugar and butter in large bowl with electric mixer at medium speed until light and fluffy. Beat in eggs and extracts at medium speed until blended (mixture will look grainy). Beat in 1 cup flour, baking powder and salt at medium speed until blended. Gradually add remaining 2 cups flour. Beat at low speed until soft dough forms. Form dough into 3 discs. Wrap discs in plastic wrap; refrigerate 2 hours or until firm.

**2.** Preheat oven to 375°F. Working with 1 disc at a time, unwrap dough and place on lightly floured surface. Roll out dough to ⅛-inch thickness. Cut dough with lightly floured 3- to 4-inch cookie cutters. Place cutouts 1 inch apart on *ungreased* cookie sheets. Gently press dough trimmings together; reroll and cut out more cookies. (If dough is sticky, pat into disc; wrap in plastic wrap and refrigerate until firm.)

**3.** To paint cookies before baking, prepare Egg Yolk Paint. Divide paint among several bowls; tint with liquid food coloring, if desired. Paint yolk paint onto unbaked cookies with paint brush.

**4.** Bake 7 to 9 minutes or until cookies are set. Remove cookies with spatula to wire rack; cool completely.

**5.** To sponge paint cooled cookies, prepare Royal Icing. Divide icing among several bowls; tint with liquid or paste food coloring. For best results, use 2 to 3 shades of the same color. (If icing is too thick, stir in water, 1 drop at a time, with spoon until desired consistency.) Spread thin layer of icing on cookies to within ⅛ inch of edges with small spatula. Let stand 30 minutes at room temperature or until icing is set.

**6.** Cut clean kitchen sponge into 1-inch squares with scissors. Dip sponge into tinted icing, scraping against side of bowl to remove excess icing. Gently press sponge on base icing several times until desired effect is achieved. Let stand 15 minutes or until icing is set.

**7.** To pipe additional decorations on cookies, prepare Decorator Frosting. Tint frosting as directed in Step 5, if desired. Place each color frosting in piping bag fitted with small writing tip or resealable plastic freezer bags with one small corner cut off. Decorate as desired. Let cookies stand at room temperature until piping is set.

**8.** Store loosely covered at room temperature up to 1 week.

*Makes about 3 dozen cookies*

**EGG YOLK PAINT**
2 egg yolks
2 teaspoons water

Combine egg yolks and water in small bowl with fork until blended.

*Makes about ⅓ cup*

**NOTE:** Only brush this paint onto unbaked cookies.

## HOLIDAY HAPPENINGS

### ROYAL ICING
**4 egg whites***
**4 cups powdered sugar, sifted**
**1 teaspoon lemon extract or clear vanilla
extract****

Beat egg whites in clean, large bowl with
electric mixer at high speed until foamy.
Gradually add sugar and lemon extract. Beat
at high speed until thickened.

*Makes 2 cups*

*\*Use only grade A clean, uncracked eggs.*

*\*\*Icing remains very white when clear flavorings are
used.*

**NOTE:** When dry, Royal Icing is very hard
and resistant to damage that can occur
during shipping.

### DECORATOR FROSTING
**¾ cup butter, softened**
**4½ cups powdered sugar, sifted**
**3 tablespoons water**
**1 teaspoon vanilla**
**¼ teaspoon lemon extract**

Beat butter in medium bowl with electric
mixer at medium speed until smooth. Add
2 cups sugar. Beat at medium speed until
light and fluffy. Add water and extracts. Beat
at low speed until well blended. Beat in
remaining 2½ cups sugar until mixture is
creamy. *Makes 2 cups*

**NOTE:** This frosting is perfect for piping, but
is less durable than Royal Icing. Bumping,
stacking and handling may damage
decorations.

*Sugar Cookies*

## 295 GREETING CARD COOKIES

½ cup butter or margarine, softened
¾ cup sugar
1 egg
1 teaspoon vanilla extract
1½ cups all-purpose flour
⅓ cup HERSHEY'S Cocoa
½ teaspoon baking powder
½ teaspoon baking soda
¼ teaspoon salt
Decorative Frosting (recipe follows)

In large bowl, beat butter, sugar, egg and vanilla until light and fluffy. Stir together flour, cocoa, baking powder, baking soda and salt; add to butter mixture, blending well. Refrigerate about 1 hour or until firm enough to roll. Cut cardboard rectangle for pattern, 2½×4 inches; wrap in plastic wrap.

Preheat oven to 350°F. On lightly floured board or between two pieces of waxed paper, roll out half of dough to ¼-inch thickness. Place pattern on dough; cut through dough around pattern with sharp paring knife. (Save dough trimmings and reroll for remaining cookies.) Carefully place cutouts on lightly greased cookie sheet; bake 8 to 10 minutes or until set. Cool 1 minute on cookie sheet. (If cookies have lost their shape, trim irregular edges while cookies are still hot.) Carefully transfer to cooling rack. Repeat procedure with remaining dough. Prepare Decorative Frosting; spoon into pastry bag fitted with decorating tip. Pipe names or greetings onto cookies; decorate as desired.

*Makes about 12 cookies*

DECORATIVE FROSTING
3 cups powdered sugar
⅓ cup shortening
2 to 3 tablespoons milk
Food color (optional)

In medium bowl, beat sugar and shortening; gradually add milk, beating until smooth and slightly thickened. Divide frosting into two bowls; tint with food color, if desired. Cover.

## 296 CHOCOLATE CHIP SHAMROCKS

1 cup (2 sticks) butter or margarine, softened
½ cup packed brown sugar
⅓ cup granulated sugar
2 teaspoons vanilla extract
½ teaspoon salt
1 egg yolk
2½ cups all-purpose flour
2 cups (12-ounce package) NESTLÉ® TOLL HOUSE® Semi-Sweet Chocolate Mini Morsels
1 container (16 ounces) prepared vanilla frosting, colored green if desired
Green coarse sugar or candies

**BEAT** butter, sugars, vanilla and salt in large mixer bowl until creamy. Beat in egg yolk. Gradually beat in flour. Stir in morsels. Shape dough into 2 flat round discs. Cover; chill for about 1 hour or until firm. **ROLL** each disc to ¼-inch thickness Cut into shamrock shapes; place on ungreased baking sheets. **BAKE** in preheated 350°F. oven for 9 to 11 minutes or until golden brown. Cool on baking sheets for 2 minutes. Remove to wire racks to cool completely. Spread with frosting; sprinkle with green sugar.

*Makes about 3 dozen cookies*

*Greeting Card Cookies*

## HOLIDAY HAPPENINGS

## 297 EASTER COOKIE POPS

1 cup FLEISCHMANN'S® Margarine
1 cup sugar
1 egg
1 teaspoon lemon extract
   Red, yellow or green food coloring, optional
3 cups all-purpose flour
2 teaspoons DAVIS® Baking Powder
   Colored sprinkles or sugars
12 (6-inch) lollipop or wooden pop sticks*
1 (16-ounce) can prepared vanilla frosting
   Assorted candies and colored decorator gels

*If desired, omit lollipop or wooden pop sticks.

With mixer, beat margarine and sugar until creamy. Beat in egg and lemon extract. Tint with food coloring if desired. Mix flour and baking powder; blend into margarine mixture. Beat at medium speed until mixture forms a ball. Let dough rest 15 minutes; do not refrigerate.

On floured surface, roll dough to a ⅛-inch thickness. With floured 4-inch cookie cutter, cut dough into desired shapes, rerolling scraps as necessary. Place on lightly greased baking sheet. Lightly press lollipop or wooden pop stick into half of the cookies, making sure the stick extends to center of cookie. Bake at 400°F for 5 to 7 minutes. Do not brown. Cool completely on wire rack.

To assemble, spread the top of each cookie with 1 tablespoon frosting; place cookies without sticks on top of cookies with sticks to form sandwich. Decorate as desired with assorted candies and gels. Store in airtight container for up to 2 weeks.

*Makes about 1½ to 2 dozen pops*

## 298 EASTER EGG COOKIES

1 package DUNCAN HINES® Golden Sugar Cookie Mix
¼ cup CRISCO® Oil or CRISCO® PURITAN® Canola Oil
1 egg
1 tablespoon water
   Assorted colored decors
   Corn syrup
   Food coloring

**1.** Preheat oven to 375°F.

**2.** Combine cookie mix, oil, egg and water in large bowl. Stir with wooden spoon until thoroughly blended.

**3.** Place 1 level *measuring* teaspoonful dough on ungreased baking sheet about 2 inches apart for each cookie. Flatten dough into egg shape (an oval with one narrow end and one wide end). Decorate half the eggs with assorted decors. Press lightly into cookie dough. Bake at 375°F for 6 to 7 minutes or until cookies are light golden brown around the edges. Cool 1 minute on baking sheets. Remove to cooling racks. Cool completely.

**4.** To decorate plain cookies, combine 1 tablespoon corn syrup and 1 or 2 drops food coloring in small bowl for each color. Stir to blend. Paint designs with tinted corn syrup using clean artist paint brushes. Sprinkle painted areas with colored decors, if desired. Store between layers of waxed paper in airtight container.

*Makes 5 dozen cookies*

**TIP:** Keep cookie dough an even thickness when shaping for more even baking.

*Easter Egg Cookies*

## HOLIDAY HAPPENINGS

### 299 FROSTED EASTER CUT–OUTS

**COOKIES**

1¼ cups granulated sugar
  1 BUTTER FLAVOR* CRISCO® Stick or
      1 cup BUTTER FLAVOR CRISCO
      all-vegetable shortening
  2 eggs
¼ cup light corn syrup or regular pancake
      syrup
  1 tablespoon vanilla
  3 cups all-purpose flour (plus
      4 tablespoons), divided
¾ teaspoon baking powder
½ teaspoon baking soda
½ teaspoon salt

**ICING**

  1 cup confectioners sugar
  2 tablespoons milk
    Food color (optional)
    Decorating icing

*\*Butter Flavor Crisco is artificially flavored.*

**1.** Place sugar and shortening in large bowl. Beat at medium speed of electric mixer until well blended. Add eggs, syrup and vanilla; beat until well blended and fluffy.

**2.** Combine 3 cups flour, baking powder, baking soda and salt. Add gradually to shortening mixture, beating at low speed until well blended.

**3.** Divide dough into 4 equal pieces; shape each into disk. Wrap with plastic wrap. Refrigerate 1 hour or until firm.

**4.** Heat oven to 375°F. Place sheets of foil on countertop for cooling cookies.

**5.** Sprinkle about 1 tablespoon flour on large sheet of waxed paper. Place disk of dough on floured paper; flatten slightly with hands.

Turn dough over; cover with another large sheet of waxed paper. Roll dough to ¼-inch thickness. Remove top sheet of waxed paper. Cut into desired shapes with floured cookie cutter. Place 2 inches apart on ungreased baking sheet. Repeat with remaining dough.

**6.** Bake one baking sheet at a time at 375°F for 5 to 7 minutes or until edges of cookies are lightly browned. *Do not overbake.* Cool 2 minutes on baking sheet. Remove cookies to foil to cool completely.

**7.** For icing, combine confectioners sugar and milk; stir until smooth. Add food color, if desired. Stir until blended. Spread icing on cookies; place on foil until icing is set. Decorate as desired with decorating icing.
*Makes about 3½ dozen cookies*

### 300 HALLOWEEN COOKIE PIZZA

¾ cup packed light brown sugar
½ cup butter flavor shortening
  1 egg
  1 tablespoon water
  1 teaspoon vanilla extract
1¼ cups all-purpose flour
½ teaspoon baking soda
¼ teaspoon salt
  1 cup REESE'S® Peanut Butter Chips
  1 cup miniature marshmallows
½ cup HERSHEY'S Semi-Sweet Chocolate
      Chips
½ cup chopped pecans
    CHOCOLATE DRIZZLE (page 273)
    ORANGE DRIZZLE (page 273)

**1.** Heat oven to 350°F. Lightly grease 12-inch round pizza pan.

## HOLIDAY HAPPENINGS

**2.** In large bowl, beat brown sugar and shortening until creamy. Add egg, water and vanilla; beat well. Stir together flour, baking soda and salt; add to sugar mixture, beating on low speed of electric mixer until well blended. Stir in peanut butter chips. Spread batter into prepared pan to within ½ inch of edge.

**3.** Bake 11 to 13 minutes or until set. Remove from oven. Sprinkle marshmallows, chocolate chips and pecans over top. Return to oven. Bake 5 to 7 minutes or until marshmallows are lightly browned. Cool completely.

**4.** Prepare CHOCOLATE DRIZZLE and ORANGE DRIZZLE. Drizzle CHOCOLATE DRIZZLE over top. Drizzle ORANGE DRIZZLE over chocolate. Let stand about 1 hour until drizzles set. Cut into wedges.
*Makes about 16 to 20 servings*

**CHOCOLATE DRIZZLE:** In small microwave-safe bowl, place ¼ cup HERSHEY'S Semi-Sweet Chocolate Chips and 1½ teaspoons butter flavor shortening. Microwave at MEDIUM (50%) 1 minute; stir. If necessary, microwave at MEDIUM an additional 15 seconds at a time, stirring after each heating, just until chips are melted when stirred.

**ORANGE DRIZZLE:** In small bowl, stir together ½ cup powdered sugar, 1 tablespoon water, 3 drops yellow food color and 2 drops red food color; stir until well blended.

*Halloween Cookie Pizza*

## 301 GIANT CANDY CORN COOKIES

1 cup FLEISCHMANN'S® Margarine
⅔ cup sugar
⅔ cup light corn syrup
1 teaspoon orange extract
1 egg, beaten
4 cups all-purpose flour
2 teaspoons DAVIS® Baking Powder
¼ teaspoon yellow food coloring
¼ teaspoon red food coloring

In 3-quart saucepan, over medium heat, stir margarine, sugar and corn syrup, until margarine melts and sugar dissolves. Remove from heat; stir in orange extract. Cool 5 minutes; blend in egg.

In bowl, mix flour and baking powder; slowly blend in egg mixture to make a stiff dough. Shape ¼ of dough into 12×1½-inch log; set aside. On waxed paper, knead yellow food coloring into remaining dough; divide in half. On waxed paper, knead red food coloring into one piece of yellow dough to make orange. Shape both yellow and orange doughs into separate 12×2½-inch logs. On waxed paper, stack orange log over yellow log; top with plain log. Wrap; chill several hours or until firm.

Let dough stand at room temperature 10 minutes. Cut stacked log into 24 (½-inch thick) slices; place on lightly greased baking sheet. Flatten each piece, shaping into a triangle about ⅛-inch thick.

Bake at 350°F for 9 to 11 minutes until lightly brown. Do not overbake. Cool on wire rack; store in airtight container.

*Makes 2 dozen*

## 302 HUGE SCARY SPIDERS

2 ounces of unsweetened chocolate
1¼ cups all-purpose flour
1½ teaspoons baking powder
¼ teaspoon salt
¼ cup margarine
1 cup sugar
1 egg, beaten
1 teaspoon vanilla
Red baking candies or "red hots"

Preheat oven to 375°F. Lightly grease baking sheet.

Melt chocolate over low heat in small saucepan. Let cool. Mix flour, baking powder and salt in small bowl. Beat margarine in medium bowl on low speed of electric mixer until smooth. Add sugar; beat until creamy. Stir in egg, vanilla and chocolate. Add flour mixture; mix well forming a stiff dough.

To make spider, shape 2-inch flat oval for the body. Make spider's head by flattening a circle about ½-inch wide. Shape dough for eight legs each about two inches long and less than ¼ inch wide. Attach the head and legs to body. Put two red candies into head for eyes. Bake 5 to 8 minutes or until lightly browned. Let spiders cool on baking sheet to avoid breaking when removing.

*Makes 20 spiders*

## 303 JACK O'LANTERN COOKIES

1 cup butter or margarine, softened
$\frac{1}{2}$ cup firmly packed light brown sugar
$\frac{1}{2}$ cup granulated sugar
2 eggs
1 teaspoon vanilla extract
1$\frac{1}{3}$ cups all-purpose flour
1 teaspoon baking soda
1$\frac{1}{2}$ cups rolled oats (quick or old-fashioned), uncooked
1 package (6 ounces) dried fruit bits
1$\frac{1}{2}$ cups (6 ounces) Gjetost cheese, cut into $\frac{1}{4}$-inch cubes
1 cup chopped walnuts
2 cups confectioners' sugar
2 to 3 tablespoons milk
   Orange and green food coloring

Preheat oven to 375°F. In small bowl with electric mixer, cream butter and sugars until light and fluffy. Blend in eggs and vanilla. In another small bowl, combine flour and baking soda; stir into dough. Blend in oats, fruit, cheese and walnuts. Shape tablespoons of dough into balls and place 2 inches apart on ungreased cookie sheets. Press down lightly with glass. Bake 10 minutes or until golden. Cool on wire racks.

In medium bowl, blend confectioners' sugar with enough milk to make a thick frosting. Divide in half. Color one-half with green food coloring and the remainder with orange food coloring. Decorate cookies in pumpkin design. *Makes about 4$\frac{1}{2}$ dozen cookies*

*Favorite recipe from* **Norseland Foods**

## 304 OATS 'N' PUMPKIN PINWHEELS

1$\frac{1}{2}$ cups all-purpose flour
1 cup QUAKER® Oats (quick or old fashioned, uncooked)
$\frac{1}{4}$ teaspoon baking soda
1$\frac{1}{2}$ cups sugar, divided
$\frac{1}{2}$ cup (1 stick) margarine or butter, softened
2 egg whites
1 cup canned pumpkin
$\frac{1}{2}$ teaspoon pumpkin pie spice
$\frac{1}{4}$ cup sesame seeds

In small bowl, combine flour, oats and baking soda; set aside. In large mixing bowl, beat 1 cup sugar and margarine until fluffy; mix in egg whites. Stir in dry ingredients. On waxed paper, press dough into 16×12-inch rectangle. In small bowl, combine pumpkin, remaining $\frac{1}{2}$ cup sugar and the pumpkin pie spice; mix well. Spread mixture over dough to $\frac{1}{2}$-inch of edge. Roll dough, beginning at narrow end. Sprinkle sesame seeds over roll, pressing gently into dough. Wrap in waxed paper; freeze until firm or overnight.

Preheat oven to 400°F. Spray cookie sheet with non-stick cooking spray. Cut frozen dough into $\frac{1}{4}$-inch slices; place on cookie sheet. Bake 9 to 11 minutes or until golden brown. Remove to wire rack; cool completely.

*Makes about 4 dozen cookies*

## 305 FALL HARVEST OATMEAL COOKIES

1¼ cups firmly packed light brown sugar
¾ BUTTER FLAVOR* CRISCO® Stick or
  ¾ cup BUTTER FLAVOR CRISCO
  all-vegetable shortening
1 egg
⅓ cup milk
1 tablespoon grated orange peel
1½ teaspoons vanilla
3 cups quick oats, uncooked
1 cup all-purpose flour
1½ teaspoons cinnamon
½ teaspoon baking soda
½ teaspoon salt
¼ teaspoon nutmeg
¼ teaspoon ground cloves
1 cup coarsely chopped, peeled apples
1 cup raisins
1 cup coarsely chopped walnuts

*Butter Flavor Crisco is artificially flavored.*

**1.** Heat oven to 375°F. Grease baking sheets. Place sheets of foil on countertop for cooling.

**2.** Place brown sugar, shortening, egg, milk, orange peel and vanilla in large bowl. Beat at medium speed of electric mixer until well blended.

**3.** Combine oats, flour, cinnamon, baking soda, salt, nutmeg and cloves. Add to shortening mixture; beat at low speed until blended. Stir in apples, raisins and walnuts.

**4.** Drop dough by rounded measuring tablespoonfuls 2 inches apart onto prepared baking sheets.

**5.** Bake one baking sheet at a time at 375°F for 10 to 12 minutes or until cookies are lightly browned. *Do not overbake.* Cool 2 minutes on baking sheet. Remove cookies to foil to cool completely.
  *Makes about 2½ dozen cookies*

## 306 CRANBERRY NUT OATMEAL COOKIES

1¼ cups firmly packed light brown sugar
¾ BUTTER FLAVOR* CRISCO® Stick or
  ¾ cup BUTTER FLAVOR CRISCO
  all-vegetable shortening
1 egg
⅓ cup milk
1½ teaspoons vanilla
1 teaspoon grated orange peel
3 cups quick oats, uncooked
1 cup all-purpose flour
½ teaspoon baking soda
½ teaspoon salt
¼ teaspoon cinnamon
1 cup dried cranberries
1 cup coarsely chopped walnuts

*Butter Flavor Crisco is artificially flavored.*

**1.** Heat oven to 375°F. Grease baking sheets. Place sheets of foil on countertop for cooling cookies.

**2.** Place brown sugar, shortening, egg, milk, vanilla and orange peel in large bowl. Beat at medium speed of electric mixer until well blended.

**3.** Combine oats, flour, baking soda, salt and cinnamon. Add to shortening mixture; beat at low speed just until blended. Stir in cranberries and walnuts.

**4.** Drop dough by rounded measuring tablespoonfuls 2 inches apart onto prepared baking sheets.

**5.** Bake one baking sheet at a time at 375°F for 10 to 12 minutes or until cookies are lightly browned. *Do not overbake.* Cool 2 minutes on baking sheet. Remove cookies to foil to cool completely.
  *Makes about 2½ dozen cookies*

*Fall Harvest Oatmeal Cookies*

## 307 IRRESISTIBLE PEANUT BUTTER JACK O' LANTERNS

### COOKIES

1¼ cups firmly packed light brown sugar
¾ cup creamy peanut butter
½ CRISCO® Stick or ½ cup CRISCO all-vegetable shortening
3 tablespoons milk
1 tablespoon vanilla
1 egg
1¾ cups all-purpose flour
¾ teaspoon baking soda
¾ teaspoon salt

### ICING

1 cup (6 ounces) semisweet chocolate chips
2 teaspoons BUTTER FLAVOR* CRISCO® all-vegetable shortening**

*Butter Flavor Crisco is artificially flavored.*

**Crisco all-vegetable shortening can be substituted for Butter Flavor Crisco.*

1. Heat oven to 375°F. Place sheets of foil on countertop for cooling cookies.

2. For cookies, place brown sugar, peanut butter, shortening, milk and vanilla in large bowl. Beat at medium speed of electric mixer until well blended. Add egg; beat just until blended.

3. Combine flour, baking soda and salt. Add to shortening mixture; beat at low speed just until blended.

4. Pinch off pieces of dough the size of walnuts. Shape into balls. Place 3 inches apart on ungreased baking sheet. Flatten each ball with bottom of glass to approximately ⅜-inch thickness. Form into pumpkin shape, making indentation on top of round. Pinch off very small piece of dough and roll to form small stem. Attach to top of cookie. Score dough with vertical lines with small, sharp knife to resemble pumpkin.

5. Bake one baking sheet at a time at 375°F for 7 to 8 minutes or until cookies are set and just beginning to brown. *Do not overbake.* Cool on baking sheet 2 minutes. Remove cookies to foil to cool completely.

6. For icing, place chocolate chips and shortening in heavy resealable sandwich bag; seal bag. Microwave at 50% (MEDIUM) for 1 minute. Knead bag. If necessary, microwave at 50% for another 30 seconds at a time until mixture is smooth when bag is kneaded. Cut small tip off corner of bag. Pipe lines and faces on cookies to resemble jack o' lanterns.

*Makes about 3 dozen cookies*

## 308 FROST–ON–THE–PUMPKIN COOKIES

2 cups all-purpose flour
1 teaspoon baking powder
1 teaspoon ground cinnamon
½ teaspoon baking soda
½ teaspoon ground nutmeg
1 cup butter, softened
¾ cup JACK FROST® Granulated Sugar
¾ cup firmly packed JACK FROST® Brown Sugar
1 cup canned pumpkin
1 egg
2 teaspoons vanilla
½ cup raisins
½ cup chopped walnuts
Cream Cheese Frosting (recipe follows)

Preheat oven to 350°F. In small mixing bowl, combine flour, baking powder, cinnamon, baking soda and nutmeg. Set aside. In large mixer bowl, beat butter for 1 minute. Add granulated sugar and brown sugar; beat until fluffy. Add pumpkin, egg and vanilla; beat well. Add flour mixture to pumpkin mixture; mix until well blended. Stir in raisins and walnuts. Drop by teaspoonfuls 2 inches apart onto greased cookie sheet.

Bake 10 to 12 minutes. Cool on cookie sheet for 2 minutes. Transfer to wire rack; cool completely. Frost with Cream Cheese Frosting. Garnish with chopped nuts, if desired.    *Makes about 4 dozen cookies*

**CREAM CHEESE FROSTING:** In medium mixing bowl, beat 3 ounces softened cream cheese, ¼ cup softened butter and 1 teaspoon vanilla until light and fluffy. Gradually add 2 cups JACK FROST® Powdered Sugar, beating until smooth.

## 309 GRAPE JACK–O'–LANTERN COOKIES

¾ cup dark molasses
¾ cup packed brown sugar
¼ cup water
3 tablespoons butter or margarine
3 cups all-purpose flour
1 teaspoon baking soda
1 teaspoon ground ginger
½ teaspoon salt
½ teaspoon ground allspice
½ teaspoon ground cinnamon
¼ teaspoon ground cloves
Orange Icing (recipe follows)
2 cups California seedless grapes

Combine molasses, sugar, water and butter in large bowl; mix well. Combine flour, baking soda, ginger, salt, allspice, cinnamon and cloves in medium bowl; mix well. Add to molasses mixture. Cover and refrigerate 2 hours or longer. Roll dough ⅛ to ¼ inch thick on floured surface. Cut dough into pumpkin shapes, 4½ to 5 inches in diameter—using a cutter or handmade cardboard pattern and a knife. Place on lightly greased cookie sheet. Bake in preheated 350°F oven 10 to 12 minutes or until firm when lightly touch with finger. Cool. Ice with Orange Icing and decorate with grapes.

*Makes 18 to 20 large cookies*

**ORANGE ICING:** Beat 6 cups powdered sugar and about ⅓ cup orange juice until smooth and of spreading consistency. Tint with 9 drops yellow food color and 10 drops red food color or to desired orange color. Makes about 1⅔ cups.

*Favorite recipe from California Table Grape Commission*

## 310 THE BIG SPIDER WEB

1½ cups all-purpose flour
½ teaspoon baking soda
¾ cup creamy peanut butter
½ cup FLEISCHMANN'S® Margarine,
   softened
1¼ cups firmly packed light brown sugar
2 teaspoons vanilla extract
1 egg
¾ cup milk chocolate chips, divided
½ cup PLANTERS® Dry Roasted Peanuts,
   chopped
1 cup marshmallow fluff
   Assorted candies and gummy creatures

Combine flour and baking soda; set aside.

In large bowl, with electric mixer at medium speed, beat peanut butter, margarine, sugar and vanilla until creamy. Beat in egg until light and fluffy; gradually blend in flour mixture. Stir in ½ cup chocolate chips and chopped peanuts.

Press dough into greased 14-inch pizza pan. Bake at 350°F for 20 to 25 minutes or until done. Cool completely in pan on wire rack. Frost top of cookie with marshmallow fluff to within 1-inch of edge. Melt remaining chocolate chips, drizzle chocolate in circular pattern over marshmallow. Draw knife through marshmallow topping to create web effect. Decorate with assorted candies and gummy creatures.      *Makes 16 servings*

## 311 HARVEST PUMPKIN COOKIES

2 cups all-purpose flour
1 teaspoon baking powder
1 teaspoon ground cinnamon
½ teaspoon baking soda
½ teaspoon salt
½ teaspoon ground allspice
1 cup butter, softened
1 cup sugar
1 cup canned pumpkin
1 egg
1 teaspoon vanilla
1 cup chopped pecans
1 cup dried cranberries (optional)
   Pecan halves (about 36)

**PREHEAT** oven to 375°F. Combine flour, baking powder, cinnamon, baking soda, salt and allspice in medium bowl.

**BEAT** butter and sugar in large bowl with electric mixer at medium speed until light and fluffy. Beat in pumpkin, egg and vanilla. Gradually add flour mixture. Beat at low speed until well blended. Stir in chopped pecans and cranberries with spoon.

**DROP** heaping tablespoonfuls of dough 2 inches apart onto *ungreased* cookie sheets. Flatten slightly with back of spoon. Press one pecan half into center of each cookie.

**BAKE** 10 to 12 minutes or until golden brown. Let cookies stand on cookie sheets 1 minute; transfer to wire racks to cool completely. Store tightly covered at room temperature or freeze up to 3 months.
      *Makes about 36 cookies*

**NOTE:** If dried cranberries are not available, substitute raisins or currants.

*Harvest Pumpkin Cookies*

## 312 GINGER PUMPKIN FACE COOKIES

1 cup 100% bran cereal
¼ cup BRER RABBIT® Light Molasses
1 egg, beaten
1¼ cups all-purpose flour
1 teaspoon baking soda
1 teaspoon ground ginger
¼ teaspoon ground cloves
½ cup FLEISCHMANN'S® Margarine, softened
1 cup sugar, divided
½ cup PLANTERS® Pecan Halves, chopped
    Nonstick cooking spray
36 PLANTERS® Pecan Halves
    Powdered Sugar Icing, recipe follows
    Candy corn, melted chocolate, colored sprinkles, for garnish

Mix bran, molasses and egg; let stand 5 minutes. In another bowl combine flour, baking soda and spices; set aside.

In large bowl, with mixer at medium speed, beat margarine and ¾ cup sugar until creamy; blend in bran mixture. Stir in flour mixture until blended. Stir in chopped pecans. Form into 1-inch balls; roll in remaining ¼ cup sugar.

Place 2-inches apart on baking sheets greased with cooking spray. Flatten balls with bottom of glass. Insert 1 whole pecan into top edge of dough for stem. Bake at 375°F for 7 to 9 minutes. Let stand 1 minute before removing to cooling rack. Frost with Powdered Sugar Icing and decorate with candy corn, melted chocolate and colored sprinkles. *Makes about 3 dozen*

**POWDERED SUGAR ICING:** Combine 2 cups powdered sugar and 3 to 4 tablespoons milk until smooth. Tint with red and yellow food coloring to make orange tone.

## 313 OLD–FASHIONED HARVEST COOKIES

¾ BUTTER FLAVOR* CRISCO® Stick or
    ¾ cup BUTTER FLAVOR CRISCO all-vegetable shortening
1 cup firmly packed dark brown sugar
¾ cup canned solid-pack pumpkin
1 egg
2 tablespoons molasses
1½ cups all-purpose flour
1 teaspoon ground nutmeg
½ teaspoon baking powder
½ teaspoon baking soda
¼ teaspoon salt
¼ teaspoon ground cinnamon
2½ cups quick-cooking oats (not instant or old-fashioned), uncooked
1½ cups finely chopped dates
½ cup chopped walnuts

*Butter Flavor Crisco is artificially flavored.*

**1.** Preheat oven to 350°F. Grease cookie sheet with shortening.

**2.** Combine shortening and sugar in large bowl. Beat at medium speed of electric mixer until well blended. Beat in pumpkin, egg and molasses.

**3.** Combine flour, nutmeg, baking powder, baking soda, salt and cinnamon. Mix into creamed mixture at low speed until just blended. Stir in, one a time, oats, dates and nuts with spoon.

**4.** Drop rounded tablespoonfuls of dough 2 inches apart onto cookie sheet.

**5.** Bake at 350°F for 10 to 12 minutes or until bottoms are lightly browned. Cool 2 minutes on cookie sheet. Remove to wire rack. *Makes about 4 dozen cookies*

## 314 CHERRY DOT COOKIES

2¼ cups all-purpose flour
2 teaspoons baking powder
½ teaspoon salt
¾ cup margarine, softened
1 cup sugar
2 eggs
2 tablespoons skim milk
1 teaspoon vanilla
1 cup chopped nuts
1 cup finely chopped pitted dates
⅓ cup finely chopped maraschino cherries
2⅔ cups KELLOGG'S CORN FLAKES®
      cereal, crushed to 1⅓ cups
15 maraschino cherries, cut into quarters
   Vegetable cooking spray

**1.** Stir together flour, baking powder and salt. Set aside.

**2.** In large mixing bowl, beat margarine and sugar until light and fluffy. Add eggs. Beat well. Stir in milk and vanilla. Add flour mixture. Mix well. Stir in nuts, dates and the ⅓ cup chopped cherries.

**3.** Shape level measuring tablespoon of dough into balls. Roll in Kellogg's Corn Flakes® cereal. Place on baking sheets coated with cooking spray. Top each with cherry quarter.

**4.** Bake at 350°F about 10 minutes or until lightly browned. Remove to wire racks to cool. *Makes 5 dozen cookies*

## 315 LINZER TARTS

1 cup BLUE BONNET® Spread, softened
1 cup granulated sugar
2 cups all-purpose flour
1 cup PLANTERS® Slivered Almonds,
   chopped
1 teaspoon grated lemon peel
¼ teaspoon ground cinnamon
⅓ cup raspberry preserves
   Confectioners' sugar

In large bowl with electric mixer at high speed, beat Spread and granulated sugar until light and fluffy. Stir in flour, almonds, lemon peel and cinnamon until blended. Cover; refrigerate 2 hours.

Preheat oven to 325°F. Divide dough in half. On floured surface, roll out one-half of dough to ⅛-inch thickness. Using 2½-inch round cookie cutter, cut circles from dough. Reroll scraps to make additional rounds. Cut out ½-inch circles from centers of half the rounds. Repeat with remaining dough. Place on ungreased cookie sheets.

Bake 12 to 15 minutes or until lightly browned. Remove from cookie sheets; cool on wire racks. Spread preserves on top of whole cookies. Top with cut-out cookies to make sandwiches. Dust with confectioners' sugar. *Makes about 2 dozen cookies*

## 316 PEPPERMINT PUFFS

1 cup firmly packed light brown sugar
¾ BUTTER FLAVOR* CRISCO® Stick or
    ¾ cup BUTTER FLAVOR CRISCO
    all-vegetable shortening
2 tablespoons milk
1 tablespoon vanilla
1 egg
1¾ cups all-purpose flour
1 teaspoon salt
¾ teaspoon baking soda
⅔ cup crushed peppermint candy canes**

*Butter Flavor Crisco is artificially flavored.*

**To crush candy canes, break into small pieces.
Place in plastic food storage bag. Secure top. Use
rolling pin to break candy into very small pieces.*

**1.** Heat oven to 375°F. Place sheets of foil on
countertop for cooling cookies.

**2.** Combine brown sugar, shortening, milk
and vanilla in large bowl. Beat at medium
speed of electric mixer until well blended.
Beat egg into creamed mixture.

**3.** Combine flour, salt and baking soda. Mix
into creamed mixture at low speed just until
blended. Stir in crushed candy.

**4.** Shape dough into 1-inch balls. Place
2 inches apart on ungreased baking sheet.

**5.** Bake one baking sheet at a time at 375°F
for 8 to 10 minutes for chewy cookies or
11 to 13 minutes for crisp cookies. *Do not
overbake.* Cool 2 minutes on baking sheet.
Remove cookies to foil to cool completely.
*Makes about 3 dozen cookies*

## 317 MEXICAN CHOCOLATE MACAROONS

1 package (8 ounces) semisweet baking
    chocolate, divided
1¾ cups plus ⅓ cup whole almonds, divided
¾ cup sugar
1 teaspoon ground cinnamon
1 teaspoon vanilla
2 egg whites

**1.** Preheat oven to 400°F. Grease baking
sheets; set aside.

**2.** Place 5 squares of chocolate in food
processor; process until coarsely chopped.
Add 1¾ cups almonds and sugar; process
using on/off pulsing action until mixture is
finely ground. Add cinnamon, vanilla and egg
whites; process just until mixture forms
moist dough.

**3.** Form dough into 1-inch balls (dough will
be sticky). Place about 2 inches apart onto
prepared baking sheets. Press 1 almond on
top of each cookie.

**4.** Bake 8 to 10 minutes or just until set. Cool
2 minutes on baking sheets. Remove cookies
from baking sheets to wire rack to cool.

**5.** Heat remaining 3 squares chocolate in
small saucepan over very low heat until
melted. Spoon chocolate into small
resealable plastic food storage bag. Cut
small corner off bottom of bag with scissors.
Drizzle chocolate over cookies.
*Makes 3 dozen cookies*

*Mexican Chocolate Macaroons*

## 318 HOLIDAY PINEAPPLE CHEESE BARS

¼ cup butter or margarine
¼ cup packed brown sugar
¾ cup flour
¾ cup finely chopped macadamia nuts
1 (8-ounce) can crushed pineapple, undrained
1 (8-ounce) package PHILADELPHIA BRAND® Cream Cheese, softened
¼ cup granulated sugar
1 egg
1 cup BAKER'S® ANGEL FLAKE® Coconut
½ cup coarsely chopped macadamia nuts
1 tablespoon butter or margarine, melted

• Preheat oven to 350°F.

• Beat ¼ cup butter and brown sugar in small mixing bowl at medium speed with electric mixer until well blended. Add flour and ¾ cup finely chopped nuts; mix well. Press onto bottom of 9-inch square baking pan. Bake 10 minutes. Cool.

• Drain pineapple, reserving 2 tablespoons liquid.

• Beat cream cheese, reserved liquid, granulated sugar and egg in small mixing bowl at medium speed with electric mixer until well blended. Stir in pineapple. Pour over crust.

• Sprinkle with combined coconut, ½ cup coarsely chopped nuts and 1 tablespoon butter.

• Bake 18 minutes. Cool completely. Cut into bars. *Makes about 1½ dozen bars*

**Prep Time:** 20 minutes
**Cook Time:** 18 minutes

## 319 PEANUT BUTTER SPRITZ SANDWICHES

1 package DUNCAN HINES® Peanut Butter Cookie Mix
¼ cup CRISCO® Oil or CRISCO® PURITAN® Canola Oil
1 egg
4 bars (1.55 ounces each) milk chocolate

**1.** Preheat oven to 375°F.

**2.** Combine cookie mix, contents of peanut butter packet from Mix, oil and egg in large bowl. Stir until thoroughly blended. Fill cookie press with dough. Press desired shapes 2 inches apart onto ungreased baking sheet. Bake at 375°F for 7 to 9 minutes or until set but not browned. Cool 1 minute on baking sheet.

**3.** Cut each milk chocolate bar into 12 sections by following division marks on bars.

**4.** To assemble, carefully remove one cookie from cookie sheet. Place one milk chocolate section on bottom of warm cookie; top with second cookie. Press together to make sandwich. Repeat with remaining cookies. Place sandwich cookies on wire rack until chocolate is set. Store in airtight container.
*Makes 3½ to 4 dozen sandwich cookies*

**TIP:** For best appearance, use cookie press plates that give solid shapes.

*Peanut Butter Spritz Sandwiches*

## 320 PEPPERMINT REFRIGERATOR SLICES

**3 packages DUNCAN HINES® Golden Sugar Cookie Mix, divided**
**¾ cup CRISCO® Oil or CRISCO® Puritan® Canola Oil, divided**
**3 eggs, divided**
**3 tablespoons water, divided**
**3 to 4 drops red food coloring**
**¾ teaspoon peppermint extract, divided**
**3 to 4 drops green food coloring**

**1.** For pink cookie dough, combine ¼ cup oil, 1 egg, 1 tablespoon water, red food coloring and ¼ teaspoon peppermint extract in large bowl. Stir until evenly tinted. Add 1 cookie mix and stir until thoroughly blended. Set aside.

**2.** For green cookie dough, combine ¼ cup oil, 1 egg, 1 tablespoon water, green food coloring and ¼ teaspoon peppermint extract in large bowl. Stir until evenly tinted. Add 1 cookie mix and stir until thoroughly blended. Set aside.

**3.** For plain cookie dough, combine remaining cookie mix, ¼ cup oil, remaining egg, 1 tablespoon water and remaining ¼ teaspoon peppermint extract in large bowl. Stir until thoroughly blended.

**4.** To assemble, divide each batch of cookie dough into four equal portions. Shape each portion into a 12-inch-long roll on waxed paper. Lay 1 pink roll beside 1 green roll; press together slightly. Place 1 plain roll on top. Press rolls together to form 1 tri-colored roll; wrap in waxed paper or plastic wrap. Repeat with remaining rolls to form 3 more tri-colored rolls; wrap separately in waxed paper or plastic wrap. Refrigerate rolls for several hours or overnight.

**5.** Preheat oven to 375°F.

**6.** Cut chilled rolls into ¼-inch-thick slices. Place 2 inches apart on ungreased baking sheets.

**7.** Bake at 375°F for 7 to 8 minutes or until set but not browned. Cool 1 minute on baking sheets. Remove to wire racks. Cool completely. Store in airtight containers.
*Makes about 15 dozen cookies*

**TIP:** For a delicious flavor variation, substitute almond extract for peppermint extract.

## 321 PUMPKIN JINGLE BARS

**¾ cup MIRACLE WHIP® Salad Dressing**
**1 two-layer spice cake mix**
**1 (16-ounce) can pumpkin**
**3 eggs**
 **Confectioners' sugar**
 **Vanilla frosting**
 **Red and green gumdrops, sliced**

• Preheat oven to 350°F.

• Mix salad dressing, cake mix, pumpkin and eggs in large bowl at medium speed of electric mixer until well blended. Pour into greased 15½×10½×1-inch jelly-roll pan.

• Bake 18 to 20 minutes or until edges pull away from sides of pan. Cool. Sprinkle with sugar. Cut into bars. Decorate with frosting and gumdrops.
*Makes about 3 dozen bars*

**Prep Time:** 5 minutes
**Cook Time:** 20 minutes

*Pumpkin Jingle Bars*

## 322 FRUITCAKE SLICES

1 cup butter or margarine, softened
1 cup powdered sugar
1 egg
1 teaspoon vanilla extract
1½ cups coarsely chopped candied fruit (fruitcake mix)
½ cup coarsely chopped walnuts
2½ cups all-purpose flour, divided
¾ to 1 cup flaked coconut

**BEAT** butter in large bowl with electric mixer at medium speed until smooth. Add powdered sugar; beat until well blended. Add egg and vanilla; beat until well blended.

**COMBINE** candied fruit and walnuts in medium bowl. Stir ¼ cup flour into fruit mixture. Add remaining 2¼ cups flour to butter mixture; beat at low speed until blended. Stir in fruit mixture with spoon.

**SHAPE** dough into 2 logs, each about 5½ inches long and 2 inches in diameter. Spread coconut evenly on sheet of waxed paper. Roll logs in coconut, coating evenly. Wrap each log in plastic wrap. Refrigerate 2 to 3 hours or overnight, or freeze up to 1 month. (Let frozen logs stand at room temperature about 10 minutes before slicing and baking.)

**PREHEAT** oven to 350°F. Grease cookie sheets. Cut logs into ¼-inch-thick slices; place 1 inch apart on cookie sheets.

**BAKE** 13 to 15 minutes or until edges are golden brown. Transfer to wire racks to cool. Store in airtight container.

*Makes about 48 cookies*

## 323 SNOW PUFF COOKIES

1 cup (2 sticks) butter or margarine, softened
1 cup sifted powdered sugar
2 teaspoons vanilla
2 cups all-purpose flour
1 cup WHEAT CHEX® brand cereal, crushed to ⅓ cup
½ teaspoon salt
Powdered sugar

Preheat oven to 325°F. In large bowl, combine butter and sugar until well blended. Stir in vanilla. Stir in flour, cereal and salt, mixing well. Using level tablespoon, shape dough into 1-inch balls. Place on ungreased baking sheet. Bake 14 to 16 minutes or until bottoms are lightly browned. Cool. Roll in powdered sugar. *Makes 3 dozen cookies*

## 324 KRINGLE'S CUTOUTS

1¼ cups granulated sugar
1 BUTTER FLAVOR* CRISCO® Stick or 1 cup BUTTER FLAVOR CRISCO all-vegetable shortening
2 eggs
¼ cup light corn syrup or regular pancake syrup
1 teaspoon vanilla
3 cups plus 4 tablespoons all-purpose flour, divided
¾ teaspoon baking powder
½ teaspoon baking soda
½ teaspoon salt
Colored sugar, decors and prepared frosting (optional)

*Butter Flavor Crisco is artificially flavored.*

### Kringle's Cutout

**1.** Combine sugar and shortening in large bowl. Beat at medium speed of electric mixer until well blended. Add eggs, syrup and vanilla. Beat until well blended and fluffy.

**2.** Combine 3 cups flour, baking powder, baking soda and salt. Add gradually to creamed mixture at low speed. Mix until well blended.

**3.** Divide dough into 4 quarters. Cover and refrigerate at least two hours or overnight.

**4.** Heat oven to 375°F. Place sheets of foil on countertop for cooling cookies.

**5.** Spread 1 tablespoon flour on large sheet of waxed paper. Place one quarter of dough on floured paper. Flatten slightly with hands.

Turn dough over. Cover with another large sheet of waxed paper. Roll dough to ¼-inch thickness. Remove top layer of waxed paper. Cut out dough with seasonal cookie cutters. Place cutouts 2 inches apart on ungreased baking sheets. Roll and cut out remaining dough. Sprinkle with colored sugar and decors or leave plain to frost when cool.

**6.** Bake at 375°F for 5 to 9 minutes, depending on size of cookies. (Bake small, thin cookies about 5 minutes; larger cookies about 9 minutes.) *Do not overbake.* Cool 2 minutes on baking sheets. Remove cookies to foil sheets to cool completely.

*Makes 3 to 4 dozen cookies*
*(depending on size and shape)*

## 325 DUTCH ST. NICHOLAS COOKIES

½ cup whole natural almonds
¾ cup butter or margarine, softened
½ cup packed brown sugar
2 tablespoons milk
1½ teaspoons ground cinnamon
¼ teaspoon ground nutmeg
¼ teaspoon ground ginger
¼ teaspoon ground cloves
2 cups sifted all-purpose flour
1½ teaspoons baking powder
½ teaspoon salt
¼ cup coarsely chopped citron

Spread almonds in single layer on baking sheet. Bake at 375°F, 10 to 12 minutes, stirring occasionally, until lightly toasted. Cool. Chop finely. In large bowl, cream butter, sugar, milk and spices. In small bowl, combine flour, baking powder and salt. Add flour mixture to creamed mixture; blend well. Stir in almonds and citron. Knead dough slightly to make ball. Cover; refrigerate until firm. Roll out dough ¼ inch thick on lightly floured surface. Cut out with cookie cutters. Place 2 inches apart on greased cookie sheets. Bake at 375°F, 7 to 10 minutes, until lightly browned. Remove to wire racks to cool.

*Makes about 3½ dozen cookies*

*Favorite recipe from* **Almond Board of California**

## 326 MEXICAN WEDDING COOKIES

1 cup pecan pieces or halves
1 cup butter, softened
2 cups powdered sugar, divided
2 cups all-purpose flour, divided
2 teaspoons vanilla
⅛ teaspoon salt

**PLACE** pecans in food processor. Process using on/off pulse until pecans are ground, but not pasty.

**BEAT** butter and ½ cup powdered sugar in large bowl with electric mixer at medium speed until light and fluffy. Gradually add 1 cup flour, vanilla and salt. Beat at low speed until well blended. Stir in remaining 1 cup flour and ground pecans with spoon.

**SHAPE** dough into a ball; wrap in plastic wrap and refrigerate 1 hour or until firm.

**PREHEAT** oven to 350°F. Shape tablespoons of dough into 1-inch balls. Place 1 inch apart on *ungreased* cookie sheets.

**BAKE** 12 to 15 minutes or until pale golden brown. Let cookies stand on cookie sheets 2 minutes.

*Meanwhile,* **PLACE** 1 cup powdered sugar in 13×9-inch glass dish. Transfer hot cookies to powdered sugar. Roll cookies in powdered sugar, coating well. Let cookies cool in sugar.

**SIFT** remaining ½ cup powdered sugar over sugar-coated cookies before serving. Store tightly covered at room temperature or freeze up to 1 month.

*Makes about 48 cookies*

## 327 MINI CHIP SNOWBALL COOKIES

1½ cups (3 sticks) butter, softened
¾ cup powdered sugar
1 tablespoon vanilla extract
½ teaspoon salt
3 cups all-purpose flour
2 cups (12-ounce package) NESTLÉ® TOLL HOUSE® Semi-Sweet Chocolate Mini Morsels
½ cup finely chopped nuts
   Powdered sugar

BEAT butter, ¾ cup powdered sugar, vanilla and salt in large mixer bowl. Gradually beat in flour; stir in morsels and nuts. Shape level tablespoons of dough into 1¼-inch balls. Place on ungreased baking sheets.

BAKE in preheated 375°F. oven for 10 to 12 minutes or until cookies are set and lightly browned. Remove from oven. Sift powdered sugar over hot cookies on baking sheets. Cool on baking sheets for 10 minutes; remove to wire racks to cool completely. Sprinkle with additional powdered sugar if desired. Store in airtight containers.

*Makes about 5 dozen cookies*

## 328 LEBKUCHEN JEWELS

¾ cup packed brown sugar
1 egg
1 cup honey
1 tablespoon grated lemon peel
1 teaspoon lemon juice
2¾ cups all-purpose flour
1 teaspoon ground nutmeg
1 teaspoon ground cinnamon
1 teaspoon ground cloves
½ teaspoon baking soda
½ teaspoon salt
1 cup SUN-MAID® Golden Raisins
½ cup each mixed candied fruits and citron
1 cup chopped DIAMOND® Walnuts
   Lemon Glaze (recipe follows)
   Candied cherries and citron, for garnish

Preheat oven to 375°F. In large bowl, beat brown sugar and egg until smooth and fluffy. Add honey, lemon peel and juice; beat well. In medium bowl, sift flour with nutmeg, cinnamon, cloves, baking soda and salt; gradually mix into egg-sugar mixture on low speed of electric mixer. Stir in fruits and nuts. Spread batter into greased 15×10-inch jelly-roll pan.

Bake 20 minutes or until lightly browned. Cool slightly in pan; brush with Lemon Glaze. Cool; cut into diamonds. Decorate with candied cherries and slivers of citron, if desired. Store in covered container up to 1 month. *Makes about 4 dozen cookies*

LEMON GLAZE: In small bowl, combine 1 cup sifted powdered sugar with enough lemon juice (1½ to 2 tablespoons) to make thin glaze.

## 329 DOUBLE–DIPPED CHOCOLATE PEANUT BUTTER COOKIES

1¼ cups all-purpose flour
½ teaspoon baking powder
½ teaspoon baking soda
½ teaspoon salt
½ cup butter or margarine, softened
½ cup granulated sugar
½ cup packed light brown sugar
½ cup creamy or chunky peanut butter
1 egg
1 teaspoon vanilla
  Granulated sugar
1½ cups semisweet chocolate chips
3 teaspoons shortening, divided
1½ cups milk chocolate chips

**PREHEAT** oven to 350°F. Combine flour, baking powder, baking soda and salt in small bowl.

**BEAT** butter, ½ cup granulated sugar and brown sugar in large bowl with electric mixer at medium speed until light and fluffy. Beat in peanut butter, egg and vanilla. Gradually stir in flour mixture until blended.

**SHAPE** heaping tablespoonfuls of dough into 1½-inch balls. Place balls 2 inches apart on *ungreased* cookie sheets. (If dough is too soft, refrigerate 30 minutes.)

**DIP** table fork into granulated sugar; press criss-cross fashion onto each ball, flattening to ½-inch thickness.

**BAKE** 12 minutes or until set. Let cookies stand on cookie sheets 2 minutes; transfer to wire racks to cool completely.

**MELT** semisweet chocolate chips and 1½ teaspoons shortening in heavy small saucepan over low heat. Dip one end of each cookie in mixture; place on waxed paper. Let stand until chocolate is set, about 30 minutes. Repeat with milk chocolate chips and remaining 1½ teaspoons shortening, dipping opposite ends of cookies. Store cookies between sheets of waxed paper in cool place or freeze up to 3 months.

*Makes about 24 (3-inch) cookies*

## 330 YULETIDE LINZER BARS

1⅓ cups butter or margarine, softened
¾ cup sugar
1 egg
1 teaspoon grated lemon peel
2½ cups all-purpose flour
1½ cups whole almonds, ground
1 teaspoon ground cinnamon
¾ cup raspberry preserves
  Powdered sugar

**PREHEAT** oven to 350°F. Grease 13×9-inch baking pan.

**BEAT** butter and sugar in large bowl with electric mixer until creamy. Beat in egg and lemon peel until blended. Mix in flour, almonds and cinnamon until well blended.

**PRESS** 2 cups dough into bottom of prepared pan. Spread preserves over crust. Press remaining dough, a small amount at a time, evenly over preserves.

**BAKE** 35 to 40 minutes until golden brown. Cool on wire rack. Sprinkle with powdered sugar; cut into bars. *Makes 36 bars*

*Yuletide Linzer Bars*

## 331 WALNUT CHRISTMAS BALLS

1 cup California walnuts
⅔ cup powdered sugar, divided
1 cup butter or margarine, softened
1 teaspoon vanilla
1¾ cups all-purpose flour
    Chocolate Filling (recipe follows)

Preheat oven to 350°F. In food processor or blender, process walnuts with 2 tablespoons of the sugar until finely ground; set aside. In large bowl, cream butter and remaining sugar. Beat in vanilla. Add flour and ¾ cup of the walnut mixture; beat until blended. Roll dough into about 3 dozen walnut-size balls. Place 2 inches apart on ungreased cookie sheets.

Bake 10 to 12 minutes or until just golden around edges. Remove to wire racks to cool completely. Prepare Chocolate Filling. Place generous teaspoonful of filling on flat side of half the cookies. Top with remaining cookies, flat side down, forming sandwiches. Roll chocolate edges of cookies in remaining ground walnuts.

*Makes about 1½ dozen sandwich cookies*

**CHOCOLATE FILLING:** Chop 3 squares (1 ounce each) semisweet chocolate into small pieces; place in food processor or blender with ½ teaspoon vanilla. In small saucepan, heat 2 tablespoons *each* butter or margarine and whipping cream over medium heat until hot; pour over chocolate. Process until chocolate is melted, turning machine off and scraping sides as needed. With machine running, gradually add 1 cup powdered sugar; process until smooth.

*Favorite recipe from **Walnut Marketing Board***

## 332 HOLIDAY WREATH COOKIES

1 package (20 ounces) refrigerated sugar
    cookie dough
2 cups shredded coconut
2 to 3 drops green food color
1 container (16 ounces) ready-to-spread
    French vanilla frosting
    Green sugar and small cinnamon
    candies

**1.** Preheat oven to 350°F. Divide cookie dough in half (keep half of dough refrigerated until needed). Roll dough out on well-floured surface to ⅛-inch-thick rectangle. Cut with cookie cutters to resemble wreaths. Repeat with remaining half of dough.

**2.** Place cookies about 2 inches apart onto ungreased baking sheets. Bake 7 to 9 minutes or until edges are lightly browned. Remove cookies from baking sheets to wire rack to cool completely.

**3.** Place coconut in plastic food storage bag. Add food color; seal bag and shake until coconut is evenly colored. Frost cookies with frosting and decorate with coconut or green sugar and cinnamon candies.

*Makes about 2 dozen cookies*

*Holiday Wreath Cookies*

## 333 CHRISTMAS COOKIE HOUSE

**COOKIE DOUGH:**

2¾ cups flour
1 teaspoon ground ginger
½ teaspoon cinnamon
¼ teaspoon salt
⅔ cup KARO® Light Corn Syrup
½ cup packed brown sugar
6 tablespoons MAZOLA® Margarine
   or Butter

   Gingerbread House Cookie Mold*
   MAZOLA NO STICK® Corn Oil Cooking
   Spray
   Decorator Icing (page 299)
   Assorted candy for decorations such as
     colored sugar crystals, spearmint
     leaves, various small colored candies
     or peppermint candies

*All Occasion Gingerbread House Cookie Mold is
available in Williams Sonoma retail stores. To order,
dial 1-800-541-2233.

**1. FOR COOKIE DOUGH:** In large bowl
stir flour, ginger, cinnamon and salt. In
1-quart saucepan combine corn syrup,
brown sugar and margarine; stir over
medium heat until margarine is melted. Stir
into flour mixture until well blended. On
waxed paper, press dough into a rectangle;
cut into three equal parts. (Do not
refrigerate dough before molding.)

**2.** Preheat oven to 350°F. Spray Gingerbread
House Cookie Mold with cooking spray.
Firmly press one-third of dough into mold
sections. Bake 25 minutes or until lightly
browned. Cool 5 minutes. Carefully remove
pieces from mold. Cool on wire racks. Cool
cookie mold until it can be handled. Repeat
to make second half of house.

**3.** On waxed paper-lined cookie sheet, roll
remaining dough ⅛ inch thick. Cut into
people, trees, animals or desired shapes with
cookie cutters. Remove dough trimmings
and reroll; arrange cookies on ungreased
cookie sheets. Bake 10 to 13 minutes or until
lightly browned. Remove from cookie
sheets; cool on wire racks.

**4. TO ASSEMBLE HOUSE:** Cover 13-inch
square of heavy cardboard with foil. In
center draw 5×4½-inch rectangle to serve as
guide for base of house. Fill pastry bag fitted
with plain tip with Decorator Icing.

**5.** On one wall of house, pipe icing along
inside of one side and along bottom edge.
On one side wall of house, pipe icing along
bottom edge. Following guidelines, carefully
stand front and side wall pieces on
cardboard base, placing edge of side wall
against inside edge of front wall. Pipe extra
icing on inside seams for extra strength.
Front and side walls should stand alone. If
necessary, hold in place a few minutes until
icing sets. Repeat with remaining back and
side walls, piping icing along ends of side
walls. Carefully press walls together to form
the house. Let stand 10 minutes to set.

**6. TO ATTACH ROOF:** Pipe icing along top
edge of front wall, and front half of side
walls. Place one roof piece on top of house;
hold or prop in place about 5 minutes or
until set. Pipe icing along top edge of back
wall and back half of side walls. Pipe icing
along roof edges where roof pieces will
meet. Place remaining roof section on house
so that roof pieces meet to form peak; hold
or prop in place about 5 minutes or until set.
Use icing to fill in any spaces along peak of
house. Attach chimney with icing.

**7.** Use icing to attach candies to roof and chimney. Add spearmint leaf "shrubs" to sides of house and a candy pathway. Decorate cookie trees and people with icing, colored sugars and candies. Attach to base with icing.

**Prep Time:** 3 hours
**Bake Time:** 50 minutes, plus cooling

**DECORATOR ICING:** In large bowl with mixer at low speed, beat 1 pound confectioners' sugar, ½ cup warm water, 3 tablespoons meringue powder** and ½ teaspoon cream of tartar until blended. Beat at high speed 7 to 10 minutes or until knife drawn through mixture leaves a path. Divide and color as desired. Keep covered with damp cloth at all times. Makes about 2 cups.

*\*\*Meringue powder is available from specialty cake decorating suppliers or by contacting Wilton Industries, 2240 West 75th Street, Woodridge, IL 60517. Phone: (708) 963-7100, ext. 320.*

*Christmas Cookie House*

## 334 SANTA'S CHOCOLATE COOKIES

1 cup margarine or butter
⅔ cup semisweet chocolate chips
¾ cup sugar
1 egg
½ teaspoon vanilla
2 cups all-purpose flour
   Apricot jam, melted semisweet
      chocolate, chopped almonds, frosting,
      coconut or colored sprinkles

Preheat oven to 350°F. Melt margarine with ⅔ cup chocolate chips in small saucepan over low heat stirring until completely melted, or place in microwavable bowl and microwave at HIGH 2 to 2½ minutes, stirring after every minute. Combine chocolate mixture and sugar in large bowl. Add egg and vanilla; stir well. Add flour; stir well. Refrigerate, covered, 30 minutes or until firm.

Shape dough into 1-inch balls or 2-inch logs. Place 1 inch apart on ungreased cookie sheets. If desired, flatten balls with bottom of drinking glass; make a depression in center and fill with jam.

Bake 8 to 10 minutes or until set. Remove to wire racks; cool completely. Decorate as desired with melted chocolate, almonds, frosting, coconut and colored sprinkles.

*Makes about 3 dozen cookies*

## 335 PFEFFERNÜSSE

3½ cups all-purpose flour
  2 teaspoons baking powder
1½ teaspoons ground cinnamon
  1 teaspoon ground ginger
  ½ teaspoon baking soda
  ½ teaspoon salt
  ½ teaspoon ground cloves
  ½ teaspoon ground cardamom
  ¼ teaspoon freshly ground black pepper
  1 cup butter, softened
  1 cup granulated sugar
  ¼ cup dark molasses
  1 egg
    Powdered sugar

**COMBINE** flour, baking powder, cinnamon, ginger, baking soda, salt, cloves, cardamom and pepper in large bowl.

**BEAT** butter and granulated sugar in large bowl with electric mixer at medium speed until light and fluffy. Beat in molasses and egg. Gradually add flour mixture. Beat at low speed until dough forms. Shape dough into disk; wrap in plastic wrap and refrigerate until firm, 30 minutes or up to 3 days.

**PREHEAT** oven to 350°F. Grease cookie sheets. Roll dough into 1-inch balls. Place 2 inches apart on prepared cookie sheets.

**BAKE** 12 to 14 minutes or until golden brown. Transfer cookies to wire racks; dust with sifted powdered sugar. Cool completely. Store tightly covered at room temperature or freeze up to 3 months.

*Makes about 60 cookies*

## 336 BASIC HOLIDAY RAISIN COOKIES

½ cup butter or margarine, softened
⅓ cup sugar
1 egg yolk
⅛ teaspoon salt
1 cup all-purpose flour
½ cup raisins
    Semisweet or white chocolate
    Colored sprinkles, raisins, nuts or
        candied fruit pieces, for decoration

Cream butter and sugar; beat in egg yolk and salt. Add flour just to blend thoroughly. Mix in raisins. On lightly floured surface, roll into 12-inch log. Wrap securely and refrigerate at least 1 hour or up to 1 week.

Preheat oven to 350°F. With sharp knife, slice cookies ⅓ inch thick; place 1 inch apart on ungreased baking sheets. Bake 15 to 20 minutes until cookies are set and bottoms are lightly browned. Remove to racks to cool completely. Decorate as desired with melted semisweet or white chocolate and top with colored sprinkles, raisins, nuts or candied fruit pieces. Cool; store between sheets of waxed paper in airtight container.

*Makes 3 dozen cookies*

*Favorite recipe from* **California Raisin Advisory Board**

## 337 MAPLE WALNUT MERINGUES

⅓ cup powdered sugar
½ cup plus ⅓ cup ground walnuts, divided
¾ cup packed light brown sugar
3 egg whites, at room temperature
    Pinch salt
⅛ teaspoon cream of tartar
1 teaspoon maple extract

**PLACE** 1 oven rack in the top third of oven and 1 oven rack in the bottom third of oven; preheat oven to 300°F. Line 2 large cookie sheets with aluminum foil, shiny side up.

**STIR** powdered sugar and ½ cup walnuts with fork in medium bowl; set aside. Crumble brown sugar into small bowl; set aside.

**BEAT** egg whites and salt in large bowl with electric mixer at high speed until foamy. Add cream of tartar; beat 30 seconds or until mixture forms soft peaks. Sprinkle brown sugar, 1 tablespoon at a time, over egg white mixture; beat at high speed until each addition is completely absorbed. Beat 2 to 3 minutes or until mixture forms stiff peaks. Beat in maple extract at low speed. Fold in walnut mixture with large rubber spatula.

**DROP** level tablespoonfuls of dough to form mounds about 1 inch apart on prepared cookie sheets. Sprinkle cookies with remaining ⅓ cup ground walnuts. Bake 25 minutes or until cookies feel dry on surface but remain soft inside. (Rotate cookie sheets from top to bottom halfway through baking time.)

**SLIDE** foil with cookies onto wire racks; cool completely. Carefully remove cookies from foil. Store in airtight container with waxed paper between layers of cookies. Cookies are best the day they are baked.

*Makes about 36 cookies*

## 338 FESTIVE RUGELACH

1½ cups (3 sticks) butter or margarine, softened
12 ounces cream cheese, softened
3½ cups all-purpose flour, divided
½ cup powdered sugar
¾ cup granulated sugar
1½ teaspoons ground cinnamon
1¾ cups "M&M's"® Chocolate Mini Baking Bits, divided
Powdered sugar

Preheat oven to 350°F. Lightly grease cookie sheets; set aside. In large bowl cream butter and cream cheese. Slowly work in *3 cups flour*. Divide dough into 6 equal pieces and shape into squares. Lightly flour dough, wrap in waxed paper and refrigerate at least 1 hour. Combine remaining *½ cup flour* and ½ cup powdered sugar. Remove one piece of dough at a time from refrigerator; roll out on surface dusted with flour-sugar mixture to 18×5×⅛-inch-thick strip. Combine granulated sugar and cinnamon. Sprinkle dough strip with 2 tablespoons cinnamon-sugar mixture. Sprinkle about *¼ cup "M&M's"® Chocolate Mini Baking Bits* on wide end of each strip. Roll dough starting at wide end to completely enclose baking bits. Cut strip into 1½-inch lengths; place seam-side down about 2 inches apart onto prepared cookie sheets. Repeat with remaining ingredients. Bake 16 to 18 minutes or until golden. Cool completely on wire racks. Sprinkle with powdered sugar. Store in tightly covered container.

*Makes about 6 dozen cookies*

VARIATION: For crescent shapes, roll each piece of dough into 12-inch circle. Sprinkle with cinnamon-sugar mixture. Cut into 12 wedges. Place about *½ teaspoon "M&M's"® Chocolate Mini Baking Bits* at wide end of each wedge and roll up to enclose baking bits. Place seam-side down on prepared baking sheet and proceed as directed.

## 339 FRUIT BURST COOKIES

1 cup margarine or butter, softened
¼ cup sugar
1 teaspoon almond extract
2 cups all-purpose flour
½ teaspoon salt
1 cup finely chopped nuts
SMUCKER'S® Simply Fruit

Preheat oven to 400°F. Cream margarine and sugar until light and fluffy. Blend in almond extract. Combine flour and salt; add to margarine mixture and blend well. Shape level tablespoons of dough into balls; roll in nuts. Place 2 inches apart on ungreased cookie sheets; flatten slightly. Indent centers; fill with fruit spread.

Bake 10 to 12 minutes or just until lightly browned. Cool on wire racks.

*Makes about 2½ dozen cookies*

*Festive Rugelach*

## 340 CHUNKY BUTTER CHRISTMAS COOKIES

1¼ cups butter, softened
1 cup packed brown sugar
½ cup dairy sour cream
1 egg
2 teaspoons vanilla
1½ cups all-purpose flour
1 teaspoon baking soda
1 teaspoon salt
1½ cups old fashioned or quick oats, uncooked
1 (10-ounce) package white chocolate pieces
1 cup flaked coconut
1 (3½-ounce) jar macadamia nuts, coarsely chopped

Beat butter and sugar in large bowl until light and fluffy. Blend in sour cream, egg and vanilla. Add combined flour, baking soda and salt; mix well. Stir in oats, white chocolate pieces, coconut and nuts. Drop rounded teaspoonfuls of dough, 2-inches apart, onto ungreased cookie sheet. Bake in preheated 375°F oven 10 to 12 minutes or until edges are lightly browned. Cool 1 minute; remove to cooling rack. *Makes 5 dozen*

*Favorite recipe from* **Wisconsin Milk Marketing Board**

## 341 CRISPY THUMBPRINT COOKIES

1 package (18.25 ounces) yellow cake mix
½ cup vegetable oil
1 egg
3 cups crisp rice cereal, crushed
½ cup chopped walnuts
Raspberry or strawberry preserves

**1.** Preheat oven to 375°F.

**2.** Combine cake mix, oil, egg and ¼ cup water. Beat at medium speed of electric mixer until well blended. Add cereal and walnuts; mix until well blended.

**3.** Drop by heaping teaspoonfuls about 2 inches apart onto ungreased baking sheets. Use thumb to make indentation in each cookie. Spoon about ½ teaspoon preserves into center of each cookie. (Or, place ½ of mint candy in center of each cookie).

**4.** Bake 9 to 11 minutes or until golden brown. Cool cookies 1 minute on baking sheet; remove from baking sheet to wire rack to cool completely.
*Makes 3 dozen cookies*

*Crispy Thumbprint Cookies*

## 342 SPRITZ COOKIES

1¼ cups granulated sugar
  1 BUTTER FLAVOR* CRISCO® Stick or
    1 cup BUTTER FLAVOR CRISCO
    all-vegetable shortening
  2 eggs
¼ cup light corn syrup or regular pancake
    syrup
  1 tablespoon vanilla
  3 cups all-purpose flour
¾ teaspoon baking powder
½ teaspoon baking soda
½ teaspoon salt
    Colored sugar crystals (optional)
    Nonpareils (optional)
    Chocolate jimmies (optional)

*Butter Flavor Crisco is artificially flavored.*

**1.** Heat oven to 375°F. Place sheets of foil on
countertop for cooling cookies.

**2.** Place sugar and shortening in large bowl.
Beat at medium speed of electric mixer until
well blended. Add eggs, syrup and vanilla;
beat until well blended and fluffy.

**3.** Combine flour, baking powder, baking
soda and salt. Add gradually to shortening
mixture; beat at low speed until well
blended.

**4.** Fill cookie press with dough, following
manufacturer's directions. Press dough
about 1½ inches apart on ungreased baking
sheet. Sprinkle with colored sugar,
nonpareils or chocolate jimmies, if desired.

**5.** Bake one sheet at a time at 375°F for 7 to
9 minutes or until bottoms of cookies are
golden. *Do not overbake.* Cool 2 minutes on
baking sheet. Remove cookies to foil to cool
completely.

*Makes about 7½ dozen cookies*

## 343 FROSTY'S COLORFUL COOKIES

1¼ cups firmly packed light brown sugar
¾ BUTTER FLAVOR* CRISCO® Stick or
    ¾ cup BUTTER FLAVOR CRISCO
    all-vegetable shortening
  2 tablespoons milk
  1 tablespoon vanilla
  1 egg
1¾ cups all-purpose flour
  1 teaspoon salt
¾ teaspoon baking soda
  2 cups red and green candy-coated
    chocolate pieces

*Butter Flavor Crisco is artificially flavored.*

**1.** Heat oven to 375°F. Place sheets of foil on
countertop for cooling cookies.

**2.** Place brown sugar, shortening, milk and
vanilla in large bowl. Beat at medium speed
of electric mixer until well blended. Add egg;
beat well.

**3.** Combine flour, salt and baking soda. Add
to shortening mixture; beat at low speed just
until blended. Stir in candy-coated chocolate
pieces.

**4.** Drop dough by rounded measuring
tablespoonfuls 3 inches apart onto
ungreased baking sheets.

**5.** Bake one baking sheet at a time at 375°F
for 8 to 10 minutes for chewy cookies, or
11 to 13 minutes for crisp cookies. *Do not
overbake.* Cool 2 minutes on baking sheet.
Remove cookies to foil to cool completely.

*Makes about 3 dozen cookies*

*Snow-Covered Almond Crescents*

## 344 SNOW–COVERED ALMOND CRESCENTS

1 cup (2 sticks) margarine or butter,
   softened
¾ cup powdered sugar
½ teaspoon almond extract *or* 2 teaspoons
   vanilla extract
2 cups all-purpose flour
¼ teaspoon salt (optional)
1 cup QUAKER® Oats (quick or
   old-fashioned, uncooked)
½ cup finely chopped almonds
   Additional powdered sugar

Preheat oven to 325°F. Beat margarine,
¾ cup powdered sugar and almond extract
until fluffy. Add flour and salt; mix until well
blended. Stir in oats and almonds. Shape
level measuring tablespoonfuls of dough
into crescents. Place on ungreased cookie
sheet about 2 inches apart.

Bake 14 to 17 minutes or until bottoms are
light golden brown. Remove to wire rack.
Sift additional powdered sugar generously
over warm cookies. Cool completely. Store
tightly covered.

*Makes about 4 dozen cookies*

## 345 CHOCOLATE–FROSTED LEBKUCHEN

4 eggs
1 cup sugar
1½ cups all-purpose flour
1 cup (6 ounces) pulverized almonds*
⅓ cup candied lemon peel, finely chopped
⅓ cup candied orange peel, finely chopped
1½ teaspoons ground cinnamon
1 teaspoon grated lemon rind
½ teaspoon ground cardamom
½ teaspoon ground nutmeg
¼ teaspoon ground cloves
Bittersweet Glaze (recipe follows)

*To pulverize almonds, place in food processor or blender. Process until thoroughly ground with a dry, not pasty, texture.*

In large bowl of electric mixer, combine eggs and sugar. Beat at high speed for 10 minutes. Meanwhile, in separate bowl, combine flour, almonds, lemon and orange peels, cinnamon, lemon rind, cardamom, nutmeg and cloves. Blend in egg mixture, stirring until evenly mixed. Cover; refrigerate 12 hours or overnight.

Preheat oven to 350°F. Grease cookie sheets and dust with flour or line with parchment paper. Drop dough by rounded teaspoonfuls 2 inches apart onto prepared cookie sheets. Bake 8 to 10 minutes or until just barely browned. Do not overbake. Remove to wire racks. While cookies bake, prepare Bittersweet Glaze. Spread over tops of warm cookies using pastry brush. Cool until glaze is set. Store in airtight container.

*Makes about 5 dozen cookies*

### BITTERSWEET GLAZE

3 squares (1 ounce each) bittersweet or semisweet chocolate, chopped
1 tablespoon butter or margarine

Melt chocolate and butter in small bowl over hot water. Stir until smooth.

## 346 JINGLE JUMBLES

¾ cup butter or margarine, softened
1 cup packed brown sugar
¼ cup molasses
1 egg
2¼ cups unsifted all-purpose flour
2 teaspoons baking soda
1 teaspoon ground ginger
1 teaspoon ground cinnamon
½ teaspoon salt
½ teaspoon ground cloves
1¼ cups SUN-MAID® Raisins
Granulated sugar

In large bowl, cream butter and sugar. Add molasses and egg; beat until fluffy. In medium bowl, sift together flour, baking soda, ginger, cinnamon, salt and cloves. Stir into molasses mixture. Stir in raisins. Cover and chill about 30 minutes.

Preheat oven to 375°F. Grease cookie sheets. Form dough into 1½-inch balls; roll in granulated sugar, coating generously. Place 2 inches apart on prepared cookie sheets.

Bake 12 to 14 minutes or until edges are firm and centers are still slightly soft. Remove to wire rack to cool.

*Makes about 2 dozen cookies*

## HOLIDAY HAPPENINGS

### 347 HONEY NUT RUGELACH

1 cup butter or margarine, softened
3 ounces cream cheese, softened
½ cup honey, divided
2 cups all-purpose flour
1 teaspoon lemon juice
1 teaspoon ground cinnamon, divided
1 cup finely chopped walnuts
½ cup dried cherries or cranberries

Cream butter and cream cheese until fluffy. Add 3 tablespoons honey; mix well. Mix in flour until dough holds together. Shape dough into a ball. Wrap tightly with plastic wrap; refrigerate at least 2 hours. Divide dough into quarters. Place one quarter on lightly floured surface and roll into 9-inch circle. Combine 2 tablespoons honey and lemon juice; mix well. Brush dough with honey mixture; sprinkle ¼ teaspoon cinnamon over entire surface. Combine walnuts and cherries. Drizzle remaining honey over walnut mixture; mix well. Spread ¼ of the walnut mixture onto dough, leaving ½-inch border. Cut into 8 triangular pieces. Roll each piece starting at wide outer edge rolling towards tip. Gently bend ends to form crescent. Place rugelach on greased parchment paper-lined baking sheet; refrigerate at least 20 minutes. Repeat process with remaining dough and filling. Bake at 350°F 20 to 25 minutes or until golden brown. Cool on wire racks.

*Makes 32 cookies*

*Favorite recipe from* **National Honey Board**

### 348 HOLIDAY CHOCOLATE SHORTBREAD COOKIES

1 cup (2 sticks) butter, softened
1¼ cups powdered sugar
1 teaspoon vanilla extract
½ cup HERSHEY'S European Style Cocoa or HERSHEY'S Cocoa
1¾ cups all-purpose flour
1⅔ cups (10-ounce package) HERSHEY'S Premier White Chips

**1.** Heat oven to 300°F.

**2.** In large bowl, beat butter, powdered sugar and vanilla until creamy. Add cocoa; blend well. Gradually add flour, stirring until smooth.

**3.** On lightly floured surface or between 2 pieces of wax paper, roll or pat dough to ¼-inch thickness. With 2-inch cookie cutters, cut into holiday shapes. Reroll dough scraps, cutting cookies until dough is used. Place on ungreased cookie sheet.

**4.** Bake 15 to 20 minutes or just until firm. Immediately place white chips, flat side down, in decorative design on warm cookies. Cool slightly; remove from cookie sheet to wire rack. Cool completely. Store in airtight container.

*Makes about 4½ dozen cookies*

**NOTE:** For more even baking, place similar shapes and sizes of cookies on same cookie sheet.

## 349 JOLLY PEANUT BUTTER GINGERBREAD COOKIES

1⅔ cups (10-ounce package) REESE'S® Peanut Butter Chips
¾ cup (1½ sticks) butter or margarine, softened
1 cup packed light brown sugar
1 cup dark corn syrup
2 eggs
5 cups all-purpose flour
1 teaspoon baking soda
½ teaspoon ground cinnamon
¼ teaspoon ground ginger
¼ teaspoon salt

1. In small microwave-safe bowl, place peanut butter chips. Microwave at HIGH (100%) 1 to 2 minutes or until chips are melted when stirred. In large bowl, beat melted peanut butter chips and butter until well blended. Add brown sugar, corn syrup and eggs; beat until light and fluffy. Stir together flour, baking soda, cinnamon, ginger and salt. Add half of flour mixture to butter mixture; beat on low speed of electric mixer until smooth. With wooden spoon, stir in remaining flour mixture until well blended. Divide into thirds; wrap each in plastic wrap. Refrigerate at least 1 hour or until dough is firm enough to roll.

2. Heat oven to 325°F.

3. On lightly floured surface, roll 1 dough portion at a time to ⅛-inch thickness; with floured cookie cutters, cut into holiday shapes. Place on ungreased cookie sheet.

4. Bake 10 to 12 minutes or until set and lightly browned. Cool slightly; remove from cookie sheet to wire rack. Cool completely. Frost and decorate as desired.
*Makes about 6 dozen cookies*

## 350 APPLE SAUCE GINGERBREAD COOKIES

4 cups all-purpose flour
2 teaspoons ground ginger
2 teaspoons ground cinnamon
1 teaspoon baking soda
½ teaspoon salt
¼ teaspoon ground nutmeg
½ cup margarine, softened
1 cup sugar
⅓ cup light (gold label) molasses
1 cup MOTT'S® Natural Apple Sauce
Decorator Icing (recipe follows)

Sift together flour, ginger, cinnamon, baking soda, salt and nutmeg; set aside. In bowl, with electric mixer at high speed, beat margarine, sugar and molasses until creamy. Alternately blend in dry ingredients and apple sauce. Cover and chill dough for several hours or overnight.

Preheat oven to 375°F. On floured surface, roll dough out to ⅛-inch thickness with lightly floured rolling pin. Cut with floured gingerbread man cutter or other shapes. Place on greased baking sheet. Bake 12 minutes or until done. Remove from sheet; cool on wire rack. Frost with Decorator Icing as desired. After icing dries, store in airtight container.
*Makes 2½ dozen (5½-inch) cookies*

**DECORATOR ICING:** Mix 2 cups confectioners' sugar and 1 tablespoon water. Add more water, 1 teaspoon at a time, until icing holds its shape and can be piped through a decorating tube.

*Jolly Peanut Butter Gingerbread Cookies*

## 351 DATE–NUT COOKIES

    1 cup chopped dates
    ½ cup water
 1¾ cups all-purpose flour
    ½ teaspoon baking powder
    ⅛ teaspoon salt
    ½ cup butter, softened
    ½ cup packed dark brown sugar
    1 egg
    2 teaspoons rum extract
    ½ cup walnut pieces, chopped

**SOAK** dates in water in small bowl at least 30 minutes or up to 2 hours.

**PREHEAT** oven to 350°F. Grease cookie sheets. Combine flour, baking powder and salt in medium bowl.

**BEAT** butter in large bowl at medium speed until smooth. Gradually beat in sugar; increase speed to high and beat until light and fluffy. Beat in egg and rum extract until fluffy. Gradually stir in flour mixture alternately with date mixture, mixing just until combined after each addition. Stir in walnuts until blended.

**DROP** level tablespoonfuls of dough about 1½ inches apart onto prepared cookie sheets. Bake 14 minutes or until just set. Transfer to wire racks to cool completely. Store in airtight container.

*Makes 24 cookies*

## 352 BUTTERY ALMOND COOKIES

 1¼ cups all-purpose flour
    ½ teaspoon baking powder
    ⅛ teaspoon salt
 1¼ cups slivered almonds, divided
  10 tablespoons butter, softened
    ¾ cup sugar
    1 egg
    1 teaspoon vanilla

**PREHEAT** oven to 350°F. Grease cookie sheets. Combine flour, baking powder and salt in small bowl.

**FINELY CHOP** ¾ cup almonds; set aside.

**BEAT** butter in large bowl with electric mixer at medium speed until smooth. Gradually beat in sugar until blended; increase speed to high and beat until light and fluffy. Beat in egg until fluffy. Beat in vanilla until blended. Stir in flour mixture until blended. Stir in chopped almonds just until combined.

**DROP** rounded teaspoonfuls of dough about 2 inches apart onto prepared cookie sheets. Top each cookie with several slivered almonds, pressing into dough.

**BAKE** 12 minutes or until edges are golden brown. Let cookies stand on cookie sheets 5 minutes; transfer to wire racks to cool completely. Store in airtight container.

*Makes about 42 cookies*

*Date-Nut Cookies*

## 353 PEANUT BUTTER GINGERBREAD MEN

5 cups all-purpose flour
1½ teaspoons ground cinnamon
1 teaspoon baking soda
½ teaspoon ground ginger
¼ teaspoon salt
¾ cup (1½ sticks) MAZOLA® Margarine, softened
¾ cup SKIPPY® Creamy Peanut Butter
1 cup packed brown sugar
1 cup KARO® Dark Corn Syrup
2 eggs
Frosting for decorating (optional)

**1.** In large bowl, combine flour, cinnamon, baking soda, ginger and salt; set aside.

**2.** In separate large bowl, beat margarine and peanut butter until well blended. Add brown sugar, corn syrup and eggs; beat until smooth. Gradually beat in 2 cups of the dry ingredients. With wooden spoon, beat in remaining dry ingredients, 1 cup at a time, until well blended. Divide dough into thirds. Wrap each portion; refrigerate until firm, at least 1 hour.

**3.** Preheat oven to 300°F. Roll out dough, one third at a time, ⅛ inch thick on lightly floured surface. Cut out with 5½-inch gingerbread cutter. Place 2 inches apart on ungreased cookie sheets.

**4.** Bake 10 to 12 minutes or until very lightly browned. Remove to wire racks to cool completely. If desired, pipe frosting on cookies to make eyes and buttons.

*Makes about 2½ dozen cookies*

## 354 CANDY CANE & WREATH ORNAMENTS

1 cup sugar
½ cup shortening
½ cup butter or margarine
1 teaspoon salt
1 egg
2 teaspoons vanilla
2½ cups all-purpose flour
½ teaspoon almond extract
¼ teaspoon liquid green food coloring
¼ teaspoon peppermint extract
½ teaspoon liquid red food coloring, divided
Decorator Frosting (page 315)

**EQUIPMENT AND DECORATIONS:**
Assorted red candies
Ribbon

**1.** Beat sugar, shortening, butter and salt in large bowl with electric mixer at medium speed until light and fluffy. Beat in egg and vanilla until well blended. Beat in flour at low speed until soft dough forms. Remove half of dough from bowl. Set aside. Divide remaining dough evenly between 2 medium bowls. Stir almond extract and green food coloring into one portion with wooden spoon until well blended. Stir peppermint extract and ¼ teaspoon red food coloring into remaining portion until well blended.

**2.** Place level teaspoonfuls of each dough on large baking sheet. Cover; refrigerate 15 minutes or until slightly firm.

**3.** Preheat oven to 375°F. Place 1 teaspoon red dough, 1 teaspoon green dough and 2 teaspoons uncolored dough on lightly floured surface. Roll out each portion into 6- to 7-inch rope with lightly floured hands. Place 1 green rope next to 1 uncolored rope and 1 red rope next to remaining uncolored rope. Twist each pair of ropes together 7 or 8 times; place on *ungreased* baking sheet.

**Candy Cane & Wreath Ornaments**

**4.** Shape red and white rope into candy cane and green and white rope into wreath. Repeat with remaining dough.

**5.** Bake 7 to 9 minutes or until cookies are firm. *Do not allow to brown.* Transfer cookies with spatula to wire racks; cool completely.

**6.** Prepare Decorator Frosting. Tint half of frosting with remaining ¼ teaspoon red liquid food coloring. Spoon frostings into piping bags fitted with writing tips. Pipe cluster of berries onto wreaths with red frosting. Glue candies onto wreaths with white frosting. Let stand 1 hour or until icing is set. Tie ribbon loops or bows onto each cookie for hanging.

*Makes about 4 dozen cookies*

**DECORATOR FROSTING**
   ¾ **cup butter, softened**
4½ **cups powdered sugar, sifted**
   3 **tablespoons water**
   1 **teaspoon vanilla**
   ¼ **teaspoon lemon extract**

Beat butter in medium bowl with electric mixer at medium speed until smooth. Add 2 cups sugar. Beat at medium speed until light and fluffy. Add water and extracts. Beat at low speed until well blended. Beat in remaining 2½ cups sugar until mixture is creamy.                                    *Makes 2 cups*

**NOTE:** This frosting is perfect for piping, but is less durable than Royal Icing (page 267). Bumping, stacking and handling may damage decorations.

## 355 YULETIDE TOFFEE SQUARES

4½ cups quick or old-fashioned oats
1 cup packed brown sugar
¾ cup (1½ sticks) butter or margarine, melted
½ cup light corn syrup
1 tablespoon vanilla extract
½ teaspoon salt
2 cups (12-ounce package) NESTLÉ® TOLL HOUSE® Semi-Sweet Chocolate Morsels
⅔ cup chopped nuts

**COMBINE** oats, brown sugar, butter, corn syrup, vanilla and salt in large bowl; mix well. Firmly press mixture into greased 15½×10½-inch jelly-roll pan.

**BAKE** in preheated 400°F. oven for 18 minutes or until mixture is browned and bubbly. Remove from oven. Immediately sprinkle chocolate morsels evenly over toffee. Let stand 10 minutes.

**SPREAD** chocolate evenly over toffee; sprinkle with nuts. Cool completely; cut into squares. Store tightly covered in cool, dry place.          *Makes 6 dozen squares*

## 356 FROSTY CHERRY COOKIES

½ cup (1 stick) butter or margarine
1 cup plus 3 tablespoons sugar, divided
1 egg, slightly beaten
½ teaspoon almond extract
1½ cups all-purpose flour
½ teaspoon salt
½ teaspoon baking soda
½ teaspoon baking powder
2 cups RICE CHEX® brand cereal, crushed to 1 cup
½ cup chopped green and red glace cherries

Preheat oven to 350°F. In large bowl, combine butter and 1 cup sugar. Stir in egg and almond extract. Stir in flour, salt, baking soda and baking powder; mix well. Stir in cereal and cherries. Shape into ¾-inch balls. In small bowl, place remaining 3 tablespoons sugar. Roll balls in sugar. Place, 2 inches apart, on baking sheet. Bake 8 to 10 minutes or until bottoms are lightly browned.          *Makes 6 dozen cookies*

## HOLIDAY HAPPENINGS

### 357 BASIC BANANA HOLIDAY COOKIES

2¾ cups all-purpose flour
1 teaspoon baking soda
¼ teaspoon salt
1 cup margarine, softened
1¼ cups granulated sugar, divided
¼ cup packed brown sugar
1 egg
1 large, ripe DOLE® Banana, mashed (about ½ cup)
½ teaspoon ground cinnamon

• **Combine** flour, baking soda and salt in medium bowl; set aside.

• **Beat** together margarine, 1 cup granulated sugar and brown sugar in large bowl until creamy. Beat in egg and banana until blended. Stir in flour mixture until combined. Cover and chill 2 hours or overnight until dough is firm enough to handle.

• **Combine** remaining ¼ cup granulated sugar and cinnamon in small bowl.

• **Shape** dough into 1-inch balls. Roll in cinnamon mixture; place two inches apart on ungreased baking sheets.

• **Bake** at 350°F 10 to 12 minutes or until lightly browned. Carefully remove cookies to wire rack to cool completely.

*Makes 4½ dozen*

**Prep:** 15 min.
**Bake:** 12 min.

VARIATIONS:
**CHOCOLATE BANANA STARS:** Prepare, shape and bake dough as directed except roll dough in 1 cup finely chopped DOLE Almonds instead of cinnamon mixture. Immediately after baking, press unwrapped individual milk chocolate pieces into center of each cookie. Cool as directed.

**BANANA CHIPPERS:** Prepare and shape dough as directed except stir in 1 package (10 ounces) peanut butter chips and 1 cup chopped pecans or walnuts into dough and omit cinnamon mixture. Bake and cool as directed.

**ZANA KRINGLES:** Stir 1 teaspoon ground ginger into flour mixture and replace brown sugar with 2 tablespoons molasses. Prepare, shape, bake and cool as directed.

## 358 DANISH LEMON–FILLED SPICE COOKIES (MEDALJEKAGER)

2¼ cups all-purpose flour
1 teaspoon ground cinnamon
½ teaspoon ground allspice
½ teaspoon ground ginger
½ teaspoon ground nutmeg
¼ teaspoon salt
1 large egg yolk
¾ cup butter, softened
¾ cup sugar
¼ cup milk
1 teaspoon vanilla
Lemon Filling (recipe follows)

**1.** Grease cookie sheets; set aside. Place flour, cinnamon, allspice, ginger, nutmeg and salt in medium bowl; stir to combine.

**2.** Place egg yolk in large bowl; add butter, sugar, milk and vanilla. Beat with electric mixer at medium speed until light and fluffy. Gradually add flour mixture. Beat at low speed until dough forms. Form dough into a disc; wrap in plastic and refrigerate 30 minutes or until firm.

**3.** Preheat oven to 350°F. Roll teaspoonfuls of dough into ½-inch balls; place 2 inches apart on prepared cookie sheets. Flatten each ball to ¼-inch thickness with bottom of glass dipped in sugar. Prick top of each cookie using fork.

**4.** Bake 10 to 13 minutes or until golden brown. Remove cookies with spatula to wire racks; cool completely.

**5.** Prepare Lemon Filling. Spread filling on flat side of half of cookies. Top with remaining cookies, pressing flat sides together. Let stand at room temperature until set. Store tightly covered at room temperature or freeze up to 3 months.
*Makes about 3 dozen sandwiches*

**LEMON FILLING**
2¼ cups sifted powdered sugar
1½ tablespoons butter, softened
3 tablespoons lemon juice
½ teaspoon lemon extract

Beat all ingredients in medium bowl with electric mixer at medium speed until smooth. *Makes about 1 cup filling*

## 359 SNOWBALLS

1 cup butter or margarine, softened
½ cup DOMINO® Confectioners 10-X Sugar
¼ teaspoon salt
1 teaspoon vanilla extract
2¼ cups all-purpose flour
½ cup chopped pecans
Additional DOMINO® Confectioners 10-X Sugar

In large bowl, beat butter, ½ cup sugar and salt until fluffy. Add vanilla. Gradually stir in flour. Blend nuts into dough. Cover and refrigerate until firm.

Preheat oven to 400°F. Form dough into 1-inch balls. Place 1 inch apart on ungreased cookie sheets.

Bake 8 to 10 minutes or until set, but not brown. Immediately roll in additional sugar. Cool on wire racks. Roll in sugar again. Store in airtight container.
*Makes about 5 dozen cookies*

*Danish Lemon-Filled Spice Cookies (Medaljekager)*

## 360 HOLIDAY HIDEAWAYS

**COOKIES**
- ⅔ BUTTER FLAVOR* CRISCO® Stick or ⅔ cup BUTTER FLAVOR CRISCO all-vegetable shortening
- ¾ cup sugar
- 1 egg
- 1 tablespoon milk
- 1 teaspoon vanilla
- 1¾ cups all-purpose flour
- 1 teaspoon baking powder
- ½ teaspoon salt
- ½ teaspoon baking soda
- 48 maraschino cherries, well drained on paper towels

**DIPPING CHOCOLATE**
- 1 cup white or dark melting chocolate, cut in small pieces
- 2 tablespoons BUTTER FLAVOR CRISCO all-vegetable shortening
- Finely chopped pecans
- Slivered white chocolate

*Butter Flavor Crisco is artificially flavored.*

Preheat oven to 350°F. For Cookies, cream shortening, sugar, egg, milk and vanilla in large bowl at medium speed of electric mixer until well blended. Combine flour, baking powder, salt and baking soda; beat into creamed mixture at low speed. Press dough in very thin layer around well-drained cherries. Place 2 inches apart on ungreased cookie sheet. Bake 10 minutes. Cool on cookie sheet 1 minute; remove to cooling rack. Cool completely.

For Dipping Chocolate, melt chocolate of choice and shortening in small saucepan over very low heat or 50% power in microwave; stir. Transfer chocolate to glass measuring cup. Drop one cookie at a time into chocolate. Use fork to turn, covering cookie completely in chocolate. (If chocolate becomes too firm, microwave on low to reheat.) Lift cookie out of chocolate on fork, allowing excess to drip off. Place on waxed paper-lined cookie sheet. Before chocolate sets, sprinkle chopped pecans on top of white chocolate cookies or white chocolate on top of dark chocolate cookies. Chill in refrigerator to set chocolate.

*Makes about 4 dozen cookies*

## 361 FESTIVE FUDGE BLOSSOMS

- 1 box (18.25 ounces) chocolate fudge cake mix
- ¼ cup butter or margarine, softened
- 1 egg, slightly beaten
- ¾ to 1 cup finely chopped walnuts
- 48 chocolate star candies

**1.** Preheat oven to 350°F. Cut butter into cake mix in large bowl until mixture resembles coarse crumbs. Stir in egg and 2 tablespoons water until well blended.

**2.** Shape dough into ½-inch balls; roll in walnuts, pressing nuts gently into dough. Place about 2 inches apart onto ungreased baking sheets.

**3.** Bake cookies 12 minutes or until puffed and nearly set. Place chocolate star in center of each cookie; bake 1 minute more. Cool 2 minutes on baking sheet. Remove cookies from baking sheets to wire rack to cool completely. *Makes 4 dozen cookies*

*Festive Fudge Blossoms*

## 362 CHRISTMAS SPRITZ COOKIES

2¼ cups all-purpose flour
¼ teaspoon salt
1¼ cups powdered sugar
1 cup butter, softened
1 large egg
1 teaspoon vanilla
1 teaspoon almond extract
   Green food coloring (optional)
   Candied red and green cherries and
      assorted decorative candies, as
      desired

**1.** Preheat oven to 375°F. Place flour and salt in medium bowl; stir to combine.

**2.** Beat powdered sugar and butter in large bowl with electric mixer until light and fluffy. Beat in egg, vanilla and almond extract. Gradually add flour mixture. Beat at low speed until well blended. Divide dough in half. If desired, tint half the dough green with food coloring.

**3.** Fit cookie press with desired plate (or change plates for different shapes after first batch). Fill press with dough; press dough 1 inch apart onto *ungreased* cookie sheets. Decorate with cherries and assorted candies.

**4.** Bake 10 to 12 minutes or until just set. Remove cookies with spatula to wire racks; cool completely. Store tightly covered at room temperature or freeze up to 3 months.
*Makes about 5 dozen cookies*

## 363 CHRISTMAS ORNAMENT COOKIES

2¼ cups all-purpose flour
¼ teaspoon salt
1 cup granulated sugar
¾ cup butter or margarine, softened
1 large egg
1 teaspoon vanilla
1 teaspoon almond extract
   Icing (page 323)
   Assorted food coloring
   Assorted candies or decors

**1.** Place flour and salt in medium bowl; stir to combine.

**2.** Beat sugar and butter in large bowl with electric mixer at medium speed until light and fluffy. Beat in egg, vanilla and almond extract. Gradually add flour mixture. Beat at low speed until well blended. Form dough into 2 discs; wrap in plastic wrap and refrigerate 30 minutes or until firm.

**3.** Preheat oven to 350°F. Working with 1 disc at a time, unwrap dough and place on lightly floured surface. Roll out dough with lightly floured rolling pin to ¼-inch thickness. Cut dough into desired shapes with assorted floured cookie cutters. Place cutouts on *ungreased* cookie sheets. Using drinking straw or tip of sharp knife, cut a hole near top of cookie to allow for piece of ribbon or string to be inserted for hanger. Gently press dough trimmings together; reroll and cut out more cookies.

**4.** Bake 10 to 12 minutes or until edges are golden brown. Let cookies stand on cookie sheets 1 minute. Remove cookies with spatula to wire racks; cool completely.

**5.** Prepare Icing. Spoon Icing into small resealable plastic food storage bag. Cut off very tiny corner of bag with white Icing; pipe decoratively over cookies. Decorate with additional Icing colors and candies as desired. Let stand at room temperature 40 minutes or until set. Thread ribbon through cookie hole to hang as Christmas tree ornament.

*Makes about 2 dozen cookies*

**ICING**
   **2 cups powdered sugar**
   **2 tablespoons milk or lemon juice**

Place powdered sugar and milk in small bowl; stir with spoon until smooth. (Icing will be very thick. If it is too thick, stir in 1 teaspoon additional milk.) If desired, Icing may be divided into small bowls and tinted with food coloring.

***Christmas Ornament Cookies***

## 364 DANISH RASPBERRY RIBBONS (HINDBAERKAGER)

1 cup butter, softened
½ cup granulated sugar
1 large egg
2 tablespoons milk
2 tablespoons vanilla
¼ teaspoon almond extract
2⅔ cups all-purpose flour
6 tablespoons seedless raspberry jam
   Glaze (recipe follows)

**1.** Beat butter and sugar in large bowl with electric mixer at medium speed until light and fluffy. Beat in egg, milk, vanilla and almond extract until well blended. Gradually add 1½ cups flour. Beat at low speed until well blended. Stir in enough remaining flour to form stiff dough. Form dough into a disc; wrap in plastic wrap and refrigerate until firm, at least 30 minutes or overnight.

**2.** Preheat oven to 375°F. Cut dough into 6 equal pieces. Rewrap 3 dough pieces and return to refrigerator. With floured hands, shape each piece of dough into 12-inch-long, ¾-inch-thick rope. Place ropes 2 inches apart on *ungreased* cookie sheets. Make a lengthwise ¼-inch-deep groove down center of each rope with handle of wooden spoon. (Ropes will flatten to ½-inch-thick strips.)

**3.** Bake 12 minutes. Take strips out of oven; spoon 1 tablespoon jam along each groove. Return to oven; bake 5 to 7 minutes longer or until strips are light golden brown. Cool strips 15 minutes on cookie sheet.

**4.** Prepare Glaze. Drizzle strips with Glaze; let stand 5 minutes to dry. Transfer strips to cutting board. Cut cookie strips at 45° angle into 1-inch slices. Remove cookies with spatula to wire racks; cool completely.

Repeat with remaining dough. Store tightly covered between sheets of waxed paper at room temperature.

*Makes about 5½ dozen cookies*

**GLAZE**
½ cup powdered sugar
1 tablespoon milk
1 teaspoon vanilla

Place all ingredients in small bowl; stir with spoon until smooth.

*Makes scant ¼ cup glaze*

## 365 EGGNOG CRISPS

½ cup (1 stick) butter or margarine, melted
1 cup granulated sugar
1 large egg
1½ teaspoons brandy extract
1½ cups cake flour
½ cup ground pecans
½ teaspoon ground nutmeg
1¾ cups "M&M's"® Chocolate Mini Baking Bits
36 pecan halves

Preheat oven to 375°F. Lightly grease cookie sheets. Cream butter and sugar until light and fluffy; add egg and brandy extract. Combine flour, ground pecans and nutmeg; blend into creamed mixture. Stir in baking bits. Drop by heaping tablespoonfuls onto cookie sheets; top each cookie with 1 pecan half, pressing down gently. Bake 10 to 11 minutes or until edges turn light golden. Cool 1 minute on cookie sheets; cool completely on wire racks.

*Makes about 3 dozen cookies*

*Danish Raspberry Ribbons (Hindbaerkager)*

## ACKNOWLEDGMENTS

**The publisher would like to thank the companies and organizations listed below for the use of their recipes and photographs in this publication.**

Arm & Hammer Division, Church & Dwight Co., Inc.

Best Foods Division, CPC International Inc.

Blue Diamond Growers

California Apricot Advisory Board

California Prune Board

California Raisin Advisory Board

California Table Grape Commission

California Tree Fruit Agreement

Cherry Marketing Institute, Inc.

Del Monte Corporation

Diamond Walnut Growers, Inc.

Dole Food Company, Inc.

Domino Sugar Corporation

Grandma's Molasses, a division of Cadbury Beverages Inc.

Hershey Foods Corporation

Kahlúa® Liqueur

Kellogg Company

Kraft Foods, Inc.

Leaf®, Inc.

M&M/Mars

McIlhenny Company

MOTT'S® Inc., a division of Cadbury Beverages Inc.

Nabisco, Inc.

National Honey Board

Nestlé USA

Norseland, Inc.

Ocean Spray Cranberries, Inc.

Oregon Washington California Pear Bureau

The Procter & Gamble Company

Quaker® Kitchens

Ralston Foods, Inc.

Refined Sugars, Inc.

Roman Meal Company

Sargento® Foods Inc.

The J.M. Smucker Company

Sokol & Company

The Sugar Association, Inc.

Sunkist Growers

Sun•Maid Growers of California

Walnut Marketing Board

Washington Apple Commission

Wesson/Peter Pan Foods Company

Wisconsin Milk Marketing Board

## INDEX

# INDEX

# INDEX

# INDEX

## INDEX

# INDEX

# METRIC CONVERSION CHART

## VOLUME MEASUREMENTS (dry)

1/8 teaspoon = 0.5 mL
1/4 teaspoon = 1 mL
1/2 teaspoon = 2 mL
3/4 teaspoon = 4 mL
1 teaspoon = 5 mL
1 tablespoon = 15 mL
2 tablespoons = 30 mL
1/4 cup = 60 mL
1/3 cup = 75 mL
1/2 cup = 125 mL
2/3 cup = 150 mL
3/4 cup = 175 mL
1 cup = 250 mL
2 cups = 1 pint = 500 mL
3 cups = 750 mL
4 cups = 1 quart = 1 L

## VOLUME MEASUREMENTS (fluid)

1 fluid ounce (2 tablespoons) = 30 mL
4 fluid ounces (1/2 cup) = 125 mL
8 fluid ounces (1 cup) = 250 mL
12 fluid ounces (1 1/2 cups) = 375 mL
16 fluid ounces (2 cups) = 500 mL

## WEIGHTS (mass)

1/2 ounce = 15 g
1 ounce = 30 g
3 ounces = 90 g
4 ounces = 120 g
8 ounces = 225 g
10 ounces = 285 g
12 ounces = 360 g
16 ounces = 1 pound = 450 g

## DIMENSIONS

1/16 inch = 2 mm
1/8 inch = 3 mm
1/4 inch = 6 mm
1/2 inch = 1.5 cm
3/4 inch = 2 cm
1 inch = 2.5 cm

## OVEN TEMPERATURES

250°F = 120°C
275°F = 140°C
300°F = 150°C
325°F = 160°C
350°F = 180°C
375°F = 190°C
400°F = 200°C
425°F = 220°C
450°F = 230°C

## BAKING PAN SIZES

| Utensil | Size in Inches/Quarts | Metric Volume | Size in Centimeters |
|---|---|---|---|
| Baking or | 8×8×2 | 2 L | 20×20×5 |
| Cake Pan | 9×9×2 | 2.5 L | 23×23×5 |
| (square or | 12×8×2 | 3 L | 30×20×5 |
| rectangular) | 13×9×2 | 3.5 L | 33×23×5 |
| Loaf Pan | 8×4×3 | 1.5 L | 20×10×7 |
| | 9×5×3 | 2 L | 23×13×7 |
| Round Layer | 8×1½ | 1.2 L | 20×4 |
| Cake Pan | 9×1½ | 1.5 L | 23×4 |
| Pie Plate | 8×1¼ | 750 mL | 20×3 |
| | 9×1¼ | 1 L | 23×3 |
| Baking Dish | 1 quart | 1 L | — |
| or Casserole | 1½ quart | 1.5 L | — |
| | 2 quart | 2 L | — |